TERESA DEEVY RECLAIMED

VOLUME ONE

TERESA DEEVY RECLAIMED

VOLUME ONE

TEMPORAL POWERS

KATIE ROCHE

WIFE TO JAMES WHELAN

EDITED BY

JONATHAN BANK,
CHRISTOPHER MORASH,
AND
JOHN P. HARRINGTON

Jonathan Bank
Mint Theater Company
311 West 43rd Street, Suite 307
New York, NY 10036
jbank@minttheater.org

ISBN: 978-0-9718262-4-3
Library of Congress Control Number: 2011936088

Book designed by Nita Congress
nita@njccommunications.com

CONTENTS

THE TERESA DEEVY PROJECT

For a writer to achieve lasting fame it is not always enough to create great work—they must also have a champion—a sympathetic and passionate advocate. Mint Theater Company has claimed that role on behalf of a brilliant, but now voiceless writer. Teresa Deevy is a great writer with a great personal story—"one of the most undeservedly neglected and significant Irish playwrights of the 20th century" (the *Irish Times*). The Teresa Deevy Project is intended to bring this neglected writer the attention and acclaim she deserves.

In the spring of 2010, Mint Artistic Director Jonathan Bank traveled to Ireland to meet with members of the Deevy family and to see Landscape, the Deevy family home where Teresa was born and spent her final years. All of Teresa's remaining papers were stored there, including complete and incomplete typescripts of both produced and unproduced plays. Every page was carefully scanned and/or copied and brought back to New York. The original papers were donated in 2011 by Deevy's literary executor, Jacqui Deevy, to the National University of Ireland, Maynooth, where they are preserved in the university's manuscript collection for future generations of scholars. While they have been saved, other Deevy manuscripts appear to be lost for good (like Deevy's first Abbey play, *Reapers*.)

Mint launched the Deevy Project in July 2010 with a highly regarded production of *Wife to James Whelan*. The project continued with readings of her short plays *The King of Spain's Daughter*, *Strange Birth*, and *Light Falling*. In 2011 came a full production of *Temporal Powers* and a reading of her unpublished and unproduced short play *In the Cellar of My Friend*. In 2012, Mint will produce Deevy's best-known play, *Katie Roche*, and publish Volume Two of *Teresa Deevy Reclaimed*, which will include all of her short dramatic works as well as her full-length play *The Wild Goose*. Video recordings have been or will be made of all the full-length plays.

Teachers and universities interested in obtaining copies of this book and/or the video recordings should contact Jonathan Bank, Mint Theater Company (jbank@minttheater.org; www.minttheater.org).

TERESA DEEVY: BETWEEN THE LINES

Christopher Morash

One way to begin to understand Teresa Deevy's work is to put her in the context of the generation of Irish writers who came before her. She was born in 1894, three years before W. B. Yeats, Lady Gregory, and Edward Martyn founded the Irish Literary Theatre (later the Abbey Theatre). She entered University College Dublin as one of the first female students just a few years before the Easter Rising in 1916—what Yeats would call that moment of "terrible beauty"—in which writers played such a prominent role. Teresa Deevy would have been in her mid-thirties when the Abbey became the first state-subsidized theater in the English-speaking world in 1926. Thus, Teresa Deevy grew up simultaneously with both the Abbey and the new Irish state. She comes just after the heroic generation that, as the critic Declan Kiberd puts it in relation to Yeats, believed themselves to be in a position "to invent Ireland *ex nihilo*."[1]

Yet she was never really a part of that generation. A series of personal events would shape Deevy's own life in the years during which Yeats and O'Casey were writing for the theater and the new state was coming into being. In 1913, while attending university, she contracted Ménière's disease and lost her hearing. At around the same time, the family fortunes began to decline, keeping her increasingly at the family home, Landscape, in Waterford, with her mother and sisters.

If Deevy's life during this period was removed from the historic events taking place in Dublin and elsewhere, she was by no means living in isolation. She began attending the theater in London, where she had gone to learn lip-reading. In the late 1920s, she began to write plays,

---

[1] Declan Kiberd, *Inventing Ireland: The Literature of the Modern Nation* (London: Vintage, 1995), p. 123.

and on March 18, 1930 (after at least one encouraging rejection), the Abbey Theatre staged *Reapers*. This was followed in rapid succession by a one-act comedy, *A Disciple*, in 1931, and her first major play, *Temporal Powers*, staged by the Abbey in 1932. The latter won the Abbey's new play competition that year, so it was little surprise that it was eager to stage her next play, a powerful one-act work, *The King of Spain's Daughter*, in 1935. She quickly followed this with the play for which she is best known today, *Katie Roche*, in 1936—a play that John Harrington, later in this volume, describes as mapping "an innovative path for the Abbey Theatre." Another full-length play followed quickly, this time a sprawling historical play, *The Wild Goose*.

All told, the middle years of the 1930s saw an impressive burst of creativity on Deevy's part—six plays in as many years—and, as a result, hopes for her future were high. Reading through reviews from this period, as the Abbey's founding generation passed or moved on (Lady Gregory died in 1932 and Yeats in 1939; O'Casey went into self-imposed exile in 1926), there was a palpable hope that Teresa Deevy would be among those who would take up the mantle as part of a new generation of Irish playwrights for a theater whose reputation had always rested on its writers.

However, it was not to be. Even at the height of her success, it was clear that Deevy was far from comfortable with the Abbey. In a January 1935 letter to her friend Florence Hackett in Kilkenny, Deevy wrote: "Something will have to be done about the theatre in Ireland. It's appalling." These were difficult years in which to be critical of the theater. In the 1920s, the Irish Free State government had introduced stringent regimes of literary and cinematic censorship, with the result that many of Ireland's leading literary figures of the time found themselves unable to publish their work in their own country. Irish theater had been left out of the censorship net; however, there were those who argued that there was a need to bring it under tighter control. "Any work which does not show Ireland as a land of saints and scholars," commented the *Irish Times* in 1935, "any play which ventures to attack or to satirise an aspect of Irish life, is condemned at once as a treacherous onslaught on the national prestige."[2] As the battle lines in the Irish culture wars of the 1930s were drawn with increasing clarity, Teresa Deevy made it clear where she stood. "Who are the censors?" she demanded in an open letter to the *Irish Times* in 1936. "By what right do they hold office? And how, in case of proved incompetence, can they be removed?"[3]

---

[2] "The Nation's Prestige," *Irish Times* (Aug. 28, 1935), p. 6.

[3] Teresa Deevy, "The Censorship," *Irish Times* (Oct. 20, 1936), p. 4.

If Deevy was outspoken in her personal capacity, it was not immediately obvious that her plays were in any way subversive. For instance, when the curtain had risen on her first major success, *Temporal Powers*, the audience would have been faced with a set that reminded them of many peasant dramas of the Abbey's first decade: "The action of the play takes place in the interior of an old ruin on a hillside in Ireland." By the middle decades of the twentieth century, there was strong official sanction for the idea that Irish culture was defined by the values of peasant society, evoked in Irish Taoiseach Éamon de Valera's famous St. Patrick's Day speech as "that Ireland of which we dreamed...the home of a people who valued material wealth only as a basis for right living, of a people who, satisfied with frugal comfort, devoted their leisure to the things of the spirit." And yet, while *Temporal Powers* may look as if it belongs to this world of idealized noble peasants, it becomes clear as the play unfolds that they are not: they are simply poor and, in their struggle for subsistence, they may find ethics expendable when the alternative is hunger. It was little wonder that the *Irish Times* wrote: "Throughout the performance [one] is haunted by the feeling of some unfamiliar quality in the atmosphere."[4]

Similarly, it is worth remembering that Deevy's short play *The King of Spain's Daughter* and her best-known work, *Katie Roche*, were on the stage of Ireland's national theater at the same time that the debates were taking place that would lead to the drafting of the 1937 Irish Constitution. In *The King of Spain's Daughter*, the character of Annie Kinsella must chose between loveless marriage and a life of drudgery in a factory on a stage dominated by a large sign reading "Road Closed." *Katie Roche* develops this theme of the limited opportunities that the new state presented to Irish women; the overwhelming feeling in *Katie Roche* is of watching a woman who has been trapped by domestic life. All of this is in sharp contrast to the official view of the role of women in the 1937 Constitution, which declares: "The State recognises that by her life within the home, woman gives to the State a support without which the common good cannot be achieved." In contrast, as the *Irish Times* noted, "All through the play, one seems to see an almost imperceptible change in the ordinary values of life."[5] As with *Temporal Powers*, Deevy was putting herself at odds with the dominant values of Irish society.

This critical stance was to make Deevy's position in the theater increasingly precarious after 1935, as the writers who had always run the theater

---

[4] "Thought-Provoking Play: 'Temporal Powers,'" *Irish Independent* (Sept. 13, 1932), p. 9.

[5] "Miss Deevy's New Play," *Irish Times* (March 17, 1936), p. 5.

gave way to a cadre of much more politically orthodox administrators. The most powerful of these would be Ernest Blythe, a former finance minister and ardent supporter of the Irish language revival movement. Throughout the early 1930s, as Yeats spent less and less time in Ireland, and grew older and frailer (even as his writing blazed with a final strange intensity), control slipped increasingly to Blythe. In a particularly scathing history of the Abbey written in 1950, Peter Kavanagh concluded that with the death of Yeats in 1939, the Abbey had died: "The Abbey Theatre was a dream in the mind of Yeats... when he died the reality returned to the dream and passed away with its creator."[6] Even decades later, playwrights who had suffered bruising encounters with Blythe still harbored resentments: playwright Hugh Leonard (author of the Tony-winning *Da*) recalled him as "a despot without any knowledge of or even liking for the theatre."[7]

It was into this heated and embittered atmosphere that Teresa Deevy came of age as a dramatist—to her cost. In 1939, a new play, *Holiday House,* was accepted by the Abbey and a contract issued. However, the play was never staged, and any attempt by Deevy to find out why was met, in her words, "with evasive replies."[8] Similarly, she later wrote to Florence Hackett about the rejection of *Wife to James Whelan*:

> Blythe's letter, when returning it, showed clearly that he has no use for my work—never asked to see any more... it may be a good thing to be finished with the Abbey. Yet I love the Abbey, & their actors are fine.[9]

From that point onwards, apart from one play performed on the Abbey's experimental stage (*Light Falling*, 1948), Deevy was effectively finished with the Abbey Theatre.

With the major Irish theater for new playwrights closed to her, Teresa Deevy turned increasingly after 1940 to writing for radio. From one point of view, this was remarkable, given that the first radio broadcast in Ireland took place in 1926, more than a decade after Deevy had become deaf. And yet, in this medium that she could never experience directly, she excelled, both writing specifically for the airwaves and adapting her stage plays. It would thus be on radio that *Wife to James Whelan* would finally reach an audience when it was broadcast on the BBC in 1946,

---

[6] Peter Kavanagh, *The Story of the Abbey Theatre* (1950; rpt. Orono, ME: National Poetry Foundation, 1984), p. 184.

[7] Hugh Leonard, "Theatrical Bricks and Mortar," *Sunday Independent* (March 3, 2002), p. 77.

[8] "The White Steed," *Irish Times* (May 8, 1939), p. 8.

[9] Teresa Deevy, Letter to Florence Hackett, (undated; *ca.*1941/2) TCD Ms. 10722.

and the following year on Radio Éireann. However, writing for radio in Ireland in the 1940s was not easy, and much of Deevy's surviving correspondence from the period attests to her constant struggle to make a living as a writer. "I am very pleased to think you would like to do *Katie Roche*," Deevy responded to a producer with Radio Éireann in the mid-1940s, "but must ask for a higher free than you have offered."[10]

In spite of her sometimes straitened financial circumstances, Deevy continued to write throughout the 1940s and 1950s. In this regard, her life began to echo the situation of a character like Katie Roche, insofar as a vivid life of the imagination became a necessity in a world of material constraints. Indeed, if we are looking for the distinguishing feature of Teresa Deevy's theater, it may well be this: the quest for a theatrical form that could accommodate the essential privacy of an inner life. In *Katie Roche*, the title character may be trapped in marriage to a man to whom she seems indifferent; nonetheless, there is triumph in her final lines: "I *will* be brave!... I was looking for something great to do—sure now I have it." Likewise, in *Wife to James Whelan*, she brings together a group of characters who live closely with one another in a small Irish town, but who each maintain a deeply private self from which the others are excluded. Developing this idea later in a short play called *In the Cellar of My Friend*, one character observes: "It do seem to me there is no two people can to the full com-pre-hend one another. Not fully... not as I sees it."[11] In these gaps of comprehension, Teresa Deevy stakes out her theatrical territory.

Deevy's own deafness in the world of the hearing may have contributed to a heightened consciousness of language, and of its failures. And, writing as a woman in a society that offered women very limited choices may have helped attune her to the need to maintain an inner life separate from the strictures of society. Or it may have been that, like many of her generation in Ireland coming after a generation that had seen its historical role in heroic terms and seeing those heroic dreams tempered by the cold exigencies of reality, she had a mistrust of language. It would likely be a mistake to reduce her work to any one of these factors. Teresa Deevy was first and foremost a writer for the theater, fascinated by what stage language could, and could not, do.

In the years just before her death in 1963, there was a brief, belated, flurry of interest in her work. The script of *Wife to James Whelan* that had gathered dust for almost a decade after the radio broadcasts of the mid-1940s was finally produced in October 1956. That same year,

---

[10] Teresa Deevy, Letter to Larry McDonagh (undated; *ca.* 1945?), TCD Ms. 33,665.

[11] Teresa Deevy, *In the Cellar of My Friend*, NLI Ms. 29,169.

John Jordan, one of the most respected Irish literary critics of the time, published an influential reassessment of her work in which he argued that she should be seen as a key figure in an Irish dramatic tradition:

> Synge and O'Casey are our dramatic geniuses in this century. But there is a distinguished class of those who are only less than great. I believe that Teresa Deevy should be counted among that select band. And, within her chosen field, she is incomparable.[12]

Today, we can begin to place her even more precisely. Just as her plays do their work with what happens between the lines, Deevy's writing as a whole exists between two generations of Irish playwrights. If some aspects of her dramaturgy look back to those who preceded her, her ability to create characters with fully realized private lives that are partly obscured from the audience (and from the other characters) anticipates the Irish playwright Brian Friel, who was only just coming to prominence at Deevy's death. It could be argued that Friel's whole career has been an attempt to find a dramatic form to stage the privacies between people—and the same could be said of Teresa Deevy. Considered in this light, she begins to take her proper place as a pivotal figure in Irish theater, not simply the successor of the founding generation of Abbey playwrights, but the precursor of the vibrant Irish theater of today.

Christopher Morash is Professor and Head of English at National University of Ireland, Maynooth, where he founded the Centre for Media Studies. His most recent book is A History of the Media in Ireland *(Cambridge, 2009). Earlier publications include* A History of Irish Theatre 1601–2000 *(Cambridge, 2002), which won the Theatre Book Prize from the Society for Theatre Research, and* Writing the Irish Famine *(Oxford, 1996).*

[12] John Jordan, "Teresa Deevy: An Introduction," *Irish University Review* I:8 (Spring, 1956), p. 26.

EDITORS' NOTE

Our intention is to provide the most accurate and reliable texts for all of Teresa Deevy's plays—but that's not so easy. Some of them exist only as multiple draft typescripts filled with cross-outs and handwritten additions. And her typescripts are idiosyncratic. For example, ellipses vary from the usual three dots all the way up to nine—and there's no way to know how intentional this was. Some scripts appear to have been typed professionally, possibly after Deevy died in 1963; the punctuation in these is more "normal"—the first step in an editing process which we continue here.

Even the plays that were previously published present editorial problems; Deevy tinkered continuously. For example, her one-act play *Strange Birth* was published twice, and the two editions have real differences. She even changed the title of her first short play twice: it was produced at the Abbey in 1931 as *A Disciple* and published under that title in 1937, then republished as *The Enthusiast* a year later and finally as *In Search of Valour* in 1947.

Of the three plays in this volume, *Katie Roche* is the only one that was published while Teresa Deevy was still alive. Victor Gollancz selected it for the 1935–36 edition of his annual *Famous Plays* anthology (adding a note justifying its inclusion, "even though it cannot yet be called famous"). It was published again in 1939, this time by Macmillan. There are differences between the two published versions—not major differences and not many, but differences all the same. We used Macmillan as the basis for our text; it was the later text and the changes to the play seem consistent with Deevy's rewriting process: she was always on the lookout for the simplest and most dramatic line. For example, near the end of the play Reuben says to Stanislaus:

Gollancz	*Macmillan:*
You must see the danger for her.	She's in great danger.

The Deevy papers were stored for decades in two suitcases under a bed at Landscape, the family home in Waterford. Among these, we found several different typescripts for *Temporal Powers*, but none match the play as it was published in 1984 in the *Journal of Irish Literature*. That text is the leanest, making it the obvious choice as a basis for ours. The differences are barely noticeable, one draft being just ten or fifteen words shorter than the previous.

Wife to James Whelan was first published in 1995 by the *Irish University Review*. Its text was taken from the only script that exists, a clean, professionally typed version that was missing for decades (and ultimately turned up at Landscape). Given that this play was under revision for years (at least), it's unfortunate that there were no earlier drafts preserved. At least it was not lost for good, like Deevy's first Abbey play, *Reapers*. It appears she lent her only manuscript to John Jordan in 1956 when he was writing an article on her work. It has been missing ever since.

TEMPORAL POWERS

A Play in Three Acts

INTRODUCTION

Jonathan Bank

Temporal Powers was the third of Teresa Deevy's plays produced by the Abbey Theatre. Deevy shared first prize in 1932 (with Paul Vincent Carrol for *Things That Are Caesar's*) in the playwriting competition started by the company in an effort to encourage new work and new writers—even though, as it happens, neither writer was new to the Abbey. The judges' report called Deevy's drama "strikingly original and of fine literary quality."

Opening night was "filled to overflowing," according to the *Irish Times*, which called *Temporal Powers* "one of the most thoughtful works seen for some time at the Abbey." This sentiment was echoed in the other reviews of the time. "There seems little doubt that *Temporal Powers* will figure often in the Abbey repertory" predicted the *Stage*.

Frank O'Connor, a brilliant short story writer who was later to become an Abbey director, wrote an effusive note to Deevy after seeing *Temporal Powers*:

> Nothing since the "Playboy" has excited me so much. It's a grand thing to think that Ireland is stepping into the limelight once more; we've had so many books, so many plays, and so little of Ireland in them. I congratulate you heartily and wish you all the success you deserve.

If nothing else, what Deevy deserved was a revival of her prize-winner after its initial week long run. O'Connor, Deevy noted in a letter to her friend Florence Hackett, had told her that "Yeats does not care at all for my plays." W.B. Yeats, of course, was the driving force at the Abbey. "Not very encouraging," she continued, "but it is better to know. He said that is the reason my work is not brought on at the Abbey more. He got some friends of his to write and ask for a revival of *Temporal Powers*, but it came to nothing."

O'Connor was appointed to the Abbey Board in the fall of 1935, and in 1937 *Temporal Powers* was finally revived for a week, in preparation for that year's American tour. Deevy was undoubtedly surprised at its inclusion in the tour repertory but less surprised when it was dropped.

The Dublin correspondent to the *Christian Science Monitor* reported:

> It is a happy thought that led to the play's inclusion in the repertory selected for this year's American tour, as Miss Deevy's work is deserving a wider, and possibly more appreciative audience than Dublin provides. Its coming presentation in the United States prompted its

> recent staging before large audiences of which visitors composed the majority. Its reception reflected the novelty of Miss Deevy's style as well as its analytical qualities. In other words, the author has earned a recognition which she has not wholly received.

This was ever the case. In *Teresa Deevy: An Introduction*, published by the *Irish University Review* in 1956, critic John Jordan calls *Temporal Powers* "a great play," and writes, "One wishes that some publisher would provide a text of this play, if only to correct the vulgar impression of Miss Deevy as a one-theme dramatist." Jordan is referring to the notion of Deevy as preoccupied with the romantic fancies of young girls, as in *Katie Roche*, *The King of Spain's Daughter*, and *In Search of Valour*.

It is gratifying to here present *Temporal Powers* together with Deevy's *Wife to James Whelan*. They both dramatize the struggle between ambition and contentment (among other themes), but Deevy gives each play's female protagonist a different side of the argument—perhaps revealing the extent to which she herself struggled with the question.

In *Temporal Powers*, Min ridicules Michael for his lack of ambition: "What good is any man if he don't outdo who's living beside of him?" Michael's unwillingness to follow anything other than the dictates of his heart leads to eviction and ultimately emigration. In *Wife to James Whelan*, Nan berates James for seeking to improve himself: "...whatever good there is in betterment," she jeers in response to his plans to start a business. Nan, like Michael, is content with the life she has, but things don't work out well for her either—she ends up desperately poor, a widow with a young son to feed. Both Nan and Michael resort to stealing and both spend time in jail. Shame over the loss of reputation casts a long shadow over them both.

On the other side of the coin, James Whelan achieves material success, but he is never at peace; ambition seems a curse that may have cost him a chance at happiness. Things are even more desperate for Min in *Temporal Powers*; she is left with less than nothing at the end of the play.

Both plays are love stories that end badly. Both hinge on moments where rage, resentment, and pride conquer vulnerability and honesty. In each, two people who love each other are left separated by a silence that neither is willing to pierce. "That is what have the whole world addled—trying to make one out of two," Min cries, "You might give it up!"

Lennox Robinson, Deevy's director and champion at the Abbey, wrote in a 1939 review of her *Three Plays* for the *Dublin Magazine*, "It is right and easy to criticize her achievement, she has, so far, practically only one subject—disillusionment; love, life, glory, all end in mud." He nevertheless goes on to call her "the most important dramatist writing for the Irish theatre since 1930. Perhaps I should say will be—" he quibbles, lamenting that "Teresa Deevy has not yet found for herself a strong, popular, dramatic subject. She may never have the luck to do so. These subjects come the wind's way, the boy's way..."

In *Temporal Powers*, Deevy found for herself a strong, dramatic subject, without doubt—whether it will ever prove to be popular is another matter entirely.

Jonathan Bank has been the Artistic Director of Mint since 1996 where he has unearthed and produced dozens of lost or neglected plays, many of which he has also directed. He is also the editor of three additional volumes in the Reclaimed *series (Harley Granville Barker, St. John Hankin, and Arthur Schnitzler) as well as* Worthy But Neglected: Plays of the Mint Theater Company.

Mint Theater Company's production of *Temporal Powers,* written by Teresa Deevy, began performances on August 3, 2011, at the Mint Theater, 311 West 43rd Street, in New York City, with the following cast and credits:

Michael Donovan....................Aidan Redmond
Min Donovan....................Rosie Benton
Moses Barron....................Eli James
Lizzie Brennan....................Wrenn Schmidt
Daisy Barron....................Fiana Toibin
Ned Cooney....................Con Horgan
Maggie Cooney....................Bairbre Dowling
Jim Slattery....................Paul Carlin
Father O'Brien....................Robertson Carricart

Directed by: Jonathan Bank
Set Design by: Vicki R. Davis
Costume Design by: Andrea Varga
Lighting Design by: Jeff Nellis
Sound Design: Jane Shaw
Props Design: Joshua Yocom
Production Stage Manager: Lisa McGinn
Assistant Stage Manager: Andrea Jo Martin, Lauren McArthur
Dramaturgy: Heather J. Violanti
Dialect and Additional Dramaturgy: Amy Stoller
Assistant to the Director: Natalia Schwein
Press Representative: David Gersten & Associates
Advertising and Marketing: The Pekoe Group

CHARACTERS

MIN DONOVAN
MOSES BARRON
DAISY BARRON
NED COONEY
FATHER O'BRIEN
MICHAEL, her husband
LIZZIE BRENNAN
MAGGIE COONEY
JIM SLATTERY

SETTING

The action of the play takes place in the interior of an old ruin on a hillside in Ireland.

Act I. Afternoon in the early autumn of 1927.
Act II. A few hours later.
Act III. The following morning.

ACT I

Part of the interior of an old ruin. The place is now scarcely habitable; the walls are broken and crumbling: moss and tufts of grass are plentiful in the crevices. A great gap in the wall at the back shows where a large low window has fallen away. Beside this, to the left, is the doorway, without a door. The fireplace is at the right side of the room: a kettle has been left on the hearth-stone, and in the corner, on a wooden stool, are two cups and a plate. In another corner there is a mattress, roped up, and near it, on the floor, are an old hairbrush, a piece of a looking-glass, a child's battered drum, and a picture—"Bubbles"—framed.

Near the fireplace, part of a low broken wall juts into the room: on this a woman is sitting. She is MIN DONOVAN, thirty-two years of age, poorly dressed but wearing her shawl with a distinctive grace. She may be full of despair. She is never merely depressed.

At the other side of the room her husband, MICHAEL, is trying to fix a hinge to an old shutter which he hopes to use as a door. MICHAEL is a gaunt man, with a meditative air; toil-worn and, though only five years older than MIN, is aged beyond his years. He cannot manage the shutter very well now: each time it slips, MIN laughs—a short, scornful laugh.

MIN: Try again! Ha!... Ha! Keep on tryin'! *(Again the shutter slips, and she turns to the fire as though tired watching.)* It would be as good for you to leave off from it. What great hand will you make at that—no more than at what you ever done? *(Half affectionate through her contempt.)* Oh, he'll keep on tryin'... like he was diggin' in the field till they had us evicted. *(MICHAEL looks at her, a silencing look.)* So, I shouldn't say that! Well, it was true for me then—maybe that's why I shouldn't—you were diggin' and diggin' an' it done us no good! *(The shutter slips.)* Ha! Ha! *(Then, as MICHAEL starts once more:)* "The King of Scotland—he thrun himself down... he was tryin' an' tryin'..."

MICHAEL: Will you stop quiet! *(Low tone, but nearly at the end of his patience.)*

MIN: *(Aggrieved.)* To stop quiet I must?—A thing I never done! It isn't enough we'd be evicted out from below but when I'd come here for a shelter I must keep a quiet tongue in my mouth—what he wouldn't ask had I a roof over my head! Quiet! *(Forced resignation. A pause. MICHAEL bends over his work; MIN watches, then:)* It is grand for the men can be passin' the time pleasant with work, but myself must stop without a word outer me… Don't be killin' yourself—we wouldn't be much better off… An' what now can I do seein' you won't leave me talk? If they'll leave us stop here the night that's as much as they'll do, so there's no call for killin' yourself. *(The shutter slips.)* Ha! "The King of Scotland—"

MICHAEL: *(Blazing.)* If you don't stop quick, I'll put you inside! *(Jerks his head in the direction of a small door in the wall at the left side.)*

MIN: *(Amazed.)* What? The first time y'ever said a right word! *(He turns away, but she keeps looking at him with fresh interest.)* The eviction'll do that good if it'll make you feel like another… *(A pause. She gets up, goes to the small door, examines the place inside, then:)* I'd as lief be in it. Come on, let you, an' put me in! *(When he takes no notice, she goes to him, affectionate.)* Poor Michael Donovan…a pity but you were different. What was on me that I ever took up with you? I am lookin' for that answer day an' night. What was on the two of us seein' you never had sense?

MICHAEL: It'll do now. *(Takes the shutter to the doorway and fixes it there.)*

MIN: *(Back at the fire.)* Too full of feelin' I was…till the poverty dried me. *(Bitterly. Then looks down at her own clothes and grows angry.)* If my mother'd see me now! An' I loved what was neat! The wan in the school would keep herself the best ever! *(MICHAEL, in turning from the doorway, brushes against the picture frame.)* Mind me "Bubbles"! *(Springs up, takes the picture, dusts it lovingly with her shawl. Then, looking at it:)* Though it wasn't what I'd want. What I'd want most was that woman asleep in the Dublin gallery… The whole school was took up to see the gallery in Dublin. It was then I knew life. We had our lunch in our pocket, but I forgot—

MICHAEL: *(Testily.)* You tolt me before—

MIN: *(After a silence.)* I would be better to be th' ole brick lyin' there without pain or feelin' or any thoughts goin' through me. *(MICHAEL, sympathetic, comes over and pats her shoulder a little awkwardly. But she turns on him, her sorrow lost now in anger.)* Great good are your big hands to me! An' they wore to the bone diggin' in a field that is but stone an' thistle!

MICHAEL: I had to do the work before me!

MIN: Why had you? Is it like th' ole cows we should be only munchin' what's under our nose?

MICHAEL: I did me best.

MIN: *(Quiet, accusing.)* Your best! Michael Donovan, it was never in your heart to make money. Now, what worse thing could be said of any man?

MICHAEL: I worked—I didn't spare myself—

MIN: 'Tis that 'ud anger me—workin' an' no thought of what profit was in it! Like an ole cart horse draggin' at a load until he'd drop! An' myself lookin' ever at the bones stickin' out through your body an' sayin' to myself in the night how we were neither a step this way nor that.

MICHAEL: I'll go over to my sister Maggie tomorra, an' see—

MIN: You might as well not! 'Tis th' inside of you is wrong! *(A pause.)* Look back, let you, an' see did j'ever at all dream of bein' rich? *(MICHAEL looks back, but does not speak, knowing that his dreams would meet no sympathy.)* No! You did not. Contented you'd be as long as you could tire yourself!

MICHAEL: *(Quietly.)* I was content while we were below.

MIN: *(Quietly too.)* It was when I seen that despair took a hold of me.

MICHAEL: A good life it was, an' hard.

MIN: I think you'd never ask better than a day's hard work that 'ud give no profit! No, you would not—so long as you could be moonin' on the hill in the evenin'.

MICHAEL: I'd ask no better, now or ever, than to live out me life where we were.

MIN: That is what has us evicted this day.

MICHAEL: I'd ask no better than to be on the hill of a summer evening, me work done, and you inside, and the evening falling quiet.

MIN: The hill was me enemy ever. *(She looks across the room, catches sight of the child's drum, and, turning quickly away from it, says bitterly:)* Isn't it well for little Seamus that we buried him the time—a child that his father would put an old hill before.

MICHAEL: I worked to keep you in that place!

MIN: A hole of a place! And I'm better thrun out! *(MICHAEL goes away to the other side of the room. MIN glances over her shoulder, and, after a moment says, in a lighter tone:)* The kinda man I'd ask is wan that would stand behind a shop counter quiet and easy the day long, and could be smoking his pipe in the evening if he'd like, and myself, as was meant, ornamenting the house. *(MICHAEL has knocked a loose stone from the wall, and now, stretching up, discovers that something has been hidden in the wall, behind this stone. MIN goes to him.)* What's there? What?

MICHAEL: *(Pulls out a packet, carefully wrapped up.)* Look at that! I wonder...what?...

MIN: Open it! Quick!

MICHAEL: 'Twas hid up there... *(Turns it over in his hand, slowly.)*

MIN: Can't you open it! *(He hesitates.)* Don't be looking at it! Go on! *(MICHAEL opens the packet. They see a number of notes and some silver. They stare at it, then at each other, then back again at the money.)* Money! A pile!

MICHAEL: What do it mean? Money...what—?

MIN: Good luck coming our way in the last! Mick, 'tis like what you'd dream! Show! *(But he instinctively draws back from her.)* What? What are you shaking your head for?

MICHAEL: Min, that money don't belong to us! *(Holding it from her.)*

MIN: What? Is it to the old ruin it belongs?

MICHAEL: *(Slowly.)* Wait till we'll think—

MIN: Till judgment we'd think without thinking the same! What are you at? *(He has turned away, and now puts the money back in the hole in the wall.)* Great good is it to the old wall up there.

MICHAEL: Give me time... That money must be stole.

MIN: If it is aself it isn't us stole it! Michael, have sense! What have we a chance for if we don't use it?

MICHAEL: *(Slowly.)* Some wan left that money there.

MIN: 'Twas the angels of God put it in their head to leave it there! 'Tis the hand of God I see in this as clear as me own... A wonder but you'd see! What would it be but the Providence of God looking down on His poor children and they destitute—

MICHAEL: We have no claim—

MIN: I have a feeling it was left there thousands and thousands of years back, so there is no one living now with a claim on it at all—

MICHAEL: If it were there very long, it wouldn't be the kind of money it is.

MIN: Leave us see is there a name on any part of it.

MICHAEL: What name could be on it?

MIN: Only one look—

MICHAEL: It is what I'll do—to bring it down to Father O'Brien and see what will he say.

MIN: *(After a moment.)* Michael Donovan, you won't take that money out of this and you alive.

MICHAEL: Would you ask I'd do wrong?

MIN: Wrong! What is wronger I ask you than crawling through life with tattered rags on your back?

MICHAEL: So you're asking we rob?

MIN: And what did you ever do but rob? Maybe you didn't take money wasn't yours—but worse. Robbing me you are since you laid eyes on me! Oh *(With growing anger.)* he couldn't commit sin at all! Sure he should tell it if he did! Running to Father O'Brien! *(Then more quietly.)* Michael, Father O'Brien won't be standing beside of you the last day. 'Tis what you'll find out for yourself will stand there, and not what you were told.

MICHAEL: Is there no heed of God's law in you?

MIN: *(Pleading.)* It wasn't us took this. Out of the cabin they hunted us, and it was yourself thought of this place for a shelter, and it was yourself put your hand on the money now—Oh, Micky, who but you'd see wrong in keeping it? If you ever felt for me, don't drown the hope of new life for me now. 'Twould start us new in the States...only to take what we found, and start decent...I'm young yet—so are you—you could make a fine woman of me out there—

MICHAEL: No matter what wonder I could do, it wouldn't be right.

MIN: You! With your right and your wrong! *(Tries to push him aside in hope of getting at the money.)* Keep out of that! *(Struggles.)*

MICHAEL: *(Questioning her.)* Can't you turn into your heart and rest there awhile.

MIN: A bitter place to rest!

MICHAEL: If we'd climb to the top of the world, what more would we have than what our heart would hold? Take heed now of God being in your heart.

MIN: And a great chance you'd give Him to stop there! Hatred and evil is in me heart, and is your doing! *(Struggles again to push him aside.)*

MICHAEL: Sh—sh—now.

MIN: Leave me go!

MICHAEL: What good would our life be and the weight of that money on our heart and soul? Min, them things are only temporary and shifting.

MIN: And what is ourself but temporary and shifting? *(Then in quiet bitterness:)* Let you go off now and tell this in confession—that never once since Min Power married you had she a finger of lace to stretch on the window. Window! It wasn't but a hole stuffed with rags! But sure that is all right—so long as it isn't a thing he should tell!

MICHAEL: What good is your jeering? Some are rich, and some poor, and it must be the poverty was meant for us, seeing no matter how hard I'd work—

MIN: Meant! Oh, sure it was meant! Oh, you're a wonder for the reading of God's mind.

(As they look at each other, a low mournful whistle is heard—then another, coming nearer.)

MICHAEL: This will be Moses Barron.

MIN: Bringing food to us they can't well spare!

(MICHAEL puts the stone back in the wall, hiding the money. MOSES BARRON comes in. He is twenty-one but already quite old. His thin, sensitive face has a withered look, his body seems shrunken; but his personality is amazingly vital.)

MICHAEL: Come in, Moses, and we're glad to see you.

MIN: What brought you up, Moses Barron?

MOSES: Following me profession—knocking down time. *(He leaves a small tin near the fireplace, then turns to examine MICHAEL's handiwork.)* You're not far behind meself for doing a good job.

MIN: *(Having looked into the tin.)* You can tell the truth. It won't shame Michael Donovan to know he's taking the bit out of a neighbour's mouth. *(She takes a potato from the tin, and eats ravenously.)* That is what he would think right.

MOSES: That would pickle it nice for me if the neighbour'd be the landlord.

MIN: *(To MICHAEL.)* Maybe you'll bring yourself to take some. *(He does. She then holds the tin out to MOSES.)* Go on, Moses.

(MOSES takes a little and nibbles.)

MICHAEL: *(Enjoying it.)* You brought better than we had a long while... thank you, Moses.

MOSES: You may thank Liz Brennan.

MICHAEL: Liz Brennan?

MOSES: That little one is sweet on me and goes as a daily to the house beyond... District Justice what's-his-name. They gives her what is over.

MIN: He was afraid it was stole. He don't like stealing from the rich!

MOSES: That's gaining popular now—stealing and robbing. Did ye hear the big lot was took from Coolbarry Post Office the other day?

MICHAEL: What was that? I didn't hear.

MOSES: They walked in, and they walked out, and that was all: revolvers they had.

MIN: I don't believe it! I don't believe a penny was took!

MOSES: Right you are! Neither would I if I didn't like! *(Then to MICHAEL.)* We'd all do the same were we made over again, and I'm not sure would that be a misfortune.

MICHAEL: Was the money got back? Or what way did it end?

MOSES: To be continued next week—no trace at all yet.

MIN: Maybe you'll tell me is this the law now—don't be robbing from them you never laid eyes on, but take what you'll like from them must live with you? What would you think, Moses Barron?

MOSES: I am not able to think. It might be me mother, and it might be the school I was. They were telling me things you never heard, telling and telling, and it was only the day leaving school I remembered no one had told me how to think.

MIN: Hm! Was there ever fool knew himself for a fool? There was not!... I dunno what is the meaning of the word "right."

MOSES: Oh, the word "right" is a powerful grand word that don't need meaning put on it.

MIN: Michael Donovan is fond of his own meaning for that word.

MOSES: Very few are that wise. They'd believe any lie was told before they'd believe theirself. Can't you take a bit more, man? *(To MICHAEL, friendly, understanding.)*

MIN: Right and wrong—them two words I am hearing come and go this ten year.

MOSES: *(Talking to pass off her bad feeling.)* Well, there is a kind of comfort about the word "right"—like wrapping a blanket around you. Wouldn't you think? *(To MICHAEL.)*

MICHAEL: Maybe. *(Gruff: turns away and goes to the door.)*

MIN: An excuse for not thinking—"right"—that's all.

MOSES: Oh, a real comfit-ble word... when you'd have "right an' jooty" around you, you could put out your tongue at who you'd like. Them are the two big drums to drowned all. *(Then quickly, as MIN is about to speak:)* He is too tired for this now. *(A low tone.)*

MIN: And is meself rested? I wouldn't mind if he'd do what I want! He had a right to go into the town and get work.

MOSES: He couldn't live in the town, no more than a fish.

MIN: And so meself must die!

MOSES: You will not: you've too much sense! Very few would be as gentle as Mick.

MIN: Great good was his gentleness and the world hard! He had a right to get on like another.

MOSES: Yah—he had a right to be like himself and like another! He had a right to outdo the sun in the heaven, and be in the east and the west at the one time.

MIN: I'm not asking he'd outdo the sun, but only his neighbour! What good is any man if he don't outdo who's living beside of him? *(Then as MICHAEL comes back from the door, for his benefit:)* All I'd ask that he wouldn't stand in me light, with his long shadow ever spreading before me—

(MICHAEL catches her, and before she knows what is happening has her almost inside the small door. He does this, not angrily, but with a quick decision that surprises MOSES even more than MIN.)

MIN: Mick! Don't take it! *(The money. Her eyes go to the hole in the wall.)* Don't take it away! Mick! *(Clinging to him.)* Don't give it to Father O'Brien!

MOSES: *(Very quietly.)* Father O'Brien is ten mile away, and will until tomorrow.

(MICHAEL succeeds in disengaging himself and pushes MIN in, then bolts the door.)

MICHAEL: *(Turning to MOSES.)* Is that so? Father O'Brien being away?

MOSES: If she'd like that she might as well believe it.

MICHAEL: Is it so I'm asking?

MOSES: It is as like to be true as not: he was going to the out-parish.

MICHAEL: I'll go down and find out. *(Pulls out the stone, takes the packet from the hole in the wall, looks at MOSES.)* It is this has herself upset.

MOSES: That so?

(No anxiety to hear more. MICHAEL, relieved, slips the packet into his hip pocket.)

MICHAEL: Would you stop here awhile? I wouldn't be long.

MOSES: I will to be sure.

MICHAEL: Not to leave the place and she shut in be herself. *(Wanting to make the place more comfortable for MOSES, he takes an old board that is resting against the wall, and fixes this in the great low window gap. The board does not cover the top part of the gap.)*

MOSES: When you're a while gone, you won't hear her, so I might open the door?

MICHAEL: Do not!

MOSES: Only if she'd have eased her mind to a third party, she'd be the better to live with before you'd come back.

MICHAEL: Can I count you won't open that until I come?

MOSES: You can.

(MICHAEL goes out. MOSES bends over the fire; he is sorry for MICHAEL and MIN. His face is drawn and troubled. MIN bangs angrily on the door. When she stops, MOSES whistles—a long low whistle, for company. She bangs again. There is silence. MOSES stares into the fire, thinking. After a moment a step is heard from outside. A girl comes to the window gap—her head and shoulders showing above the board. This is LIZZIE BRENNAN, eighteen years of age.)

LIZZIE: *(Eagerly.)* Moses! *(When he does not answer, raises her voice a little.)* Moses!

MOSES: *(Without moving.)* So you followed me up...you little devil!

LIZZIE: If I climbs up here, will you lift me in?

MOSES: I will not, you'd be too heavy! Come round and come in.

(LIZZIE disappears, and the next moment comes in through the doorway. She is a placid little thing, better clothed and better fed than any of the others. Now she looks all round, eagerly curious.)

LIZZIE: Michael Donovan has settled the place great. They are better off than below. Are they pleased?

MOSES: *(Sardonic.)* Oh, mighty pleased.

LIZZIE: It is grand for the two of them up here, isn't it?

MOSES: Tremendous grand!

LIZZIE: *(Seeing the tin that the food has been in.)* So it was to them you brought it! And I'll be bound Min Donovan had your share with her own.

MOSES: She had not.

LIZZIE: If you would eat a bit more! *(Goes over and kneels down beside him.)* Moses, when will you leave us get married?

MOSES: What would we do that for?

LIZZIE: Oh, gwan now. If you and me was living in a place like this!

MOSES: A grand place surely!

LIZZIE: Good enough for me if there were the two of us... Moses, I'm tired with the wishing...it is long now...

MOSES: Aren't we bad enough, don't you think, without worse?

LIZZIE: How would we be worse? It is only yourself is hindering us.

MOSES: *(Decisive.)* There is no way for us to marry. A man would get married must have money or work. What am I living on but the food you brings out?

LIZZIE: I was thinking how well they managed in the long past...we could too...

MOSES: How was that?

LIZZIE: When there was no one giving work, and none looking for it neither...only to shoot the birds in the air and catch the fish... We could...

MOSES: Yah—by hurling stones at the birds we'd live.

LIZZIE: We'd live the same as they did long ago in the open, just gathering whatever green things we could eat. Moses, I was planning, in me mind, how we could put a bit of a shelter, you and me, and agen the Winter was on us we could add to it...a bit here and there so's 'twould hold out with the wind and the rain. It is what I'd like, you and me up in some place like here...

MOSES: Like the birds nesting, in the treetops, and the foxes too!

LIZZIE: I would ask no better...if you would like it...we could be grand and happy.

MOSES: Perfect happy—like in Pariedice long back.

LIZZIE: *(A little shaken.)* I don't know, Moses, what you feels, but it would be heaven to me to be keeping the place and you out the day getting food, and to be cooking when you'd come.

MOSES: How cooking when you'd have no fire?

LIZZIE: A few dry sticks would make a fire good enough. And then to be together out on the hill or inside...you and me together, always, through the long Winter, and the Summer too... *(Watches his downcast face; he shakes his head.)* Wouldn't it be as good as in your mother's house, and she whining ever, and your sister's childer crowded one on another... Wouldn't it be as good, Moses? You and me together through the long evenings and...and always...

MOSES: And when the child would come—with you in want?

LIZZIE: What matter? I wouldn't mind! I wouldn't complain ever. It is what I would like beyond all.

(Again she watches, hoping. MIN bangs angrily on the door.)

MOSES: Min Donovan—to shut her inside he did in a row came between them. *(Stands up.)*

LIZZIE: *(Determined not to be interrupted.)* Moses!

MOSES: No! We're not the birds, Liz, nor the squirrels neither. *(Goes to the door, knocks on it, and calls.)* Right you are! Wait now till he come! *(Looks then towards the open doorway, and turning to LIZZIE says in a tone of despair.)* Here is me mother!

LIZZIE: *(Angrily.)* I wouldn't doubt but she'd come! *(Draws back partly behind the door.)*

(DAISY BARRON is seen in the doorway. She is a big, floppy, untidy woman, fifty-five or so.)

DAISY: *(At the door wailing.)* Poor Michael and Min! I came running to you. A terrible affliction. Nothing left to you now, only God's comfort! A bad way to be!

MOSES: Can't you see they're not in it?

DAISY: *(Coming in.)* I done me best. I tried to do me best. *(Excessively humble, looks at MOSES, and changes to an aggrieved tone.)* You were ever the bad son to me...coming here, outrunning your mother, and knowing how she like to be the first into the house of sorrow always!

MOSES: I dunno how would we pass the time if we hadn't the sorrowing to do.

DAISY: I couldn't please you! I couldn't. Whatever I'd do, it would be wrong. *(Then with curiosity.)* What are they at? *(Looks about, sees LIZZIE.)* Ah! Ah-a! Ah-a!!! *(Deeply antagonistic.)* Something was telling me, something was warning me...wherever you'd be, she wouldn't be more than a few yards away.

LIZZIE: I'll give good evening to you, Mrs. Barron.

DAISY: And a bad evening when you'd find yer neighbour thrun out, and yer only son running his head into a noose-trap was set for him. *(MOSES signs to LIZZIE to sit down.)* Moses, there is many a man is sorry he ever told a woman to sit down. *(MICHAEL is seen in the doorway. She turns to him, raising her hands and wailing.)* Poor Michael Donovan! Here's the sorrow of me heart for you! The first minute I could manage I came puffing up with it!

MICHAEL: I am grateful to you, Mrs. Barron, very grateful.

LIZZIE: *(A little shyly.)* I came too.

DAISY: *(In a low tone.)* And for why?

MICHAEL: *(Crossing to the fire.)* You need to be in trouble to know how good they are that are round you. Sit down, let you all, if you can find where.

LIZZIE: Moses and me'll do here. *(Makes room for MOSES beside her, then looks defiantly at DAISY.)*

DAISY: *(Looking towards the doorway.)* Will you look! Will you look! Maggie Cooney putting her best foot foremost!

(All, except MICHAEL, look out. MICHAEL takes advantage of this to open the small door in the wall, very quietly. MAGGIE COONEY, MICHAEL's sister, comes in. MAGGIE is about fifty, wears a good dark shawl, and is very neatly dressed, in her best. But she has not taken off the old bootlace which has been round her neck for years and which does duty as chain for a small crucifix. In moments of excitement or distress, MAGGIE fingers this crucifix lovingly.)

MAGGIE: *(To MICHAEL, with indignation.)* The one father we had! And I minded you often... *(Checking herself, turns to the others.)* God save all here.

DAISY: God help the lot of us!

MAGGIE: It is bad and plenty to have your brother evicted, but to have to walk ten mile to say you're sittin' be the fire! What was on you, that you didn't bring yourself and Min over to me?

MICHAEL: *(Grateful.)* I remembered you, Maggie. I remembered your house. *(Going over to her.)*

MAGGIE: That needn't have kept you from coming! Himself is gone out of it this long while, and I have great peace in it entirely.

DAISY: We knows where himself is! *(An audible whisper to MOSES, who signs to her to keep quiet.)*

MAGGIE: I have the place to myself now save for ten of the childer…for the three girls are in service, and the boys in the States…so there'll be no pinch at all. Let you come on now. Where is Min?

DAISY: That is what I'm wondering too!

MICHAEL: She is inside.

MOSES: She is wore out.

MAGGIE: Wore out! What good will that do? And tomorrow drawing on her, and on the lot of us. *(Then to MICHAEL.)* Rouse her up now, and come.

MICHAEL: Thank you, Maggie, but myself and Min will stop here till…till—

MIN: *(Who glides into the room again.)* Till he makes our fame and fortune! Till the world will be forgot, you may say!

DAISY: *(With a wail, rising.)* Poor Min Donovan! You're in deep sorrow this day!

MOSES: She knows that—you needn't be telling her. *(Takes his mother by the shoulder and makes her sit down.)*

DAISY: I couldn't please you, Moses! *(Miserably.)*

MAGGIE: *(To MIN.)* And how is it with you?

MIN: *(In a toneless voice.)* I am not in my right mind with the way he ill-treated me.

(General surprise.)

MAGGIE: And so my father isn't dead yet for all the praying you done! *(Then to MIN.)* That was his father, so you must only put up with it.

LIZZIE: *(Who has had a word with MOSES.)* Moses says 'tis a lie she's talking!

DAISY: Hold your tongue till we hear is there a terrible hidden suffering in this. *(Eagerly curious.)*

MOSES: *(Gets up, turns to his mother.)* Get up! We're clearing. *(Quiet, angry.)*

MICHAEL: Stay where you are, Moses.

MOSES: *(Angrily to LIZZIE.)* What do you want here? Only staring at Min?

LIZZIE: *(Timid.)* I wasn't, Moses. I bare turned me eyes on her. It is at you I was looking all the time.

MICHAEL: Sit down. Sit down.

DAISY: Sure, we couldn't go till we'd give the sorrow and sympathy of our heart to her.

MAGGIE: Sorrow and sympathy is what rooned the world.

DAISY: Whatever I'd say, they'd say it was wrong! *(Miserably.)*

MAGGIE: But it is better for the woman to have a lot listening, for when one wouldn't believe her, maybe another would.

MIN: Oh, I'm telling a lie! *(Bitterly.)* What I'll say won't hold against him; he's good!

MAGGIE: He would be better to be like another.

MIN: *(Fiercely.)* Will you tell me is it a right goodness that'll take the sap from a man and the strong purpose, and leave him like a ball of putty rolling around and thinkin' of God?

MOSES: *(In a low voice to his mother.)* If there was a decent feel in us, we'd leave the place to them are related together. *(When she will not move, he turns to MIN, quiet, deliberate.)* Michael did no rolling. If ever a man worked, it was Michael.

MIN: And that is the worst part, for if he didn't work, I'd have right on my side! He'd work till he'd drop! Like the old mare pulling the plough till her legs would give way!

MAGGIE: *(To MICHAEL.)* True for her—you had a right to keep more jaunty like, and lookin' round you—

DAISY: It may be the man tried to do his best—

MAGGIE: We can't be counting the trys now, only the wins.

DAISY: *(Whining, persistently.)* But when a body tries to do their best! *(Then, answering a look from MOSES.)* I'm siding with you... I'm trying...

MAGGIE: *(To MICHAEL.)* Look the way my father got on—

MICHAEL: I didn't like his way, Maggie.

MIN: Only what he'll like he'll do. See how he'd stick in the field.

MICHAEL: I took me choice. I don't regret it; there is something a man must follow. *(Turns to MAGGIE.)* The time I took me choice was that time there was the great talk here of making money. I was a young lad—there was factories being opened up in Dublin, and all the talk in the night, and at the crossroads would be who was going up, and how much would he be making in a week. A handful went from round-about here—

MIN: I never heard this.

MICHAEL: And before they were very long gone, I was in Dublin for a day. I met the fellows went up from here, I seen the life they were having. I came home, and looked round. —"What are they tearing and straining for? What have they in the end but what is in theirself? An' I have that myself here." It is the spirit of God I knew was in me, and I knew it for stronger in a life after me heart.

MIN: When he'd start talking of God, you might go to bed. *(Then fiercely.)* Will you tell me is it a right thing—talking of God to a miserable woman, and you not trying to lift the misery is on her?

MAGGIE: *(After a silence.)* Michael, think what you'll do now, and without more delay.

DAISY: The only thing to do now is to think of them is worse off!

MAGGIE: I'll say the gospel of St. John for the Light of the World to help us now. *(She turns aside, half screening her face: her manner is simple, intimate.)*

DAISY: *(To MIN, who takes no notice of her.)* Some suffers terrible; often I comforts meself with that thought: there was poor Mollie Power—a real handsome girl, and believed life was good, and to look at her now! But, sure, she isn't as bad off as Julia Doyle had the raving madness—screeching with torture: every night I would go up around the hill till I could hear her, and every night I would say to meself, "It is getting worse." An' I waiting to know what would be the end, but you couldn't believe as bad as what happened—

MOSES: You have enough said!

DAISY: I won't open me mouth again! *(Then seeing that LIZZIE is giggling, adds vindictively:)* But 'tis hard for a mother to sit silent seeing her only son consorting together with what is no better than poison for him—

LIZZIE: Is that to be said of me? *(To MOSES, who sighs.)* Is it? *(He shrugs his shoulders.)* Is it?

MOSES: *(Reluctantly, to his mother.)* If you'd swallow what you think might sweeten it next time.

DAISY: *(Bursting into tears.)* I would be better not to be born! For then I needn't mind when me own son would be turning against me! But, sure, the world is a place only for weeping. *(More tears.)*

MOSES: A great watering ground surely.

DAISY: That is what me old mother used say—"Let ye weep now, and sorrow all ye can, so's to have the heart for rejoicing in the life to come." *(Again LIZZIE giggles.)* I will have a laugh for every tear was squeezed out of me. *(Angrily.)*

MAGGIE: *(Disturbed at her devotions, turns to LIZZIE.)* And this is Lizzie...Lizzie...?

LIZZIE: Brennan, ma'am.

DAISY: That is working tooth and nail to make it Barron!

LIZZIE: *(Springing up.)* Am I to sit here and be insulted? Am I?

MOSES: Well, I was for going on before.

LIZZIE: *(To DAISY.)* I'll say this to you now—if there was any other man at all would look at me, I wouldn't dream any more nights of Moses Barron.

MIN: *(Addressing the room in general.)* I was thinking just now, could I walk to Belfast...by begging me bread. *(Toneless. Staring straight before her.)*

MICHAEL: *(After an awkward silence, broken by MAGGIE's cough.)* You might.

MIN: On the streets of Belfast there should be a living for a woman like myself, and it a powerful rich city.

MICHAEL: *(After a moment.)* The road is before you—

DAISY: *(Turns to go.)* But look where you'll go! If I were to get under the heel of the riches that would be a bad thing. *(Turns towards the door.)* Will you look! Look!

(All, except MIN, look out.)

LIZZIE: Who is that, Moses? Who?

DAISY: *(Nudges LIZZIE, glances towards MAGGIE, and says in a mysterious tone.)* He is a man is after serving a sentence in jail...Maggie Cooney's husband...the poor woman...

MICHAEL: Maggie, it is Ned...your Ned! *(Concerned.)*

MAGGIE: How could that be? It is surely. *(Troubled.)*

DAISY: *(To LIZZIE.)* Ned Cooney...wait till we'll see what way will he look and he only out of jail now. *(Forgets their enmity in her eager curiosity.)*

(MAGGIE's husband, NED COONEY, comes in. He is a burly, unhealthy looking man, slightly lame. He has a disagreeably would-be-pleasant manner which gives the impression of insincerity.)

MICHAEL: Well, Ned...come in. *(Not too friendly.)*

NED: A gathering together of friends and neighbours... *(Looking round at them all, rubbing his hands.)*

DAISY: Your poor wife, Maggie, is here. Come in till you'll see her.

NED: A friendly gathering, I see.

MAGGIE: *(With a brave attempt at dignity.)* I am surprised to see you, Ned. I am. *(Fingering her crucifix.)*

NED: *(Ignoring her, and smiling on the others.)* A nice thing to find your friends all around you.

MAGGIE: Maybe you were at the house after I leaving?

NED: *(Looking over at MIN.)* Paying a call of a visit on me friends I came here...

(But his eyes go to the empty hole in the wall. MOSES and MICHAEL follow his look, then their eyes meet for a moment.)

DAISY: They are in deep sorrow this day.

MICHAEL: We are without a bit to offer you.

NED: That don't matter...only for the pleasure of seeing yourself and Min. *(He crosses to where MIN has crouched down on a large stone, smiles down at her.)*

MAGGIE: The childer are all well beyond, Ned.

NED: Are they? *(Careless.)*

MAGGIE: The boys are doing well in the States.

NED: Are they?

MAGGIE: *(Her dignity breaking.)* I thought you had another week to give.

NED: *(Contemptuous.)* I am out of it this long while! There was a month took off for good behaviour.

DAISY: Did you ever!

NED: *(Bending down to MIN.)* It is long since I seen you.

MIN: I would give you welcome, Ned Cooney, had I a place of me own. I am nothing at all now but a woman sitting on the floor and *(Threateningly towards MICHAEL.)* planning what she'll do.

NED: How long are ye here?

MICHAEL: Since morning.

NED: Since morning...I see. *(His eyes are busy about the place.)* You have done a nice little job of housework on it.

LIZZIE: *(Who has been staring at NED.)* Did you ever read the *Evening Mail,* Mrs. Cooney, ma'am?

MAGGIE: I might. I wouldn't know...

LIZZIE: The *Evening Mail* is the paper does be sent to the kitchen when it is two days old. *(Eager.)*

DAISY: *(Angrily.)* Will you hear her? Giving out the *Evening Mail* for the wan and only purpose of showing up her education *(Warningly to MOSES.)* so's to knock over and swipe up any would be listening to her!

MOSES: Yah—she have no modesty—opening her mouth and men in the place.

LIZZIE: Moses, I have something to tell you about the *Evening Mail.*

MOSES: Well, I'm going now.

DAISY: *(Springs up and gets between MOSES and LIZZIE .)* So am I.

MOSES: *(To LIZZIE.)* Keep your story for another time.

LIZZIE: That would be too late. I'll do it meself. Good evening, ma'am. *(To MIN, who takes no notice. Goes out.)*

MAGGIE: We'd all want to be moving. I have ten miles before me.

DAISY: Would you stop the night with me? I suppose you would not?

MAGGIE: I would be glad. And maybe *(To MICHAEL.)* tomorrow you'll know more what you'll do. Thank you kindly, Daisy Barron.

DAISY: *(Grandly.)* Let you all come now, come down with me yourself *(To MIN.)* and you *(To NED.)* and all...

MIN: *(Getting up.)* I'm not going anywhere, and I'm not stopping here either. *(Pulls her shawl about her.)* But a stroll for meself while I'm thinking. *(Goes out.)*

MICHAEL: *(To DAISY.)* I must finish this while I have the light. *(The door.)* I'll see you later below. *(Goes to the window gap and takes down the board.)*

(DAISY and MOSES go out. NED follows slowly; at the doorway he hesitates, watching MICHAEL.)

NED: *(At the doorway.)* Good evening, Michael.

MICHAEL: *(Coolly.)* Good evening... *(Then more friendly.)* I'll be down. I won't be long.

MAGGIE: Mick, I couldn't say it and they here—you must go to the States. There is no other way you'll get on. The boys sent this. *(Holds out a purse to him.)* Take it. Don't be saying no! *(For he draws back.)* They sent it for Jerry to go out. Jerry is too young yet; I wouldn't have it.

MICHAEL: Keep the money so.

MAGGIE: What good is keeping? Take it, and have sense. I'll have no need of it. The boys are real good; they have no thought in their mind but to be mailing back money as fast as they make it.

MICHAEL: So you think I'd take what they saved?

MAGGIE: What else can you do?

(MICHAEL shakes his head, turns from her. A moment's silence.)

MICHAEL: *(Bitterly.)* I was right... I know what I prize. And yet she is right. And how can that be?

MAGGIE: Min? If she is right a self, it isn't a right time she'd take for talking against you. *(Indignant, affectionate.)* But you were never right, Mick, from the time you were a boy.

MICHAEL: I am right...but it must be I made some mistake to turn her against me...

MAGGIE: What matter about her, and she your wife! But *(With reproach.)* to turn the world against yourself and not stand up to it!

MICHAEL: A mistake...somewhere... It must be you could put all the great sayings in agreement...

MAGGIE: No good in that now—take this. *(The money.)*

MICHAEL: *(Suddenly decisive.)* I'll go to the States—let them look out for me so...and see can they get work I could do.

MAGGIE: That is good sense.

MICHAEL: I have money will take me.

MAGGIE: You have? Money?

MICHAEL: I have a little. I wasn't talking of it.

MAGGIE: Well, that's not like you! But, sure, it is grand. You were planning to go, were you, Mick?

MICHAEL: I was. *(A pause.)* There is a lot of truth in what she'd say... I'll go at once—before I'll sleep tonight I'll see Jim Slattery; he'd settle all quiet for me.

MAGGIE: He would. *(Slowly, disappointed that she cannot help.)* He settled the boys going... It will be a hard life for you, Mick, that had the fields ever in your heart. No matter, maybe you will get on and have Min go out to you before very long.

MICHAEL: Before very long! She will come with me.

MAGGIE: *(Astonished.)* Have you what will take the two of you?

MICHAEL: I have.

(A silence.)

MAGGIE: *(When she has waited for information.)* I wouldn't have thought it.

But, sure, that is good, Michael... Min is that queer now it might be she wouldn't go with you.

MICHAEL: Then she would be made to. Do you think I could live without her?

(They hear a movement outside.)

MAGGIE: I think it is Ned.

MICHAEL: With him out of gaol now, you'll have more trouble.

MAGGIE: No use thinking of that. Yourself we must think of, and how you'll get on.

MICHAEL: I'll go down with you now. I must see Jim Slattery.

(They go out. NED COONEY steps in over the low wall at the window gap. He looks all round, then drags a large stone to the wall, just beneath the empty hole, stands on this, and is searching the hole when MIN appears at the gap. She watches him, amazed.)

NED: *(Muttering.)* Gone! Nabbed! *(Turns, sees MIN. They stare at each other for a moment in silence.)*

MIN: It was you! You put it there!

NED: *(Springing at her.)* Where is it? *(Catching her.)* Where have you it put?

MIN: He took it! Michael did! Wouldn't give me any.

NED: *(Turning to go.)* He won't have it long!

MIN: No good! Father O'Brien have it now!

NED: What?

MIN: If Father O'Brien is away, it might be on Michael yet.

NED: We'll see is it.

MIN: Keeping it safe for the priest he is! *(Angrily.)*

NED: Not as safe as he'd think! Where is he gone?

MIN: Wait a minute—

NED: Do you think I'm going to let that money slip?

MIN: No good rising a noise...and the lot of them below...Moses Barron and Jim Slattery and all. If we could get it quiet, though...

NED: *(Drawing up to her.)* So, will we wait here till he'll come up?

MIN: If he'd shout, they'd be up here in a minute...but I was thinking...

NED: Well? What? What? *(Very close to her.)*

MIN: *(Drawing away, antagonistic.)* And so it is you put it there! I dunno where did you get it?

NED: Mind your business!

MIN: *(With a laugh.)* I wouldn't care if it was from the Post Office aself! Now, the best time to get it would be and he asleep...

NED: Ah-a! *(Approving.)*

MIN: *(Antagonistic.)* And only myself could do that.

NED: But if he'd wake, you might be worse off than before...save I was waiting around to help when you'd want.

MIN: I am making no plans, Ned Cooney!

NED: *(Mincing.)* You are not! 'Tis I am planning...planning what we'd share...and how you could hide it away and tell Mick I took all. Ned Cooney is hunted already...you could say what you'd like.

MIN: Are you going now?

NED: *(Moving towards the door.)* Oh, I'm going, but I'll be back later. *(Comes back to her again.)* Take yer choice. I think you have sense—are you going to stop as you are for the rest of your life? I won't be far from that window outside when Mick'll have settled. He was ever great for going to bed with the birds. Then you could find if he had it.

MIN: I'm making no promise!

NED: I'm not asking you to—but we could manage it easy. *(Watches her for a moment.)* I'll be back later. *(Goes out.)*

(MIN stands there motionless, thinking.)

(Curtain.)

ACT II

A few hours later. Part of the interior of the ruin is flooded by moonlight, which comes through the half-open door, and the window gap: part is in shadow, and part lit by the lantern MICHAEL has fixed above the fireplace.

MICHAEL sits by the flickering fire which he has kindled in the big fireplace. With him is JIM SLATTERY. JIM, whose clothes show him to be a comfortably well-off countryman, is about fifty-five, thin and dark, with an air of brooding intensity. As he sits now, staring into the fire, one feels that he has sat long in silence. MICHAEL is restless, unlike himself. He changes his position, looks at JIM, then away from him—moves uneasily: very obviously anxious that silence should be broken.

JIM: Herself don't know?

MICHAEL: Not yet. I wanted this talk with you first. I said to Maggie, "I'll settle all with Jim Slattery."

JIM: It's what she'll like, I suppose? Going off to America?— The two of you? Some have a great wish—

MICHAEL: They have. *(Low tone, then.)* The reason I didn't tell yet was—

JIM: All I asked—did she know, in case she'll come up?

MICHAEL: I'll tell her now. I wanted it settled first.

JIM: You've no wish there'd be talk.

MICHAEL: That is it. I have not.

JIM: You'll want clothes before you'll go, an' she'll want more. Have you money for that?

MICHAEL: I have. How I have so much is that—

JIM: All I asked—had you the money? Since you have and want to get away quiet, it'd be best the two of you'd set out, like looking for work, till you'd reach Cork City. There you could move around and get what you'd want.

MICHAEL: Would it be long till we could be off?

JIM: Wait till I give you the name of a man to go to in Cork. *(Rises, takes papers from his pocket and goes through them.)* I haven't it. Well, I'll see you tomorrow. *(Moves as though to go, then hesitates.)* You heard talk of the raid on Coolbary Post Office?

MICHAEL: Moses Barron was here and said something about it.

JIM: There will be a lot more said about it... So Ned Cooney was here this evening?

MICHAEL: He was.

(Another silence. Both look into the fire. NED is seen for an instant at the window gap. He peers in and, having discovered who is there, withdraws.)

JIM: Is it below at Kirwan's she is?

MICHAEL: Min? Most like it is at Kirwan's. I am not sure.

JIM: It would be well she'd come now.

MICHAEL: *(Surprised.)* It is early in the night yet.

JIM: She won't mind coming the path by herself?

MICHAEL: What would she mind? It is early, and she'll have the moon, and Kirwan's but a stone's throw.

JIM: Tomorrow then. *(He is going towards the door when it is pushed open, and MIN comes in. After a swift surprised look at JIM, she goes to the side of the room away from the fire.)* Goodnight, ma'am.

MIN: 'Night. *(Scarcely audible.)*

MICHAEL: *(To JIM.)* You'll have that name for me tomorrow so?

JIM: I will. *(Crosses the room to where MIN is.)* Someone was saying below now "it is right the women should suffer the most; they are the cause of all trouble." I think it was true for him.

(They look at each other for a moment.)

MIN: I wouldn't understand you, Jim Slattery. I was never took up with thought reading.

JIM: *(Going out, turns to MICHAEL.)* So long!

MICHAEL: So long! *(Watches MIN, who goes to the fire and sits down.)* Maybe you're guessing what brought him up? *(Eagerly, as one who has something to tell.)*

MIN: *(To the fire.)* Look at Nelson had the blind eye.

MICHAEL: What?

MIN: Blind when he'd like... And that other chap who used to be composing the music under his desk. They'd have thrown him out did they know.

MICHAEL: What matter? Jim came now because—

MIN: Moving the world the two of them are for the reason they made up their minds one day.

MICHAEL: Are you going to listen to me?

MIN: Who'd care were they born had they kept to the law?

MICHAEL: I said—are you going to listen?

MIN: Who'd believe them right and they taking the risk? Right enough when you'd win! It must be they settled it in their private mind for if they'd ask any—"Oh, that would be wrong."

MICHAEL: Well, you can go without hearing! *(Bitterly.)*

MIN: It must be they said—like meself—"the law is right enough, but I sees beyond it." Keeping the law has the world full of cripples: no other thing. It is that ruins every man's life.

MICHAEL: You are not worth raising a finger for.

MIN: *(Roused.)* I was a beautiful young thing before I was married!

MICHAEL: You were right enough to look at—

MIN: Like a young deer I was...or a fawn...stepping out beautiful across the world, and yourself coming over the field like...like...oh, like what you are. But, sure, I was blind.

MICHAEL: *(Half to himself.)* I doubt would you be better off no matter what I'd do.

MIN: What was on me that I couldn't see then? Or is it I was marked down for misfortune? Coming up now, I was asking meself, "Is it you, Min Donovan, was that young girl would think when she'd wake, 'Maybe I'll meet him going to work?' Is it you would spend the whole of the day in hoping you'd meet him on the road home?" I dunno are there many as mad as I was?

MICHAEL: *(Gently.)* Look now, I was thinking after all—

MIN: If he had to go off then with another, no great harm; I could be squeezing that wrong to meself this minute, but to get what you'd want, and find it—like that!

MICHAEL: Min, when I kept that money from you, it was because I thought first—

MIN: I don't mind what you thought: you are no more to me than the wall there, and less feeling in you when you'd like...

MICHAEL: Is that the way now? *(Coaxing.)*

MIN: To take what was mine be right of findin'—

MICHAEL: It was I found it!

MIN: *(Bitterly.)* Shut in! And knowing what would make new life was being took from me reach! It was then I knew I was be myself only, and you separate by miles from me!

MICHAEL: We'll see am I now. *(Moving closer to her, affectionately.)*

MIN: *(Moving away.)* His arm around me! Sure, that is all his wife is for! What more should she want?

MICHAEL: If you'd be better humoured, I could tell—

MIN: He'd like I'd smile! He'd like the sun shining on him...when he'd have done what he'd want!

MICHAEL: *(After a moment.)* Looking at you now, I'd near change me mind.

MIN: What need he do ever—only take what he'd like, and then come back and give me a kiss...so's to do away with the cold?

MICHAEL: I gave you ever more than you'd deserve.

(They look at each other for a moment with growing anger.)

MIN: If I had the knife in my hand, I'd near stick it in you now—the only thing you could feel!

MICHAEL: It would be well for me I never gave you the feeling I did!

MIN: Great feeling!

MICHAEL: And better you didn't anger me now—mind that!

MIN: Here is the measure of what you'll feel—where did you put that money?

MICHAEL: I'll tell you what I like, and when I like, and as much as I like!

MIN: Is it the priest below has it?

MICHAEL: He might.

MIN: Ha! He don't need the sun just now!

MICHAEL: What's that? *(Catching her.)* What did you say? *(Threatening.)*

MIN: *(Frightened.)* There is a change coming on you, Michael Donovan, and I think it is not for the better.

MICHAEL: *(Softening again.)* Tired out you are: myself too. We'll go to bed. *(Turns aside, goes to the corner, and unrolls the mattress, spreads part of a blanket and a quilt on it. MIN watches him for a moment, then turns to the fire.)*

MIN: What size boot need Nelson want—beyond medium—if he wouldn't step out?

MICHAEL: Moses didn't bring up the blanket like he said he would.

MIN: So we're taking more from Moses, are we? Sure, 'twas meant we would. *(Mocking.)* "Min, it must be that it was meant." Ha!

(MICHAEL fixes the shutter high up on the window gap, then goes to the door to settle it. MIN goes to the window gap and takes down the shutter.)

MICHAEL: What are you doing?

MIN: That way I likes it.

MICHAEL: We're not leaving it open all night.

MIN: We'll want the air: a terrible close night.

(MICHAEL puts the shutter up again, though not so high as he had put it first, then turns to attend to the lantern. MIN moves over near the window gap.)

MICHAEL: *(Blazing.)* If you touch that, you'll be sorry for it!

MIN: He's real fond of me! *(Goes back to the fire.)*

(MICHAEL takes off his boots and coat. As he does this, NED is seen at the window gap, just his head and shoulders showing, but neither MICHAEL nor MIN sees him. After an instant he disappears.)

MICHAEL: Don't stop there too long. I think you didn't shut an eye last night at all.

MIN: I'm stopping by the fire.

MICHAEL: Are you. So will I pull this over then? *(The mattress.)*

MIN: I'm hoping you'll keep the length is between us! *(MICHAEL kneels down beside the mattress, makes the sign of the cross, tries to pray. Again NED appears at the window gap, but is driven away by a frantic sign from MIN. Going over to MICHAEL, nervously, having been upset by the sight of NED:)* Michael... before you'll lie down... the... the money... is there any use asking...?

MICHAEL: There is not! *(Throws himself down on the mattress. She goes back to her place, sits down, leans over the fire, her head in her hands. MICHAEL gets up, takes the quilt and brings it over to MIN.)* There. Though you would be better to come over. *(Stands watching her for a moment.)* Rest all you can, tomorrow'll be better.

MIN: *(Her head turned away.)* Are you going to bed now?

MICHAEL: Min, we are on the start of new life—

MIN: New life? *(Looks at him, interested, half hopeful. Then, as he moves nearer wanting some sign of affection, she turns away impatiently.)* You'd think we were new married, the way you're going on in place of the fact of staring at each other for ten years without a break! And no good done by that! Maybe, though, it was meant! Meant! *(A sound outside. MICHAEL goes back, lies down again. After a moment there is a sound again. MIN listens anxiously, glancing towards MICHAEL. Then, very quietly, she gets up, takes the rope that has been thrown aside off the mattress, stands in the middle of the room, rope in hand, listening. Another movement outside. Whispering, next to the window, frightened:)* Go away, for God's sake! He's only bare lying down! *(Then, closer to the window, in altered tone.)* Oh, Moses Barron, is that yourself?

MOSES: It is the bit of a blanket I said I'd bring up.

MIN: Wait and I'll take down the window. *(Takes away the board.)*

MOSES: We have no use for it below. *(Comes in, gives the blanket to her.)*

MIN: I don't know why you'd trouble yourself. *(Softened. Pause.)* Do you think can God help it?

MOSES: Help it? *(Gesture meaning "all this?" MIN nods.)* Couldn't He put a stop to it all? Only to raise His hand if He'd like.

MIN: He could I suppose.

MOSES: It must be there's more for than against for it to go on…like at the roulette…when one loses, that's win for another.

MIN: Will you help I won't lose? *(Low, passionate.)* Will you? If I am to have life ever, I must do something now. Will you? *(Silence.)*

NED: *(From outside.)* Min, what are you waiting for? Is he asleep?

MOSES: Who was that?

MIN: I dunno. *(Sullen.)*

MOSES: If it's against Michael you're asking my help, you can hold your breath.

MIN: How smart y'are! Who said Michael's name? Oh, you're real clever, Moses Barron, you are—

MOSES: It's because I have a great wish for you I'd be sorry to see—

MIN: *(Fierce.)* I know ye all! Oh, ye'd wipe out the world with a soft word! Time you'd go home.

MOSES: I don't mind the time. I'll stay keep you company. You'd have a lonely feel here with Michael asleep.

MIN: No more lonely than when he's awake. I never mind being left to myself.

MOSES: *(Turning sharply to her.)* I gave you a fright now. You thought I was…someone…

MIN: No, I did not! I didn't think at all—why would I? It would be queer you didn't give me a fright moving round like…like…

MOSES: Like a thief in the night—that's what you're thinking.

MIN: Is it now? Are you sure? I can't abide a body that goes in for being clever!

MOSES: There are a lot of thieves going around now, did you know?

MIN: Did I know? What is in your mind, Moses Barron?

MOSES: Nothing…nothing at all. Did you see Ned Cooney this evening?

MIN: He was here with ye all, so I couldn't help but see him—whether I'd like or no, same as I'd see yourself now.

MOSES: He have a queer habit of—like—fixing his eye on the wall. Did you mind that? It was like that hole was a kind of magnet to his eye. *(Nods towards the empty hole.)*

MIN: *(After a moment.)* If there is something in your mind, 'twould be well you'd get rid of it. An' if there is not, I won't be keeping you now.

MOSES: Whisper a minute—I wouldn't mind guessing Ned could tell the whereabouts of Coolbarry Post Office.

MIN: I was told long ago it is a sin to be rash-judging of your neighbours.

MOSES: We were told too much: it is a worse sin not to see what is before you… Did you hear a step now? Like someone moving quiet?

MIN: I did not. Who would be moving?

MOSES: Yah, indeed—who? Whisper again—a man robbed a Post Office wouldn't be very long making short work of a woman!

MIN: Trying to put fright on me and I without a right shelter this night.

MOSES: Fright might be the best shelter to put round you. Is that a rope you have there?

MIN: *(Furious.)* What else would you like to see, Moses Barron? If there's a thing I can't abide it is a man standing beside of me and thoughts going through his head!

MOSES: Talk quiet. You will rouse himself, and I think you don't want to.

MIN: It is no queer thing I'd have a rope, seeing it was Michael tied together the few odds we could save.

MOSES: Poor Michael. *(Looks down at MICHAEL.)* He is that done up; he looked tonight near as tired as that time he was after nursing you through the fever. Do you mind that time? For more than a month you were on the bed, and Michael near out of his sense with the fear of losing you. He wouldn't leave any do for you but himself: like the ghost of a man he was by the time you were well.

MIN: Maybe you are finished now, seeing me feet are cold for the want of the fire.

MOSES: Sure, we'll go near the fire, will we?

MIN: We will not! For I wouldn't trust you that far I'd throw.

MOSES: Why would you? 'Tis only them are honest in their heart would trust another. Will I go now, and leave him come?

MIN: Don't be too clever at all, let you—like the man put his finger where 'twasn't wanted, and is without it this day.

MOSES: Michael, I counts me friend: and—finger or no—I won't stop short but at what I believe best. You understand now what I'm saying? *(Turns to go.)*

MIN: *(Stopping him.)* Moses Barron, I think you have no kind eye for your old mother?

MOSES: *(Surprised.)* Me mother! Why would I? Amn't I living with her?

MIN: She is a dribbly kind of a woman. I couldn't abide her. Do you think would she be more attractive—like had she fifty pound a month?

MOSES: She might. *(Doubtfully.)*

MIN: She would. Do you think would she be kind of less mean in her mind?

MOSES: I wouldn't say that.

MIN: I would. It is the poverty done it—the wear and the drib. Go home now, and don't think to come between me and what I'll do.

(MOSES goes out, stepping over the low wall of the window gap. Outside he turns again and looks at MIN.)

MOSES: *(After a silence.)* Michael is the one man will put you before himself ever.

MIN: Great good I got from wherever he'd put me!

MOSES: He gave the strength of his heart to you, don't forget.

MIN: *(After a moment's thought.)* He did not—but to God he gave it—and not to Him either, or He'd have done something. He gave the whole of his heart to what he'd be dreaming out there on the hill that I don't know.

MOSES: Goodnight, Min. Don't forget. *(Moving off.)*

MIN: Moses! Maybe you'd give me a hand up with this! *(They put up the board.)* Not the whole way up. I'll want the air.

MOSES: *(When they have fixed it.)* It will be easy took down again if you'll want...the undoing of a thing is ever easy.

MIN: What would I want?

MOSES: Oh—maybe...more air!

(When he has gone, MIN goes over near MICHAEL, and looks down at him, then nervously all about the room. Finally she kneels down and passes her hand very lightly over MICHAEL's body, feeling for the money. He moves. She draws back, gets up. MICHAEL turns over and, throwing down the covering, puts his hand back to his hip pocket.)

MIN: *(When she has seen that his pocket is bulky.)* A safe place...so's I couldn't cut it off. *(Angrily, in an undertone.)* You'd sleep better without it.

LIZZIE: *(Appearing at the window.)* Min, did you see Moses?

MIN: Lizzie Brennan! A queer time you'd come!

LIZZIE: I wouldn't, but they said Moses was coming up here.

MIN: Oh, did they? Well, himself said he was coming down.

LIZZIE: Down! Have I missed of him so?

MIN: Run, let you, quick!

LIZZIE: Ah, don't be going on at me! Was he here?

MIN: He was, and is gone.

LIZZIE: Gone!—Inside to his mother. I won't see him till morning... There is something particular I was wanting to tell him.

MIN: There will tomorrow too!

LIZZIE: It is about Ned Cooney it is...

MIN: Ned Cooney?

LIZZIE: I wouldn't like that man. I think there is few would like him.

(Pause.)

MIN: And you want to know do Moses!

LIZZIE: I dunno how Maggie would marry him, no matter what he'd look twenty years back.

MIN: *(Groaning.)* Am I to stop listening to this all the night?

LIZZIE: *(Quickly.)* Maybe you like him?

MIN: Why should I like him, Lizzie Brennan? What cause have I to like him or any man?

LIZZIE: I dunno would Maggie mind, supposing him to be took up again.

MIN: What would make her mind? Only a good riddance.

LIZZIE: *(Pleased.)* I was thinking that! I was right then...in what I done.

MIN: *(Furious.)* Right! Is there anyone will stop talking of "right." And it is a queer right surely, a young girl like you standing here be the window with Michael asleep and meself going to bed.

LIZZIE: *(Offended.)* I didn't look at him, Min Donovan. I wouldn't know he was in it only you said it. When I seen he was lying on the mattress, I kept my head turned.

MIN: Well, don't be gadding now.

LIZZIE: Only if Moses would come round again, and back.

MIN: I hope he will not. I had hard work to get rid of him.

LIZZIE: It is something I done... I would like to see what way would he take it. I'd like to know I am at one with Moses before I go to bed.

MIN: At one! If you're not at one with yourself, how can you with two?

LIZZIE: If I could only have a few words with him now—

MIN: At one! That is what have the whole world addled—trying to make one out of two! You might give it up!

LIZZIE: I could be easy and happy if he'd know.

(She moves off slowly, still looking round for MOSES. MIN goes back towards MICHAEL, and stands looking down at him.)

NED: *(At the window.)* Min, are you there?

MIN: Sh-h! *(At the window.)*

NED: Is he asleep?

MIN: He was sound, but he's moving now, and Moses Barron is about.

NED: That shrimp fellow. What matter is he? Is the money on Michael?

MIN: It is. *(A low tone.)*

NED: Have you a rope there?

MIN: I have. *(Looks miserably towards MICHAEL.)*

NED: It is plain before us so: take down the board.

MIN: *(Suddenly defiant.)* I dunno will I?

NED: *(Mincing.)* Oh, that is for yourself to say—whether you'll leave slip your chance now, and spend out the rest of your life regretting it.

MIN: Maybe I would, or would not…

NED: We've no time for stopping now: loose the board till I'll get in.

MIN: The sight of you there peering in at me!

NED: I have the cloth will cover his head; he won't know what part you took. Don't be delaying now. There'll be none to tell; you can make up what you'll like.

(He puts his hand on the board and leans in a little. The board slips down noisily. MIN jumps back, terrified. NED disappears, but MICHAEL only moves slightly.)

MIN: *(When NED appears again.)* What great hurry was on you?

NED: Someone put that board so's 'twould slip! Yourself was it? *(Is about to step over the low wall.)*

MIN: Put your leg over that, and I'll raise the dead!

NED: Easy now! I'm wanting to please you… I won't come in till you'll say…it wouldn't do we'd fall out…a loss to the both of us… He is dead asleep. It would be well we'd do it now.

MIN: I'm not siding against Mick this night!

NED: You are not! And it for his good!

MIN: And if I am itself not with the likes of you!

NED: *(Quietly.)* Michael haven't the courage to keep that money. He'd like well enough you'd have it for him later. "Here's for you, Mick," you'd say, an' he sighing for some, "here's what I saved."

MIN: I'll thank you to leave me use my own tongue!

NED: I can't wait longer. Will you help, or will I come in and take all?

MIN: See how far will you get! Only to raise my voice now, and you'd be in jail.

NED: And yourself? What's before you? To think what you'd gain had you the courage now!

MIN: How much would I gain?

NED: The half of what's there. We'll share and share alike... Honest we will.

MIN: Honest? What is your meaning for that word?

NED: Do you think I'm not honest? *(Thrusting his face close to her.)*

MIN: *(Drawing back.)* I wouldn't mind had you good eyes!

NED: This is Gobermint money, so there's no harm in taking it. All they'd have to do—sit down in Dublin Castle and stamp out more pound notes. If you'd take fifty, it wouldn't be but five minutes' trouble!

MIN: Do you think am I a child in arms? It isn't that would stop me, but yourself. *(Looking at him with distaste, then towards MICHAEL.)*

NED: Hurry, and it will be over...

(Goes to step over the wall, and in doing so touches the board. It topples over and falls noisily. NED disappears, and MIN draws back, frightened. MICHAEL starts up.)

MICHAEL: What? What's that? *(Jumps up and crosses over—then, very angrily.)* What did I tell you? What?

MIN: *(Trying to keep calm.)* Looking out I was.

MICHAEL: *(Takes the board, bangs it up, fastens it securely. Then turning to MIN again:)* Go over there! *(Jerks his head towards the fireplace.)*

MIN: Like as though I was an ould dog! *(Relieved that he has not looked out, and sure she can manage him now.)*

MICHAEL: Did you hear what I said?

(When she does not move, he strikes her. Then as she falls back a step or so, more surprised than hurt, he turns away, throws himself down on the mattress again, and pulls the covering right up.)

MIN: *(Having watched him for a moment, full of resentment, says in a low tone:)* Very well, Michael Donovan...very well. *(She now takes off her shawl, picks up the rope, makes a noose, waits for a moment, then goes to the boarded-up window, and whispers:)* Ned, are you there? I'll open the door. Go very quiet.

(Again she waits, looking in MICHAEL's direction. Then goes to the door, opens it back, very cautiously. Moonlight streams in, then comes a shadow and another shadow. MOSES appears, followed by JIM SLATTERY.)

MOSES: *(Loudly.)* Jim and myself thought we'd call in passing. *(Stops as though surprised to find MICHAEL in bed. MICHAEL starts up again.)* Are we disturbing you?

MICHAEL: Who is that? Oh...Moses!

MOSES: Were you settled in?

MIN: *(In a low angry tone.)* By the way he didn't know!

MICHAEL: I was not. I had but lain down. Come in, Jim.

JIM: I won't. I wouldn't stop now; it is too late.

MICHAEL: Not at all, it is not! We'll have a pipe by the fire. *(Then to MIN, as JIM comes further in.)* Shut the door.

(She folds her arms. MICHAEL puts on his boots and coat.)

JIM: *(Apologetically to MIN.)* A queer time we'd come.

MIN: Moses Barron is fond of queer things.

MOSES: I am fond of my friends. *(Meaningly, in a low tone.)* Next time you'd do well to look out before you'd talk: myself, and not Ned, you were inviting in.

JIM: *(To MICHAEL.)* I found that name for you, Michael.

MIN: *(Taking her shawl.)* I'm going outside for myself.

JIM: We're driving you out. I wouldn't have that—

MIN: A fine beautiful night, and it kinder outside than within. Leave me pass.

MICHAEL: *(To JIM.)* Do, if that is what she wants.

MOSES: I will go with you.

MIN: You will not, Moses Barron! You have enough done! Let you stay here now, and tell out what you'll like.

(MIN is going out as NED COONEY comes in. He looks at her angrily, believing she has played false. She gestures hopelessly and goes.)

NED: *(To MICHAEL.)* Maggie I came looking for. Is she gone home?

MICHAEL: She is below with Daisy Barron.

NED: Oh, is she now! So I needn't be troubling...she'll be right enough.

MOSES: *(Drily.)* You needn't be fretting yourself sick for her sake.

NED: It might be well you'd go home to your mother.

MOSES: It might, and it might not.

NED: *(To MICHAEL.)* Would I be in your way if I'd rest here a short while?

MICHAEL: Rest and welcome. Moses and Jim turned in for a pipe.

(They gather about the fire.)

NED: *(With a great show of friendliness.)* That is what I likes—a friendly pipe with my friends.

MICHAEL: Is that all right with you, Jim? *(The wall, where JIM sits.)*

JIM: As right as can be. *(But very noticeably he puts away his pipe when NED takes out his.)*

NED: *(Jocularly.)* A little housewarming we'll call this...a little welcome to ye, Michael, settling here...a kind welcome to myself out of jail.

JIM: *(Stern.)* You got out before you should.

NED: Ah, that is often the way. They don't mean to keep you that long—only to have it sound hard to them are in the court listening.

JIM: *(Darkly.)* A long sentence will be given to them took the big haul from the Post Office beyond...when they are got...as likely they will...

NED: What was that? I didn't hear—

MOSES: Often the nearer you'd be to a thing, the less you'd hear of it.

JIM: One hundred pounds taken by armed men, Friday morning, and the people coming for their pension.

NED: Well, now, that would surprise you.

MICHAEL: *(Troubled.)* Are you sure of that, Jim?

JIM: I am sure. *(He speaks in a slow judicial way, his eyes fixed on NED.)* It would be a pleasure to me to be the judge passing sentence.

NED: Well, that is real uncommon! I am a man has some experience and can say—most times they are like ashamed. The poor judge down below, he would make you say, "It don't matter." A well-meaning man, but he have aged quicker than myself.

MOSES: So did Maggie!

NED: Maggie? What have she to do with the judge?

MOSES: Nothing, but with you.

JIM: *(Brooding.)* Their day'll come. The arm of the law will reach out to them yet.

NED: Is it hoping you are?

JIM: Hoping. Fearing... A man is beyond that... Justice ah-a... justice... *(Lovingly.)* There is a wonder in it. The one thing that makes a man know himself to be a man.

MICHAEL: *(Troubled.)* Was it pension money they took?

(JIM nods slowly.)

NED: The pension must be given to the people all the same... only to wait till they have it made out new at Dublin Castle.

MOSES: That's like what you might say to a woman... suppose you were talking to her...

NED: Do it now?

MOSES: Suppose you were wanting she'd think it all right.

NED: *(Low tone, threatening.)* It's not safe to be clever.

MOSES: Not till the right time.

JIM: Nothing gives joy to compare with it... the watching of justice...

NED: Is it the law or the justice you're talking of now? *(A little testily.)*

JIM: *(Still brooding.)* Justice... justice... Often I strengthened my heart with it. Sure... unswerving... A crowd, or a man carousing mad, leaving to of their senses and the slow-moving machine drawing near and nearer...

NED: *(Uneasily.)* Oh, I'll grant what you say—it's nice to be watching.

JIM: *(More brusquely.)* I am watching the whole of the created world since the time I was a young lad.

MOSES: Whisper, Jim, if you ever seen justice for sure certain, you're the one man did so.

JIM: A lasting grandeur is in it... the machine of the justice... watching it, a man would know himself is made in the image of God.

NED: Where were you born, Jim Slattery? Or who was your mother?

JIM: If it were making for myself, I would oil the wheel, if it were grinding me I would be glad.

(NED gets up, opens the door, looks out. The others watch him. Then, leaving the door wide open, he comes back.)

NED: I am a man learned from them high up to be polite... smooth and polite. I am a man knows when to speak, and when not... so *(To JIM.)* I'll tell the truth now. It will surprise you *(MOSES.)* as well. *(He places a hand on MICHAEL's shoulder.)* Jim Slattery, a friend of mine was starvin'. He lifted that money from out the Post Office. *(MICHAEL pushes NED's hand from his shoulder.)* Jim Slattery, your slow-moving machine is after him now. Will we give him a start? Or down him? What?

JIM: Starving—ever their password. Lust of gold is the power drives them on.

NED: No—but the opposite—the want of a living.

MICHAEL: *(Breaking out.)* Money—the want or the having—it's all the same!

Would you care about it, Jim? Would you go mad for it like...like some?

JIM: Yourself now?

MICHAEL: I couldn't have peace with it. I couldn't have peace with the thought of it in my mind! All I would ask—never to see it...a big lot...only what would keep me living, and herself pleased... If that could be...

JIM: Fool work—trying to please any but yourself.

MICHAEL: I know that, I know it well. But when we're fond of them, we can't help but wish.

NED: Sure we can't. I broke my heart trying to please Maggie.

MOSES: Did you now?

NED: Pleasin' his Maggie, is what happened my friend.*(A hand again on MICHAEL's shoulder.)* The man was being evicted out of his house. *(Turns to MICHAEL.)* Am I saying it right for you?

MICHAEL: *(Flinging off the hand.)* I don't know what you're saying.

NED: Easy now. Jim Slattery, that Post Office money is on poor Mick!

MICHAEL: It is not!

NED: Do you say it is not? *(Then to JIM.)* He near told you himself.

MOSES: And where would it be safer if so?

NED: *(To MICHAEL.)* I'm for helping you, Mick. I'm not one to down on you.

MOSES: And for helping yourself!

NED: *(To MICHAEL.)* But don't be giving me the lie. Min it was told me: she was mad to get it, planning how she could, feeling you over, asking would I help tie you up...

MOSES: *(Shaken by MICHAEL's look of guilt, protesting too much, turns to JIM.)* Mick was giving it back to Father O'Brien. He was looking for him. I know what I'm saying...he was asking where was he. *(Then more quietly.)* Michael was only keeping that money till he'd hand it over to Father O'Brien.

JIM: From America, was it? *(Watching MICHAEL.)*

MICHAEL: True for you! I thought to get away! *(With a quick, desperate movement, he is drawing the money out of his pocket when MOSES stops him.)*

MOSES: Don't!...what he wants!

NED: To help you, Mick, is what I want, to see what'll be best done.

MOSES: To clear out I'd advise you! They're looking for raiders—and yourself can't deny—

NED: Wait now, I am coming to that... smooth and polite. *(Then to MICHAEL:)* The money you have might only be part. *(MICHAEL takes the packet from his pocket. With a very detached air:)* Maybe you'd give it to Jim. *(MICHAEL holds it out to JIM who does not take it.)* Well, leave it down. *(MICHAEL leaves it between MOSES and JIM. MOSES, watchful of NED, draws a shade nearer the money.)* Now, Jim Slattery, cast your judging eye on that. *(To MOSES.)* Stand back till he'll see what is there. *(To JIM.)* Open it now.

(There is a noise outside. JIM bends forward, opening the packet. NED and MICHAEL watch him. MOSES keeps his eyes on NED. There is a sound as of footsteps, not very near. JIM stops and looks towards the door; MICHAEL also turns his head. NED snatches the money and, wild to get away, is making for the door when MOSES jumps on

to the low wall and strikes him heavily on the head. NED staggers, then falls, dropping the money.)

MOSES: *(After a moment.)* To think I done that! *(Pleased, looking at NED helpless on the floor—then to MICHAEL.)* Shift him in here with me before they'll come.

(They pull NED across to the small door in the wall, push him inside, and come back to the fire. JIM has not moved; the money lies on the floor. They all look at it for a moment in silence, then, as the steps outside are heard coming nearer, MICHAEL bends down, takes the packet, and, very deliberately, puts it back into his hip pocket.)

DAISY: *(Outside.)* Moses! Are you there?

MOSES: *(Despairing.)* Me mother!

DAISY: *(Coming in.)* I came up—

MOSES: So can be seen.

DAISY: We came up... *(MAGGIE follows in.)* ...for the reason there is a terrible new trouble come on Maggie. *(Tragically gloating.)*

MAGGIE: Where is Ned? *(She is troubled, but very quiet.)*

MOSES: Not here at all.

MICHAEL: What is it, Maggie? *(Concerned for her.)*

DAISY: It is something terrible! *(Then to MAGGIE, very eager.)* Will I say it for you?

MOSES: Do not!

MAGGIE: *(Quiet, dignified.)* I will tell them myself...like between friends.

JIM: *(Standing up.)* You'd like I was going.

MAGGIE: Don't move from where you are. Sure it is no use to be hiding the truth.

MICHAEL: What trouble is on you? Tell me—

MAGGIE: It is Ned. He—he—

DAISY: Better you'd leave me say it now.

MOSES: No, don't!

MAGGIE: *(To JIM, who again moves to go.)* Stay where you are. *(Then to MICHAEL.)* They have a reward offered for tidings of Ned.

DAISY: *(Wailing.)* Poor Ned Cooney is being hounded like the martyrs of old time!

MAGGIE: For robbing the Post Office... If he have done wrong itself, he is me own.

MICHAEL: A reward...for robbing... *(Then to MOSES.)* How did y'know? So it was Ned...

MAGGIE: Him and another, but Ned they seen well, and have it in the paper.

DAISY: *(Wailing.)* They have put his short leg in the paper; there's no escape for him! *(MOSES tries to quiet her, but she persists.)* And with the money on his head he is like ill-fated Fenians hunted for Ireland's sake.

MOSES: He is not!

DAISY: Oh! Oh!

MAGGIE: And the boys doing their best out there in the States. *(To MICHAEL, bitterly.)*

(Nobody knows what to say. Even DAISY is silenced.)

MICHAEL: You have the boys, Maggie.

MAGGIE: I had once: there is no having, Mick; no matter how tight you'd hold, your hand would be empty.

MOSES: Maggie, if he would be took up and put in jail itself—

MAGGIE: That is true! Often I'd rest more easy to know he was in it...but...but if he would get a hard sentence—

JIM: A hard sentence will be given without doubt.

MAGGIE: And not that even would be the worst...but the hunting...Ned running the road. He have no holding in him. If he were to die in the ditch, and without the priest...

MICHAEL: *(Slowly.)* It would be better they'd get him soon.

MAGGIE: I don't know. I doubt would he last long in jail. What would be right for me to do, Jim Slattery?

JIM: Right will be done; you can but look on.

MAGGIE: He is not as strong as he was. *(Turns again to MICHAEL.)* What could I do now?

JIM: Michael is not the man to ask. *(MOSES and MICHAEL look at him, alarmed, but he adds.)* There is no man you can ask, but to go on as you are: we must drag the cart.

DAISY: ...It was that one, Moses, that Lizzie Brennan had the paper. *(He makes a sign for her to stop.)* Wait till I'll tell you. I looked in, like I do every night, to make sure she's inside, and not out around leading you astray from the right path—

MOSES: Ned we are talking of.

DAISY: She was reading about him; she was near eating the paper. "What is it?" said I, friendly like, for I wanted an answer. Down she clapped it, and out away with her! Myself and Maggie spelled it out then between the two of us.

(A knock at the door. It is pushed open. FATHER O'BRIEN comes in. He is a middle-aged, brusque-mannered priest.)

FATHER O'BRIEN: Is Michael there? Ah-a! *(Holds out his hand to MICHAEL.)* I was delayed at the out-parish, or I would be with you sooner.

MICHAEL: Thank you, Father.

FATHER O'BRIEN: Where is Min? With some of the neighbours perhaps?

MOSES: At Kirwan's she is... *(Then in a lower tone.)* It might be!

FATHER O'BRIEN: That is better, much better, for her. *(Turns to MAGGIE.)* So you came over, Maggie! A bad business this.

MAGGIE: Indeed it is, Father.

DAISY: But there is worse after happening. *(Eager.)* A worse thing than Michael being evicted...a terrible affliction—

FATHER O'BRIEN: Yes, yes. *(He knows her well, and turns quickly from her. Then to MAGGIE, kindly.)* Maggie gets more than her share of trouble. *(Turns to MICHAEL.)* You're not meaning to stay here surely?

MICHAEL: Only the night until... until...

FATHER O'BRIEN: Yes, yes, we must see what can be done. I can't delay now—but they told me below you were looking for me.

MICHAEL: I was. *(Ill at ease.)*

FATHER O'BRIEN: I thought it might be urgent.

MOSES: We're all going on now—

(MICHAEL stops him with a gesture, showing that he does not wish to be left alone with FATHER O'BRIEN.)

MICHAEL: Nothing urgent! I shouldn't have troubled you at all, Father. *(Low tone.)* Don't go, Moses...and Jim.

FATHER O'BRIEN: Don't go. Michael and I'll have a talk in the morning. I must be off now. *(Turns to the women.)* It is late for the two of you women to be here. Better come down with me.

DAISY: What brought us was Maggie's terrible trouble—

FATHER O'BRIEN: I will be down the way with you now.

MICHAEL: *(To MAGGIE, as she turns to go.)* There's nothing to be done only to wait.

(She shakes her head, and goes out, fingering her crucifix. DAISY follows out.)

FATHER O'BRIEN: Come down in the morning, Michael, and we'll see what we can do.

MICHAEL: Thank you, Father.

(When FATHER O'BRIEN goes out, MICHAEL stands for a moment at the door, then comes slowly back to the fire.)

JIM: *(Sardonic.)* "Come down and we'll see what we can do." The priest was here before him and more sense, and knew we can do nothing… Old Father Conway that would go to sleep in the bog. A well-meaning man, that Father O'Brien, but thinks that is all he need be.

(A silence. MICHAEL looks into the fire. MOSES watches him. MICHAEL looks up; their eyes meet.)

MICHAEL: *(Decisive, hard.)* I can get away with it now, and they so hot after Ned.

MOSES: *(In a low tone.)* You'd have no peace.

MICHAEL: Peace! There is more besides peace.

MOSES: Don't be in any hurry. *(With quiet intentness.)*

MICHAEL: My mind's made up! I'm not delaying!

JIM: Ned Cooney is alive, and have a tongue.

MICHAEL: I'm not forgetting him. We must leave him out of this now.

(He is going towards the small door when FATHER O'BRIEN comes in again, quickly. The men look at him, surprised.)

FATHER O'BRIEN: No cause for alarm, I'm sure, but the authorities have got word, Michael, of a man they want being here. They're coming to search. The Guards are outside.

MOSES: Ned is done! *(Goes quickly to the small door, then hesitates, looks at JIM and MICHAEL.)* Will I leave him out? Or in? Which way is his chance?

JIM: All the same now; they are here.

(But MICHAEL crosses the room, unbolts the door, and NED stumbles out.)

MICHAEL: They're after you! Quick!

(NED rushes for the door, stops, terrified, seeing the Guards, then backs into the room and stands, dazed and weak, leaning against the wall, breathing hard.)

MOSES: Mick! We'll be searched! Get rid of it now! *(Jerks his head towards FATHER O'BRIEN.)*

MICHAEL: *(Puts his hand back to his hip pocket, about to give up the money—then, changing his mind.)* No, what I said, I'll stand by. *(Waits, tense, for the Guards to come.)*

JIM: *(With grim satisfaction.)* They have us all now to work out what is right.

(Civic Guards appear at the door, right.)

(Curtain.)

ACT III

Next morning, shortly after ten o'clock. The door of the ruin has been pulled down, the board has been taken from the window gap, stones pulled from the wall are thrown about, the mattress is tossed up; and now, in the morning light, and with autumn leaves blown in, the place looks more than ever a ruin.

DAISY BARRON comes in, breathless, looks about hastily, and with some satisfaction, clambers on to the low wall at the window gap, and bending outwards, risks a fall in her anxiety to see some object away to the right and lower down. She cannot see well, so stands on her toes, keeps bending to and fro, curiosity incarnate. While these antics are going on, MOSES comes in from the left and stands just inside the door, watching his mother.

DAISY: *(Turning.)* Moses, my boy! Are you saved and alive?

MOSES: Yah, I'm alive.

DAISY: My poor little boy! Only this minute out of that den of thieves!

MOSES: I am out since early morning. I came for these now. *(Turns towards the mattress and pulls off the covering.)*

DAISY: Since early morning? Are ye all released so? And nothing more to happen? *(Disappointed.)*

MOSES: Jim was left off near at once, and myself when they found out—

DAISY: But they kept Michael Donovan? Did they? Ah! Ah-a! I was thinking...I was often thinking...

MOSES: What were you thinking?

DAISY: I would be looking at him, often, and wondering...and I would say to myself, "There might be bad in that man." How well I was right.

MOSES: Right? When were you right?

DAISY: "Daisy Barron" I would say, "stir up now, and use the wit was gave you by God to find out what bad is in him." Sure, now we have proof.

MOSES: Proof?

DAISY: Did you hear Min saying last night, "He's good!" "There you are, Daisy," said I, "if she'd believe him good, she wouldn't be saying it." *(Then a sudden change.)* I dunno where did they come by that, Moses? *(The mattress which he is roping up.)* A good bit of a bed...where would you think? *(He looks at her so disapprovingly that she turns away, and climbs onto the wall.)* I am looking to see would I see the District Judge passing like for a special court on.

MOSES: The court is started inside his house. *(With quiet fury.)*

DAISY: In the house! Did you ever!

MOSES: The District Justice have a cold in his head—so they must be brought in to him.

DAISY: The prisoners brought in! And I not to see them! *(Bitterly disappointed.)* It is because of Maggie Cooney I missed it: fearing to hurt her by looking at Ned I wouldn't stop below...and I wasn't sure would I see better up here. Was Michael Donovan brought in like...like a prisoner?

MOSES: Seeing he is not a free man, you could call him a prisoner.

DAISY: Ah-a! We'll see what'll come to the light of day now! Wait till we'll see... Oh, Moses, there is a terrible lot of winking and contriving going on—you wouldn't know. There is wheels within wheels working around of us.

MOSES: Min will be coming for these. *(Puts the blanket and quilt aside.)* I'll take this below. *(The mattress.)*

DAISY: *(Goes over to him.)* Last night was hard on me! Moses! It was then I knew the hold you had on my heart. I wouldn't mind if I'd merit the suffering—like some—but to have kept myself safe from the anger of God, then to see His Hand on my innocent son—

MOSES: What harm was done me?

DAISY: You wouldn't complain, Moses, you would never... Last night was the worst I put over this many a year. I dunno when the night was that long. I was thinking how I might die, and you wouldn't mind... There, I will stop from the crying. *(A brave attempt to cheer up.)* I will do anything will please you! Last night I made up my mind to that...so's you'll stop below with me...and maybe an odd time you'll feel for me, Moses... Look at this now—we will have all below the way you like. *(Another pause, hoping for some sign of affection.)* And you won't hear a word out of me ever.

MOSES: Won't I? *(In half hope.)*

DAISY: You will not; you have suffering enough, and there is more coming now you won't like to hear, but it is better myself would tell you. Sit down now, and I will tell you the bad is in people. Sit down and we will have a grand talk... your old mother and yourself, Moses. Wait till I'll prove clear to you what you couldn't believe. Oh, the deceit is in some! Christians!...by the way! *(MOSES draws from her.)* You're not sitting down; you have no wish for me! And I your mother!

MOSES: I know you are. Can I help what'll draw me, and what won't.

DAISY: *(Vindictive.)* See will this draw you so—it is that Lizzie Brennan had you all in jail...spying she was...and informing.

MOSES: *(Furious.)* Will you leave Liz alone? Will you stop blackening her name?

DAISY: Why would I treat her different from any? If it is I am blackening her, it will wear off! If it is herself is black, she'll be getting blacker. *(Then a change in manner.)* Would you care about her, Moses? Tell your mother now, would you care about that one?

MOSES: I would give me life for her. *(Then with more caution.)* I think I would—or very near.

DAISY: Why was I born! Bringing a son into the world would break my heart. *(Gets up.)* I will tell you all so, but...wait till I'll be moving off. *(Makes sure she is not too far from the door.)* Lizzie Brennan went up to where she do be working...to the District Judge. "I have him," said she, "I have Ned Cooney; let you come now, and put your hand on him." They gave her the Guards. It is she has you all took up; on the *Evening Mail* she seen his leg. For money she done it...like Judas. She don't care about you, Moses...only for money.

MOSES: If you have told me a lie, you needn't think to see me again, and if you haven't—

DAISY: Find out have I now... You were ever hard and cruel on your old mother, let you be hard and cruel on the one deserves it now...and that will be right. *(Moves off. Then at the doorway.)* I am breaking my heart for you, Moses. I am praying to the merciful God for you... It would be a terrible wrong on Michael, if you were ever to look at that one again. It would be like taking part in what she done. I am sorry for you. I am—

MOSES: Will you get out of that!

DAISY: I will, and I will be praying— *(As she goes out, looking back towards MOSES, she almost walks against MIN, who, coming in slowly, steps aside to avoid her.)* Ah-a, Min Donovan, ah-a! A bad day this!

MIN: What is wrong with the day? Fine and mild; the fault must be with yourself. *(Antagonistic.)*

DAISY: Ah! And with more than me! I am sorry for you—

MIN: Keep your sorrow for them has need of it! *(She goes over to where MOSES has left the blanket and quilt, and stands obviously waiting for DAISY to go.)*

DAISY: *(Delaying.)* Would I send up that one to you now, Moses? Would I? Till you'd talk to her and the anger fresh on your mind? *(Silence.)* It is her day not to be working so you'd have the time to finish with her right. If you'd like, I'd send her up here… *(MOSES looks at her, plainly saying to go.)* I couldn't please you. *(Going out.)* I couldn't… I tried to do my best…

(When DAISY has gone, MIN turns to MOSES, expecting him to speak. MOSES keeps his back to her.)

MIN: *(After a silence.)* Father O'Brien is a long time getting Mick out of it.

MOSES: Father O'Brien have nothing to say to it.

MIN: Well, he have a right to! What do he want being a priest if he can't help us now!… It is himself should be locked up, seeing it was for him Michael was keeping the money.

MOSES: They say it was not.

MIN: Who said it was not! His wife should know.

MOSES: His wife should know what she pressed for! When that would be done, how could Father O'Brien get him off?

MIN: I couldn't follow you, Moses Barron. I could never understand a word you'd say. If I had someone would talk plain.

MOSES: I will talk plain! *(With fury.)*

MIN: I only want to know what happened last night.

MOSES: *(Quietly.)* When they had us arrested, they took down what we'd say. I was first, and said Mick was looking for Father O'Brien all the evening, so's to give him the money.

MIN: And the priest standing beside of him when they walked in. Why couldn't you think to say 'twas Father Keating he wanted?

MOSES: Because I am a fool! But 'twould be no good. When one man says out the simple truth, nothing we'll make up will stand against it.

MIN: And I suppose Michael went telling the truth? He would.

MOSES: Jim was after me. He made a terrible long statement. He must be queer in his mind! He would like very much to see justice being worked—he—

MIN: Jim and yourself is nothing to me! Will you tell me what was it Michael said?

MOSES: He said—it will be in the paper, so you might as well know—he said he was keeping the money to go off away.

MIN: He was not! That's a mistake. I'll go up now, and make it plain before the court'll start.

MOSES: The court is started.

MIN: *(Angry.)* 'Tis a sin to be telling lies! Though it don't put you in the law. There was no court on and I coming up.

MOSES: They were took into the Justice's house.

MIN: *(Shaken.)* What?

MOSES: On account of his chest.

MIN: What are you saying? Is it going on now?

MOSES: Inside in the house.

(MIN stares at him for a moment, then goes to the window gap, and looks down, away to the right.)

MIN: Maybe this would be the best thing ever! *(Defiantly.)*

MOSES: Oh—maybe. *(Bitterly.)*

MIN: For they can't touch him... He did no robbing. *(Then, in spite of herself, fear increases.)* How well he couldn't hold his tongue when he was got!... They couldn't...could they? What would you think?

MOSES: I have told you before I am not able to think.

(JIM SLATTERY comes onto the scene, just outside the ruin; he stands at the window gap, also looking down towards the house.)

JIM: So they're holding the court in the house below— *(Points downwards with his stick.)*

MIN: *(On edge.)* I'll thank you not to be pointing, Jim Slattery—a thing I was told was not good-mannered.

JIM: *(To MOSES.)* When it will be over, they'll open the side door.

MOSES: That'll be a while for they have more than—

MIN: Who cares when 'twill be! Michael done right! He done no wrong! No bad will come.

JIM: There is no one can say what'll come now.

MOSES: *(To JIM.)* Would you think will he be put back for trial with Ned?

JIM: You may know he will.

MIN: For trial—

JIM: *(Looks sternly at her.)* And then will be the time for speaking up! Them responsible to own what they done!

MIN: I wouldn't know what you'd mean.

JIM: *(Turns from her.)* The law is being worked out now between them four walls.

MIN: Standing there, enjoying yourself, to know Michael Donovan is being charged with...with... Sure no matter. They can do nothing to him.

JIM: He have put himself in the power of the law.

MOSES: But I think the man below is of a fairish mind.

JIM: Fairish! To have a man standing before you was got with a hundred pound not his own, and the working of the law to be your trade.

MIN: Real amusing you are, Jim Slattery!

JIM: It would be a queer judge would let that go!

MIN: I'd like to be listening to you!

JIM: What I'd like—to be passing sentence on the one caused Michael do this!

MIN: *(Looks at him for a moment, turns to MOSES.)* When 'twasn't he robbed, they couldn't jail him, could they? Michael that would never do wrong.

JIM: Only to please who he'd be better without minding.

MIN: *(Flashing.)* I was begging him to! I'm glad he done it! I wouldn't wish any other thing!

JIM: Your day'll come.

MIN: *(Laughing wild.)* Well done, Mick! It is a right good thing you done! If they'll jail you aself, I will be cheering for you! *(Falters.)* Cheering…I'll be…I am that proud…

MOSES: That would be right enough if it would make himself proud in himself.

JIM: Better than cheering—to tell what your share is!

MIN: *(Quiet.)* Is it to the judge I'd tell?

JIM: To tell out the truth and let the Guards take you up.

MIN: And if they jail me then, would Mick be thanking you? Ha! He is not like you, Jim Slattery! He is not like any other man! Michael Donovan is too good for this earth—now he have seen right, and done what I wanted!

JIM: It would be right all was known: it might lighten his sentence.

MIN: He don't want a light sentence! He don't mind what they'll do! He have risen up out of himself! I was never proud until this day!

JIM: *(To MOSES.)* Hanging around…the shawleens…so they must know the court is on.

MIN: I would like the whole world would be watching!

MOSES: Father O'Brien…he's making up here!

MIN: Near time for him! A queer thing—surely—the priest not to be with me in the hour of trial.

MOSES: They're only charging them now; there won't be a trial till—

MIN: My own trial is going on! If I'd have the priest to myself now, I might turn a good thing out of this yet.

JIM: Turning…twisting. The mills will grind on.

FATHER O'BRIEN: *(Coming in.)* Is Maggie there?

MOSES: She stopped below at Kirwan's, Father.

FATHER O'BRIEN: Poor Maggie! Well, well! *(Looks at MIN, but she looks back at him so defiantly that he turns to MOSES.)* Well, Michael may be discharged, perhaps…information's refused…very likely.

MOSES: Would you think that likely?

JIM: I would be surprised it would go that easy.

FATHER O'BRIEN: Considering his good character—and the fact that he found this money accidentally, I think it not at all unlikely he'll be discharged. *(Turns to MIN.)* We can only hope.

MIN: Can you do nothing more! *(Silence.)* Well, maybe the Bishop could. . . .

(MOSES and JIM exchange looks. MOSES steps over the low wall, and they move off together.)

FATHER O'BRIEN: If the trial comes on, I'll do what I can, but I'm hoping Michael may be discharged.

MIN: Ah, what matter—whether or no—he done right.

FATHER O'BRIEN: *(Gravely.)* He has done right now, to acknowledge his guilt.

MIN: Guilt! Is there anyone walking this earth have a mind!… Let you go beyond to the Bishop now. "Did you hear, my Lord," says you, "the thing Michael Donovan is after doing? And who is to blame?" says you—like that.

FATHER O'BRIEN: Now, Min, that won't help—

MIN: *(Fiercely.)* Guilt! It is on them kept him poor the guilt is! *(Silence. A change.)* I was thinking now, when Michael comes out of this unless he'll get a job is well paid, he'll likely take on with the robbing… But if there was a job waiting that would steady him like—

FATHER O'BRIEN: Michael will steady himself: in ourselves we must find our strength.

MIN: I dunno would I go to the Bishop?… Would it do Michael any good, would you think, if I told 'twas myself made him keep it?

FATHER O'BRIEN: You made him keep the money?

MIN: Could I make a good thing out of that, would you think?

FATHER O'BRIEN: Is it a fact? Did you ask him to keep it?

MIN: I thought I couldn't move him when he'd hold it wrong. Wrong! He have changed his mind! That'll show you!

FATHER O'BRIEN: If it was for you—

MIN: You needn't doubt it! You need have no doubt at all! Begging I was. "Michael Donovan," said I, "it is a mortal sin for you and me to be sitting here poor. Keep a hold of that money now!" I'm real proud and glad—

FATHER O'BRIEN: For shame, Min!

MIN: He have put me above all! Above what he was told, and believed always.

FATHER O'BRIEN: He has done wrong.

MIN: Wrong! The only wrong can be done is to leave your heart go bad. Did yourself know that?

FATHER O'BRIEN: I know, and you do, that you did wrong in urging Michael to keep that money.

MIN: *(Dignified.)* 'Twas the poverty urged him—let you blame being poor. Michael done right.

FATHER O'BRIEN: You are not in your right senses: later—when you are—we'll have a talk.

MIN: Talk away let you! *(Insolently.)*

FATHER O'BRIEN: Is that the way to speak to me?

MIN: *(A quick change.)* Father O'Brien, I'm after doing a bad thing.

FATHER O'BRIEN: I'm afraid you are, Min, when instead of helping Michael you—

MIN: Is it myself is telling this now, or is it you? For it is not what you'd think at all. It is against Michael I done this: it is troubling me now. When I heard what himself was planning, it went through me…poor Mick! *(A sigh, a pause.)* I dunno if I'd go to confession would you leave me tell it my own way? *(Sighs again.)* It is pressing on me now: it is more than I can bear by myself… *(Then angrily.)* Well, I thought when the Priest would come I would have comfort!

FATHER O'BRIEN: I was thinking that was all you wanted.

MIN: And what more would I ask? Isn't it comfort will be in heaven itself? Is it looking down on heaven I should be?

FATHER O'BRIEN: In a very different frame of mind you should be.

MIN: Comfort wrong now! And last Sunday we'd have it in heaven. You couldn't mind them!

FATHER O'BRIEN: Now, Min—

MIN: Often I thought it! They'd tell you look down on the fame of the world, but when a rich man would come, "He is an ornament to the Church and the State." Would he be that if he gave heed to them and he a young fellow? Am I to be looking up with one eye, and down with the other? They'd tell you the Mother of God had beauty, but if you'd wish yourself nice, that would be wrong! "I'm sorry for you," they'd say, and on top of that, "Poverty is a blessing disguised." So for why were they sorry? Ah! You couldn't mind them! Not a mind!

FATHER O'BRIEN: *(Quietly.)* I want to do what I can for you.

MIN: You do? And I not agreeing—

FATHER O'BRIEN: But you must first see the wrong in what you've done.

MIN: Ah! Then you'd help Mick? How long must I see it? *(FATHER O'BRIEN turns from her.)* Ah, Father O'Brien, I won't be tormenting you! If you'll do something for Mick, I'll see what you like. I'll do all you'll say!

FATHER O'BRIEN: I'll see you tomorrow. *(Short.)*

MIN: Tomorrow! Can you do nothing till tomorrow? Won't I see you now until tomorrow?

FATHER O'BRIEN: I will be in the chapel from half past six tonight.

MIN: Oh!... Ah! 'Tis a long step of a way.

(LIZZIE BRENNAN comes in. FATHER O'BRIEN turns to go.)

MIN: Don't leave me now! 'Tis for Mick I'm asking, and he so good for going to Mass! I'd see what you'd like— *(FATHER O'BRIEN goes. She turns to LIZZIE:)* I made a bad job of it then.

LIZZIE: Michael will be all right.

MIN: Don't be telling lies! All right! How would he?

LIZZIE: I said a prayer he'd get off. I'm hoping he will. I...I didn't know at all Michael would be taken...it is only on Ned Cooney I told.

MIN: You told? What?

LIZZIE: I said I seen Ned round about here; they were hunting him for raiding the Post Office. I didn't think ever to harm Michael... Would you think Moses will blame what I done?

MIN: And for why would he? I would like myself had done it.

LIZZIE: You would. *(Relieved.)*

MIN: There is no one thing I'd ask now but to see Ned Cooney suffering. If he is a neighbour aself, he is a pest. He is that bad he is worse than myself. What made you tell?

LIZZIE: So's we could get married.

MIN: What?

LIZZIE: Moses and me. He said we couldn't till we had the money. Now I'll be getting the reward for Ned—

MIN: Reward! *(Drawing from her.)* For money you done it!

LIZZIE: For love of Moses I done it. Sure I couldn't be wrong and that my reason. *(Pleading.)*

MIN: He won't look at you now, Moses Barron won't.

LIZZIE: Do you think he will not?

MIN: He will; no one can help what is stronger than theirself—but he'll never give you a soft word again.

LIZZIE: He didn't ever, or very few. Do you think will he marry me? *(Looks out.)* Min! If he'd go off from me now!

MIN: *(Looks out too, turns to LIZZIE.)* Let you go before he'll come.

LIZZIE: Better he'd hear it from myself. I'll tell him now. I might as well, I can have no rest till I hear is he pleased.

MIN: I could talk better, saying you done right.

LIZZIE: With Moses talk is no good—he have a terrible mind would tear to pieces all you'd say. But *(Looking around desperately.)* if there was something high up I could get on, and be like falling off when he'd come in—

MIN: Falling off?

LIZZIE: So's he should catch hold of me—like once before; he was near kissing me—if that could happen again, and we by ourselves, it would be better than talk.

MIN: *(Angered.)* Is there anyone walking this earth you could like?

LIZZIE: If he'd kiss me he'd marry me—he is that good, he's real holy and pure: that is what I love him for.

MIN: *(Angrily.)* If it'll come to him he'll do it—fall or no—and if it don't you'll hinder him with the wanting of it!

(She goes. MOSES comes in for the mattress, sees LIZZIE, and looks away from her.)

LIZZIE: Moses. *(He keeps his back towards her, and starts to rope up the mattress.)* Will I give you a hand at that?

MOSES: I am wanting no hand! *(Fierce.)*

LIZZIE: I would like to tell you something I done... *(Goes to him.)* I dunno was it right or wrong... I will be getting money very soon...

MOSES: Money. *(Glaring.)*

LIZZIE: That is good, isn't it, Moses? For when I'll have it you and me can...you know...can do what we'd like.

MOSES: What is that?

LIZZIE: Ah, go on now, don't be acting.

MOSES: Acting...

LIZZIE: Sure you know well I had no thought ever but of you... Why should I tell a lie? It is you is at the end of all I ever done... It was looking at you long ago I made up my mind not to be so mangey-like. It was with the thought of you in my mind I gave over the grumbling. Whenever I give a hand down below I do be saying to myself, "This is what Moses would think well I'd do." *(He turns on her.)* Ah—leave me show you all now!... Often, Moses, on the day I'd have off, I'd stop watching the day crawling by, and the light changing and the cows in the field and because you'd be stirring in my heart I would be happy-like only watching... And when you'd come—

MOSES: Stop that! *(Suffering.)* I know what you done!—

LIZZIE: They told! That wasn't fair!

MOSES: Fair! Was what you done fair?! Informing!!

LIZZIE: What's on you? I done no wrong! Min Donovan is after saying she is glad! *(Frightened.)*

MOSES: Who'd mind Min Donovan—a woman not in her right senses this day!

Any other wouldn't look at the side of the road you'd be!

LIZZIE: Do you think they would not?! I was right! Moses, I was right!

MOSES: Right?!

LIZZIE: I seen on the paper the Priest in Coolbarry said off the altar all should help to find the robbers. Could the Priest be telling them do wrong?

MOSES: For money you done it!

LIZZIE: You said till we'd have it we couldn't...couldn't...

MOSES: Keep your money! Even my old mother'd know it for deep mean.

LIZZIE: So that is it—your mother! *(Angered.)* Well, you have been long enough wobbling between us. You can go back to her now I'll give good-bye to you! *(Moves towards the door, stops: waits for a moment, comes back to him.)* Don't you understand Moses...it is for you I done this...so's we could be together... *(Pleading.)* What good is it to me if it don't please you?

MOSES: *(Blazing.)* How could it please me to know you that mean? Could you look at Maggie Cooney now?

LIZZIE: She'll rest easy to have him in: they said often it is better for her.

MOSES: And will you rest easy on what is near blood payment?

LIZZIE: *(Horrified.)* Don't be saying a word like that!

MOSES: Is it worse to say a thing out or do it on the sly? Ned Cooney you could hardly call a man, but when he walked in here he risked all: you're not the only one has eyes can see. What about Michael has his name ruined? ...so's you can have money!

LIZZIE: I couldn't be thinking of all that: I was only thinking of you and me. *(Pause.)* Maybe Michael will get off, and if he would then maybe you'd—

DAISY: *(Stumbling in all excitement.)* Ned Cooney is after making a dash for it!

MOSES: What?

DAISY: *(Clambers onto the wall.)* Wait'll I see!... Wait'll I see! *(Looks down to the right.)*

(MOSES gets onto the wall also. LIZZIE stands for a moment indecisive, then, clenching her hands, as with sudden resolution, runs out.)

MOSES: There he is! *(Quiet.)*

DAISY: Oh-h...there he is! *(With relish.)*

JIM: *(Comes on, outside the window gap. Stands looking down to the right, excited.)* A fool thing he'd do!

DAISY: Will you look! Will you look!

MOSES: Desperate he is!

JIM: He might know he couldn't get off.

DAISY: Ah-a! Hiding...sure they know where he is!

MOSES: Right sport, is it? *(Angrily. Gets off the wall, disgusted.)*

JIM: He haven't a chance. *(Grim.)*

DAISY: They're only waiting now till he'll turn.

MOSES: Will you get down out of that! *(Pulls her.)*

DAISY: *(Clutches at the wall.)* Don't. Ah don't, Moses! If I'd miss it now, and nothing for a twelve month again!

MOSES: Watching them drag a man to hell!

JIM: I wouldn't turn from the sight of justice being worked... He made his own road.

MOSES: Like you'd make it had you the same start!

DAISY: It is no worse than the coursing... Oh!... Ah!... *(A glance towards MOSES.)* A pity for you to be missing it.

JIM: They can take their time now... *(Then looks at MOSES.)* Turning from hard truth—that is what have the land destroyed.

DAISY: See that! That one... Lizzie Brennen!

MOSES: What is she at?

JIM: Fighting for Ned! *(Grim enjoyment.)*

MOSES: What? *(Jumps onto the wall.)*

JIM: Hindering the Guards!

DAISY: Did you ever on earth!

JIM: She tripped that fellow clever!

DAISY: Holding his leg! She ought to be ashamed!

MOSES: The little fool—she will get hurted!

DAISY: Get down out of that, Moses—it wouldn't be right, you'd look at her!

JIM: She is fighting plucky.

DAISY: And not for Ned's sake! *(Looks at MOSES.)* That one would do anything to be in the limelight before you!... Ah-a! She is rolled in the mud!

JIM: They have him!

DAISY: Ah, she made no great show of it at all!

(They get off the wall.)

JIM: *(To MOSES.)* It is right he should be got: myself gave the word.

MOSES: The word?

JIM: When I heard he was round last evening, I called up to the Guards: no surprise when they came.

MOSES: So 'twas you gave the word... *(Looks at JIM, then at his mother.)*

DAISY: Not the only one gave it— *(MOSES stops her with a sign.)*

JIM: If he was a son of my own, I'd do the same. *(Silence.)* Look around you—the law of nature is less relenting than any: mould yourself on it.

MAGGIE: *(Coming in.)* Have they got him, do you know?

(She is followed by MIN who holds herself apart, antagonistic to all the world.)

MOSES: They have, Maggie.

MAGGIE: It is better they would.

DAISY: Oh, poor Maggie Cooney, I am breaking my heart for you

MOSES: Break it quiet! *(Low tone.)*

JIM: They must treat him fair—when there is nothing proved—that is the law.

MAGGIE: He will be better off: he would die on the road.

JIM: They must keep him in middling comfort—till the trial—that is the law.

MAGGIE: They won't have him long: I think he is not long for this world.

MOSES: Sit down now, and rest awhile. *(Gently.)*

DAISY: *(Sadly.)* Moses have sorrow for all he'd look at save for his old mother.

MOSES: Often I judged myself with that: but I feels for you, when I'm away out of it, not looking at you.

(DAISY goes out. JIM also moves off slowly.)

MAGGIE: *(To MOSES.)* Michael is left off.

MOSES: Michael? Is he? Free?

MIN: I was wondering when would you think to ask!

MAGGIE: The Justice said he had a good character, and it was likely only because—

MIN: Who cares what he said? *(Turns to MOSES.)* It might be you'd think of greeting him now, seeing what he have put over, and he coming the way by himself—

MOSES: Is he? *(Goes to window; about to step over the wall, hesitates, as though struck by something in MICHAEL's bearing.)* Often I'd like my own company better than any. I'll take this down. I'll meet him coming. *(Takes the mattress and goes out.)*

MAGGIE: *(To MIN.)* I'll stop here till he come.

MIN: I doubt he'll come here—for why would he? *(Nervous, trying to keep calm, turns from the window, then back to it again.)* Ha! I told you he'd be in no great hurry! Talking to Jim! *(Resentful.)* And to Moses Barron now... It don't matter we're waiting... It don't matter what we're feeling... *(Turns from the window, looks at MAGGIE, envious of her calm.)* Would nothing disturb you, Maggie Cooney? Would nothing? *(Goes over to MAGGIE.)* I dunno does Michael feel against me... that I put him to keep the money...?

MAGGIE: *(Sadly.)* That troubling you, and the good name he had gone.

MIN: *(Impatient.)* I doubt has he much feeling at all!

MAGGIE: *(Looks out through the window gap.)* How slow the Guards are going along the road with Ned!

MIN: They're stopping that car! Putting him in!

MAGGIE: He is done up so—God help him.

MIN: Michael might stir himself if he's coming. *(Then impatient with MAGGIE.)* I dunno how you stop that quiet!

MAGGIE: Nothing'll last: the only way of stopping quiet—to have your heart in what'll last... Would we say the Gospel of St. John with poor Ned and Michael in need of help?

MIN: I have no knowledge of it: it wasn't in the caddiechism and I going to school.

MAGGIE: The prayer after the Angelus so—I'll give it out. "Let us pray—Pour forth we beseech of Thee, O Lord, Thy grace into our hearts that we— *(They hear a step.)* ...that we..."

(MICHAEL comes in, slowly.)

MICHAEL: *(Looking at MAGGIE only.)* They're taking Ned to the hospital, Maggie.

MAGGIE: Is he hurted so?

MICHAEL: Not bad—but he is weak like.

MAGGIE: Is he dying, Mick?

MICHAEL: *(Shakes his head.)* I think he'll be kept there awhile. *(A pause. MIN watches MICHAEL, who does not look in her direction.)* You might get to see him there now, if you'd like.

MAGGIE: *(Gets up.)* I will go over. *(Draws her shawl about her.)* And maybe he'll agree to have Father O'Brien see him then, by the Grace of God.

(Going out she looks back at MIN, who is still watching MICHAEL. MICHAEL, concerned only for MAGGIE, follows her

out. MIN looks angrily after them: then picks up the blanket and quilt, is going off in the opposite direction when MOSES comes in.)

MOSES: The board, Michael... *(Sees that MICHAEL is not there, turns to MIN.)* Would I take the board too?

MIN: Do what you'll like! He is that took up with Maggie that he don't mind what you'll do! *(Goes off quickly, letting the quilt fall, and not waiting to pick it up.)*

(MOSES is taking up the board when LIZZIE comes in, rather muddy and tousled, but very eager.)

LIZZIE: I was going to the house over, to know could I see the Justice when he'd be after hearing the court, when I seen herself coming down the road by herself—so I went over and told her.

MOSES: What are you after telling now?

LIZZIE: I said, "I am above touching money," I said. *(Very pleased and expecting him to be.)* "I am wanting no reward." Wasn't that right?

MOSES: *(After a moment.)* There was no wrong in it.

LIZZIE: And she will look to get work for you at once.

MOSES: For me?

LIZZIE: She will get something for you, sure. Won't that be grand now!

MOSES: It will, if I'll keep it.

LIZZIE: Something good she'll get—she was that pleased with me. But, Moses, I didn't like to tell her the truth, you know...so I said, you know—that you were—

MOSES: What did you say I was?

LIZZIE: My brother—is that right?

MOSES: *(Relieved.)* I thought you had us married. *(Sits down.)*

LIZZIE: *(Sits down close beside him.)* Didn't I make a good job of it now? *(Holds her face to be kissed.)*

MOSES: Yah—wanting no reward! *(Bends to kiss her—then changes his mind.)*

LIZZIE: Ah! We were near in heaven then.

MOSES: I dunno were we? *(Sad, old.)*

LIZZIE: Look at this! *(Puts her arms about his neck and kisses his cheek; then, seeing that he is pleased.)* Now, we will have to get married!

MOSES: Yah—sometime. *(LIZZIE kisses him again.)* We have enough now! *(Gruffly, MOSES releases himself and stands up. LIZZIE gets up too, and for a moment they stand in silence—MOSES ill at ease. They hear a step.)* Someone, thank God! Min for the quilt.

(MIN comes in, and takes up the quilt she has dropped. MOSES takes the board.)

LIZZIE: *(To MIN.)* It is grand about Michael. *(Timid.)*

MIN: What grand is in it? The same as he ever was!

LIZZIE: Sure, I think all will be right now. I think it must.

MIN: Nothing can change the inside of any man!

(MOSES goes out, and LIZZIE follows. MIN, left alone, changes from indignation to sadness. After a moment, MICHAEL comes to the doorway. He stands looking at her, then comes in slowly.)

MICHAEL: They gave Maggie a lift on the road.

MIN: Mick, I'm real glad you done this... I—I— *(He looks steadfastly at her. She falters, but forces herself to finish.)* I am as proud as can be...

MICHAEL: *(When he has finished looking at her, looks about the place.)* So Moses took the things down below!

MIN: The most of them. *(Meek.)*

MICHAEL: *(Suddenly rough.)* Gather up the rest now! *(MIN, surprised, goes about collecting the things—cups, broken mirror, picture frame, etc. MICHAEL watches her.)* Take the shawl off you and put them in it. *(She spreads her shawl, and puts the things in it.)* The kettle! *(Pointing.)* The old stool, too—put that in! Take it up now, and come on. *(She is about to put the shawlful over her shoulder when he stops her.)* Were you talking to Ned Cooney last night?

MIN: *(Frightened.)* I wasn't! I was not!

MICHAEL: You were not? *(Silence.)* You weren't talking to him? And I lying there? *(She shakes her head, miserably.)* You weren't feeling for what was on me?

MIN: If I was aself, Ned is to blame.

MICHAEL: *(With a hopeless gesture.)* What kind of woman are you—couldn't tell the truth and the two of us face to face now?

MIN: I didn't think you'd start asking. *(Then with a flash.)* How well you should make bad worse! Trying to force the truth out of me to come between us now! And it is a queer thing surely you'd have no other word for me, and I—

MICHAEL: *(Stops her.)* You had a hold over me you won't have again! We're going below to Kirwan's now; in the evening you'll go back home with Maggie—myself to Cork City, and from there to America.

MIN: Mick! Whatever I planned I wouldn't do in the end!

MICHAEL: There is no cure for that now, but to leave it.

MIN: It is Ned is to blame! And yourself Mick! ...when you lifted your hand to me the wrong was done!

MICHAEL: There is nothing to be done now—but to go.

MIN: To go?

MICHAEL: Maggie gave me the price of one ticket.

MIN: One!

MICHAEL: The boys sent it to her.

MIN: Is it to get off from me you want?

MICHAEL: *(Shakes his head.)* It is not what I'd choose at all.

MIN: How could I stop there—looking at Maggie and the childer, and I without one of my own?

MICHAEL: The boys will look out for me... They have a place.

MIN: They have: maybe you'd get on so...and maybe...send what would bring me out?

MICHAEL: That—or to come back.

MIN: *(Realizes what the going means to him.)* Don't go, Mick! Stop here! How would you be out there? You, that had your heart ever set on the hill?

MICHAEL: Come on. *(Takes the shawlful of things from her, then stops, looks out.)* Wait till they'll move off from below.

(MIN looks at him, realizes that he feels the shame of meeting others, grows restless, angry.)

MIN: It is them robbed the Post Office is to blame for it all. *(MICHAEL looks at her—his look showing the futility of what she says. So, more angrily:)* How well you wouldn't leave me do it, that would be proud now! *(A silence. She looks furtively at MICHAEL, sorry for him.)* It is Father O'Brien is to blame seeing if he hadn't stopped in the out-parish you'd have gave him the money… *(Again MICHAEL looks at her, in the same way. She turns away, brushes aside a few tears, is silent for a moment, then—)* And Lizzie Brennan is to blame… and Maggie that she wouldn't give the ticket sooner…and…and…

MICHAEL: *(After a moment.)* We may go now.

(He takes the shawlful, and they go out slowly.)

(Curtain.)

KATIE ROCHE

A Play in Three Acts

INTRODUCTION

John P. Harrington

Teresa Deevy's play *Katie Roche* opened at Dublin's Abbey Theatre on May 16, 1936. It was her third full-length play at the national theater of Ireland. She was a recognized playwright at that time and place: a review a year earlier of a one-act play, *The King of Spain's Daughter*, observed that Deevy was "known already as the author of a couple of unusually interesting plays." In addition to *Katie Roche*, that year would also bring openings in Dublin of another new full-length play, *The Wild Goose*, and a revival of *The King of Spain's Daughter*. The latter was published in the United States that year, and *Katie Roche* was published in Victor Gollancz's annual *Famous Plays* anthology for 1935–36, where it appeared beside the work of Clifford Odets and others.

At the same time, Deevy was visible as a public figure participating in meetings and writing letters to editors urging the formation of an Irish chapter of PEN, the international organization promoting literature and freedom of expression; her personal letters refer to the "narrow view" of some writers who would "limit the artist by nationality, religion, etc." She was an ardent opponent of censorship of the arts, which had become policy in Ireland with the government's 1929 establishment of the Censorship of Publications Board.

While for the most part Deevy stayed in Ireland, her interests and audiences were international. One year after its opening in Dublin, *Katie Roche* would be the lead play of an Abbey tour of the United States, where it opened at the Ambassador Theatre on October 3, 1937—the first play in a repertory including works by Sean O'Casey and John Millington Synge.

The year 1936 was one of change at the Abbey Theatre, which was examining its repertory, reviewing its mission, and weighing the artistic benefits of innovation against the financial ones of repetition. The premiere of *Katie Roche* was directed by Hugh Hunt and designed by Tanya Moiseiwitsch, both of whom had been brought in from outside Ireland to develop a new vision for the national theater. Its first review in Dublin, in the influential newspaper the *Irish Times*, praised *Katie Roche* as having "the faint impression of unreality." And a famous diarist of the period at the Abbey, Joseph Holloway, wrote that "*Katie Roche* was a strange play about the strangest character I ever saw on the stage." Both accounts noted how engaged and delighted the audience was. Applause at the end of the opening performance included calls for the author.

The originality of the play that accounts for its "unreality" and interest is its focus on the unformed title character facing a life crisis and knowing that "I must think what I will do." Katie Roche is characterized through stage directions that note her "inward glow," while specifying that she "suddenly flies out," "nods triumphantly," and is "full of power and joy." That dynamism appears in sudden flashes during her journey over twelve months from making an unhappy marriage to resigning herself to an unhappy marriage.

Katie Roche is a problematic character who seems capable of autonomy and independence but does not achieve either. This is evident even in her name: Katie Roche is the name she was given upon her adoption. Her heritage could be recovered through use of her mother's name, Halnan, or her father's name, Fitzsimon. More control of self could be realized through her married name, Gregg. But despite momentary flashes of "power and joy," the title of the play and the identity of the character remain Katie Roche. When her parentage is revealed to her, she says, "I'll make my own goodness." But she does not, and ultimately remains within the rather dismal limitations assigned her by society.

The curtains of both Act I and Act III close on parlor-room vignettes of Katie patronized by her new family, her husband Stanislaus Gregg and his sister Amelia. Only in the middle act does her "power and joy" seem potent—and this only very briefly in the opening domestic scene with Stanislaus's architectural plans, and later with her romantic interest, Michael Maguire, when she is on a ladder, laughing and looking through the window to the sounds of cheering outside. But these mid-play interludes of personal achievement are brief and unsustainable.

With the exception of the father figure Reuben, the males in *Katie Roche* are a very passive group easily influenced by females such as Amelia or Michael's mother. Notwithstanding this passivity, these men are quite capable of domestic violence. In a scene with Katie and Reuben, Deevy puts this on stage, as she does in other works. It is remarkable how little the beating scene is commented on by early reviewers. Deevy goes beyond this simple oppression to present an even grimmer vision of Irish reality. Director Judy Friel commented on this in connection with her 1994 revival of *Katie Roche* in Dublin's Peacock Theatre. "Deevy's feminism is much more than a male-bash," Friel wrote, "because *Katie Roche* shows a patriarchy fully colluded in by women."

Deevy's ability to challenge simple expectations is both the innovation of her work and a factor that limited production until its rediscovery and revival by the Mint Theater. While directing *Katie Roche*, Friel described the end of the play as a "whitewash"; others have accused Deevy of being unable to imagine identity beyond restrictive, patriarchal, and tradition-bound roles. The innovation of the ending of *Katie Roche* is that it does not settle for a "male-bash" or a simple feminist paradigm reminiscent of Ibsen's *A Doll's House.* The play is a far sterner social critique of collusion and passivity.

Deevy's scrutiny certainly is of post-revolution and pre–World War II Ireland, and her work represents an innovative path for the Abbey Theatre that it ultimately chose not to follow. Her work is a severe examination of individual character and its limits which resonates beyond the immediate context of the play and the playwright. In trying to describe the compelling power of her work, a Mint Theater actor explained, "She writes the truth of how we make ourselves unhappy."

John P. Harrington is Dean of the Faculty of Arts and Sciences at Fordham University. He is the author of The Irish Beckett, The Irish Play on the New York Stage, *and* The Life of the Neighborhood Playhouse on Grand Street *and the editor of the W.W. Norton anthology* Modern and Contemporary Irish Drama.

CHARACTERS

STANISLAUS GREGG	KATIE ROCHE
REUBEN	MICHAEL MAGUIRE
AMELIA GREGG	JO MAHONY
MARGARET DRYBONE	FRANK LAWLOR

SETTING

The action of the play takes place in the living room of Amelia Gregg's cottage in Lower Ballycar.

Act I. An August afternoon.
Act II. Four months later.
Act III. Eight months later.

ACT I

The living room of AMELIA GREGG's cottage in Lower Ballycar. It is a pleasant little room, time-worn now and scantily furnished. There is a table in the center of the room and flowers in a bowl on the table. The afternoon sun streams through a window at the left side, throwing shadows of chairs and table. Opposite the window is the fireplace, and farther back than the fireplace, at the same side, a door leads to the rest of the house. At the center-back, the house door stands a little way open.

A man comes to the house door, pushes it more open, and comes in. This is STANISLAUS GREGG, a short stoutish man of about forty-five, dressed in light tweeds, and carrying a suitcase and raincoat. Apparently surprised to find the room empty, he stands for a moment looking about, then puts down his suitcase, leaves his hat and raincoat on the table, and strolls over to the window: stands there looking out. In his bearing there is an odd mixture of truculence and repose. At one moment he is miles from his surroundings, at the next fiercely concentrated on whoever he is speaking to. Door at right opens: KATIE ROCHE comes in carrying a tray with teacups, etc. KATIE is not quite twenty. Perhaps the most remarkable thing about her is a sort of inward glow, which she continually tries to smother and which breaks out either in delight or desperation according to circumstances. Under reproof she grows abject. Seeing STANISLAUS now she stops, surprised. He turns from the window.

STANISLAUS: Good evening, Katie.

KATIE: Good evening, Mr. Gregg.

STANISLAUS: Wasn't Miss Gregg expecting me? *(Silence, KATIE puts the tray on the table.)* Was my sister not expecting me?

KATIE: I don't rightly know that.

STANISLAUS: Did she not get my letter?

KATIE: She didn't give me the word.

STANISLAUS: Well, I've come, as you see.

KATIE: Oh, why wouldn't you? *(Long-suffering.)* Don't the place belong to yourself and your sister?

STANISLAUS: —To my sister.

KATIE: Though I wasn't counting we'd have you so soon.

STANISLAUS: No?

KATIE: No. For it isn't very long since that you were here.

STANISLAUS: No, not very long.

KATIE: But I suppose you'll be stopping on now for a while?

STANISLAUS: For a little while.

KATIE: Will you have your tea now?

STANISLAUS: I'm in no great hurry. Has Miss Gregg gone out? *(Silence. KATIE takes the tea cloth from a drawer.)* Has my sister gone out?

KATIE: She went up to the chapel at half-past five, to make the stations; she won't be long now, she'll be back very soon after the ring of the Angelus. *(STANISLAUS looks at his watch.)* Will you wait that long for her?

STANISLAUS: I will.

KATIE: I must put the sheets up to air. *(Sighs.)* Will the small bed do you?

STANISLAUS: It will.

KATIE: How well it should happen today of all days.

STANISLAUS: Today?

KATIE: Only makin' worse the chance I have for tonight.

STANISLAUS: Tonight? Today?

KATIE: Don't you know very well what day is in it?

STANISLAUS: What day?

KATIE: The regatta at Coolbeg. Isn't it held beyond always on the nineteenth of August?

STANISLAUS: Ah, yes, yes; the regatta, of course.

KATIE: Not that a body'd mind the regatta itself—only skiffin' up and down the river but the dance after if they could get the chance.

STANISLAUS: Ah, yes, I see…the dance, yes, that would be very pleasant.

KATIE: Pleasant!— *(Inadequate.)* —and it likely to be the last dance of my life.

STANISLAUS: Of your life…dear, dear…how's that?

KATIE: *(Not deigning a reply, opens out the cloth.)* Would you mind liftin' them things.

STANISLAUS: *(Takes his hat and coat from the table.)* I'm sorry…excuse me… How's this to be the last dance of your life?

KATIE: *(After a moment.)* It will if I enter the convent next month.

STANISLAUS: The convent! Are you thinking of—? *(He turns away; looks out of the window.)*

KATIE: Wouldn't it be a good thing to save my soul—and to more than save it—so what else can I do?

STANISLAUS: Dear, dear…dear me. *(Silence: KATIE moves about her work, putting cups, etc., on the table. He turns to her again.)* I think you could do something else… I mean couldn't you save it, and more than save it, some other way?

KATIE: The bread and the butter and to fill the jug… What harm but there'll be a grand moon…

STANISLAUS: Dear, dear…dear me!

KATIE: The two teams are coming across from Coolbeg. The hall at the back of Riley's—that's where it will be. That's the place has the best floor. 'Twill be near enough to us, I'll be likely to hear the dance music all night.

STANISLAUS: You mustn't miss this: you must be there.

KATIE: Do you think would she let me—if you'd ask?

STANISLAUS: Oh, she must—she'll have to, we'll tell her she must—since you're going to enter the convent next month.

KATIE: Then if I didn't—would that be a mean thing?

STANISLAUS: Not at all, not at all; we're all allowed to change our minds.

(Too accommodating. KATIE gives him a look of deep suspicion; turns to her work.)

KATIE: *(After a moment: very distant.)* 'Twould be as good for you to take a stroll down by the river while the sun'll last. It would take the dry taste off your mouth before the tea.

STANISLAUS: *(Looking out of the window.)* There's something very lovely about this little place in summer…the fields and the river…and the hills beyond.

(Silence.)

KATIE: Do you sleep cold in the night now?

STANISLAUS: Sleep cold? *(Looks round at her.)*

KATIE: Will you want the rug as well as the blanket?… *(He turns to the window again.)* Sure I'll leave it beside you on the chair. You need only stretch out your hand.

STANISLAUS: —Something very lovely… Standing here now I remember and I think— *(Checks himself, forces a matter-of-fact tone.)* Well, I think it's very pleasant…very nice little place…yes, and the garden too, very nice, very well kept…the roses, the pansies, very pretty… That rambler has come on remarkably well. *(Silence, filled with KATIE's disapproval.)* Very bright border… I wonder what's the name of that little purple flower?

KATIE: She'll be able to tell you when she'll come *(Dry.)*

STANISLAUS: *(Wheels round.)* Katie, how long have you worked here for my sister?

KATIE: Three years…come Wednesday.

STANISLAUS: "Come Wednesday!" *(Correcting.)*

KATIE: *(Nervous.)* The bread and the butter…and to fill the jug… If you *did* go you'd see were the boys coming up: I'm expecting they will for the loan of the bench.

STANISLAUS: Three years with my sister.

KATIE: 'Tis better than minding the kids at the convent beyond… When you'd be working for nuns you'd never be finished. *(Moves about her work.)* In at half-eight every night. But they had a grand library.

STANISLAUS: So you told me.

KATIE: I had the *Spiritual Maxims* off by heart. I read a lot of Saints' lives… Some of them hated the convent as much as myself, until… *(Sermonizing herself.)* … until they conquered.

STANISLAUS: Now I don't suppose you know why I'm here—because how could you?

KATIE: Sure I couldn't. Unless you were short of the money and to stop here till you'll make more.

STANISLAUS: I was not short of money. I'm thinking of buying this place.

KATIE: And what would become of me? I thought I was settled here if I'd like, to work here for Miss Gregg beside the chapel until she'd die! Would you leave me stop on?

STANISLAUS: I would.

KATIE: If you would 'tis no great matter. Would she be here too?

STANISLAUS: She might.

KATIE: Where else would she go? Isn't her life spent on her here? Is it getting married you are?

STANISLAUS: Now listen to me, it's a great shame for you not to better yourself, it's a shame—the way you speak. When I look at you I think of your mother.

KATIE: *(Humble.)* You told me that, Mr. Gregg.

STANISLAUS: Yes,— she was a wonderful woman; she spoke like I do, or Miss Gregg.

KATIE: 'Tis a shame for me, honest.

STANISLAUS: It is indeed: she was a lady; she had none of your ways.

KATIE: What height did she stand?

STANISLAUS: She...stood only a little taller than you, but she had beauty. She lived here with my sister for a while.

KATIE: Oh, I am the misfortunate girl that they'd never tell me the truth!

STANISLAUS: *(Stern.)* You are a very fortunate girl—I take a great interest in all your concerns. Better go on with your work.

KATIE: I won't stir hand or foot till I hear more of my mother. That old Roche one— you couldn't squeeze a word out of her.

STANISLAUS: Mrs. Roche very kindly brought you up.

KATIE: And who asked her at all? Or how did she get a hold of me?

STANISLAUS: Your mother died.

KATIE: That I know well. Where was...where was my father?

STANISLAUS: Katie, your mother, Mary Halnan, was a wonderful woman. She was beautiful and all that. A crowd of them, long ago, were in love with her. I loved her; I could have knocked down the world for her. But—she said I was too young.

KATIE: *(Breathless.)* And were you jilted?

STANISLAUS: She thought I was too young at the time.

KATIE: Ah, sure you were. You were only a schooleen. What sense had you then? *(This to restore his manhood,— then shrewdly.)* So she married my father?

STANISLAUS: Would you think of marrying me?

KATIE: Now is it...or...or then?

STANISLAUS: Now.

KATIE: *(After a moment.)* Ah no, Mr. Gregg. I would not.

STANISLAUS: Why not? I'd like it very much *(Reassuring.)* I know I would. You might be glad afterwards. I may seem a bit on the old side—I thought of that—but I'm strong. You'd probably age more quickly so there'd be less difference between us in a few years. *(Pause.)* Whatever you wish. I've always liked you, for your mother, for yourself—anybody would. *(Pleased at this last gallantry, he bows to her.)*

KATIE: *(Whispering.)* Who was my father?

STANISLAUS: My dear little girl— *(Pitying: a hand on her shoulder.)*

KATIE: *(Flings from him.)* If you're asking to marry me, show me respect. I won't marry you now, not if you'd go on your knees. I flout you—the same as she did!

STANISLAUS: Very well, very well: that's quite all right. Go on with your work.

KATIE: *(Fuming.)* Oh, we must be humble, but 'tis hard!... The bread and the butter and to fill the jug... And how do I know are you a good man at all? *(This last with sudden spite.)*

STANISLAUS: I'm a very good man. I always was!

KATIE: For all I could say you might have a wife up behind you in Dublin.

STANISLAUS: I have no wife, I never had. *(Quiet.)*

KATIE: For why else would you ask me?

STANISLAUS: Go on with your work!

KATIE: Oh, I will, I'm very bad. *(Abject. Moves about putting cups, etc., on the table.)* If the boys would come now... that would be nice. I like when the boys come. Do you see any Christian at all?

STANISLAUS: I see an old man crossing the field.

KATIE: Is that all you see? *(Tries to edge in beside him at the window: STANISLAUS does not make room: she sighs, stands behind him.)* Why I said now I wouldn't marry you—I was thinking in my mind—if I were to lose my soul and my body—that would be a bad thing.

STANISLAUS: It would. It certainly would.

KATIE: And how do I know would I have the grace to withstand you?

STANISLAUS: You might not. I don't think you would. *(Wheels round on her.)* Better make up your mind what you believe in! Don't be holding a match to a barrel of tar! Playing with fire, like me, and crying out to be saved!

KATIE: *(Falling back a step.)* Oh-h!... *(Catches sight of somebody outside.)* Reuben! ...He's coming! It is Reuben you seen crossing the field!

STANISLAUS: And who may Reuben be?

KATIE: Holy Reuben. He walked from Dublin. I saw him this morning down the street. I never saw him before. Oh, he's a very holy man.

STANISLAUS: He seems to be coming. What does he do?

KATIE: He listens to people. You could tell him your soul. There's many go up to Dublin for Reuben to see them... But he never came here. Do you think will he come? *(At the window.)*

STANISLAUS: He's certainly coming.

KATIE: Watch there a minute. Don't let him pass. *(Flies to the door, opens it wide.)* It would be the bad house wouldn't have the door wide when he'd be passing, or wouldn't have the glass of water ready. *(Pours water into a glass.)* That's all he'll take, and he'll never sit down.

STANISLAUS: Here he is.

KATIE: Would you like a word with him by yourself, Mr. Gregg? *(Low, excited tone.)*

STANISLAUS: I would not, thank you. I'll take up my things.

KATIE: Wait till he'll see you.

(REUBEN comes to the doorway, pauses, takes off his hat, comes in. He is old, and small, with a short grey beard and white hair. The reefer jacket he wears is too big for him, his trousers are shabby and his boots covered with dust.)

REUBEN: Is there anybody here in need of me?

KATIE: *(Nervous.)* You're welcome, very welcome. Won't you come in?

REUBEN: Is there anybody here in need of help? *(Comes farther in: stands, one delicate hand resting on his stick, his hat in the other hand.)*

KATIE: I am. I think we all are. *(Takes his hat reverently, puts it on a chair, offers him the water.)* Let you take the water first. *(Shuts the door.)*

STANISLAUS: Good evening…fine evening.

REUBEN: It is a fine evening. It is one of these golden evenings that God still lavishes on a sinful world.

(KATIE, impressed, winks at STANISLAUS.)

STANISLAUS: I expect they're very glad for the regatta.

KATIE: Do you think, would Reuben care much about the regatta? To read your heart is what he wants.

REUBEN: Speak out your heart *(To KATIE.)*

KATIE: I will. I will.

STANISLAUS: Excuse me…excuse me a moment. Would you mind letting me pass.

(KATIE stands aside. STANISLAUS takes his suitcase, goes hurriedly through the door on the right.)

KATIE: I am in great trouble of mind, Rueben. I don't know what would be right for me to do.

REUBEN: Humble yourself unto the earth.

KATIE: Is it to go down on my knees you mean? *(About to kneel down.)*

REUBEN: *(Stops her.)* Tell me what's wrong.

KATIE: I will, I will. *(Pause. She stands close to him, hands clasped. REUBEN bows his head, listening.)* Well…well… I long ago made up my mind I'd be a saint. I was trying to find one went before me in a way I'd like: the most of them entered a convent very young, and I was wondering would I— But now there's a man came here and asked me to marry him—and, I know in my heart I'd like that better. *(Silence.)* Sure if I was a good wife to him—that mightn't be an easy job! *(Silence. More defensive.)* Saint Margaret of Scotland—she wasn't a nun and didn't hold with them either.

REUBEN: Screening yourself with who did and who didn't.

KATIE: Oh, that was a mean thing I said! *(Humiliated.)* All the same…see how well she got on.

REUBEN: Do you care for this man?

KATIE: I do indeed… Wouldn't yourself if he wanted to marry you? And it isn't that only; for a long time now when he'd come to the house the power would go out of my limbs. I didn't know that was love till he asked me now, and I said to myself, "there's your convent." *(Pause.)* But—I'll tell you a queer thing— *(Lower tone.)* —I have another boy besides—Michael that works at Riley's. He asked me to go for a walk. He's a clever, handsome boy, but I don't know is he great in any way like Mr. Gregg is. Mr. Gregg draws plans for houses.

REUBEN: Katie Roche—is that what they call you?

KATIE: That's what they call me... Reuben, you know all—what was wrong with my father, or what is it is wrong with me? *(Silence.)* My mother's name was Mary Halnan.

REUBEN: Yes, your mother's name was Mary Halnan. *(Pause.)* She had this earth's changeful beauty that drew many to her. *(Pause.)* There was a man who came to spend a summer here. He came for the fishing, the trout-fishing season. He saw Mary Halnan... They met very often, down by the river on those summer evenings... He thought he was strong; he didn't know the strength of passion: it swept them both. That was how she was your mother... He went away. He was never heard of again; some said he was drowned.

KATIE: *(After a silence.)* Now I know all: I am cleared of doubt. Would Michael think less of me because of this? He would; there is no man but would... What was his name?

REUBEN: *(After a pause.)* ...Maurice Fitzsimon of Kylebeg.

KATIE: Fitzsimon! of Kylebeg! The grand house beyond! And am I—? *(Raises her arms, excitedly.)*

REUBEN: Humble yourself unto the earth!

KATIE *(Laughs wildly.)* Is it to scrub out the floor you want? Me that has better blood than you all!

REUBEN: *(Grasping his stick.)* Go down on your knees! Proud of that treacherous blood!

KATIE: *(Drawn to full height.)* Did he despise her?

REUBEN: I don't think he did.

KATIE: You don't think he did! And for why should he so? Wasn't she as good as himself if she had beauty?

REUBEN: He had wife and children before ever they met.

KATIE: And is that a fault on me? I'm done with humble. I was meant to be proud. Didn't I know always I came from great people.

REUBEN: Great people!

KATIE: 'Tis good-bye to Michael. Were the Greggs grand at one time? I think they were, though they live in this little place.

REUBEN: There's one grandeur— it belongs to God.

KATIE: Ah, you couldn't go very much by the Bible; what's said in one place is unsaid in another, and that's the great puzzle; —often you'd think you had an answer.

REUBEN: Christ left no doubt. He was at war with this world, worldly thoughts, and worldly values; you speak of "grand people" and "better blood"—

KATIE: Whisht now a minute.

(She listens. The door is pushed open. MICHAEL MAGUIRE is seen in the doorway. MICHAEL is young, somewhat uncouth, not altogether without dignity. He does not see REUBEN: the door blocks his view.)

MICHAEL: Kate, why don't you come down? I'm below at the corner since Miss Gregg went out.

KATIE: Oh!

MICHAEL: Ah, come on now, all our time will be gone—the one chance we have before she'll come back.

KATIE: There's a great beauty! *(Appeal for REUBEN's sympathy. MICHAEL stiffens.)* Come in, Michael—sure you're welcome! *(Sardonic.)*

MICHAEL: I can't come now. I'm in a great hurry.

(Moving off—KATIE dives at him, catches the lapel of his coat.)

KATIE: Come in, and make use of the eyes in your head. *(REUBEN moves from behind the door. KATIE turns to him.)* Now this is the chap I was telling you about!

MICHAEL: *(Pulls off his cap.)* I'm sorry; I'm very sorry! I didn't know you were here.

REUBEN: What is it you want?

KATIE: What brought you up at this hour?

MICHAEL: *(To REUBEN.)* Since I'm here now hope you'll excuse me... 'Tis my mother I'm thinking of. She'd be very grateful if you'd look in on her. She's killed this long time praying you'll come, and I was to say it if I got the chance. She has money put by—she wants to give it to you till you'll get a Mass said—'tis for the peace of the world and her cough to be cured that's on her chest and smothering her now for more than twelve months.

REUBEN: I'll come see your mother.

MICHAEL: I'll tell her so; she'll be very grateful. *(Moves to go.)*

KATIE: Well, Michael? *(Challenging.)*

MICHAEL: What brought me up now was the bench for tonight that Miss Gregg has promised. If we could take it now I'd call Jo Mahony—he'd give me a hand.

KATIE: Was it that brought you up?

MICHAEL: It was that surely.

KATIE: *(Gentle.)* Michael, let us have no lies now in the presence of Reuben, for he knows well what's between us.

MICHAEL: *(Alarmed.)* And what is between us? There's nothing between us, to my knowledge, and never was.

KATIE: He must hear the whole truth.

MICHAEL: Well, you couldn't mind yourself with a girl!

KATIE: *(To REUBEN, a hand on MICHAEL's arm.)* How the two of us fell to meeting so often... It is that Michael can play the melodeon grand, and I'm fond of a tune, and then one day he put his arm around me—

MICHAEL: You're very mean—

KATIE: —And said would the two of us ever suit one another.

MICHAEL: I'm not denying it! *(To REUBEN.)* But you gave me no promise, *(To KATIE.)* so there's nothing between us. And even now *(To REUBEN.)* she could do what she'd like with me. And you know that well, *(To KATIE.)* and you're very mean—

KATIE: *(Earnest.)* Reuben, would it be a mean thing now if I gave him up?

REUBEN: *(Turns to MICHAEL.)* I'll come see your mother. *(Moves towards the door, stops, looks at KATIE.)* You're quite free—isn't he saying it? Make your own choice. *(Very gruff.)* I think 'twould be better go on with your work and put all that nonsense out of head.

(Goes out. MICHAEL, following out, laughs.)

KATIE: *(With a flash.)* Is it Michael you mean?

MICHAEL: *(Delaying.)* How could you put me out of your head? What's in the heart, Kate, is in the mind.

(Goes. KATIE watches them for a moment. Crosses the room, takes her hat from the rack near the door, goes to the mirror. AMELIA GREGG comes in. AMELIA is an odd little woman of something over fifty, dressed with careful neatness, in dark things—a long dark coat and a black hat that not all her care can ever keep quite straight. Cotton gloves.)

AMELIA: Katie, I came back. I came back early because my brother's coming... I forgot to tell you. I don't know how I forgot.

KATIE: 'Tis of no great account.

AMELIA: I can't think how I forgot. For a few days. I don't know why he's coming,— but of course I'm pleased. I'm always very pleased.

KATIE: He had always a heavy hand with the butter. I'll run down to Harney's for a half pound... Upstairs he is now.

AMELIA: Upstairs? —Has he come?

KATIE: He was ashamed before Reuben, so he went up. *(Gives her hair a final touch, goes to the door, looks back.)* So long now. *(Cheerily.)* I won't make any delay, and when I come back I'll get the tea. *(Goes.)*

(AMELIA goes eagerly to the door leading to the rest of the house—hesitates, comes back a little way. Looks about the room, moves a chair here—a book there. Goes again to the door, looks round the room, and, not satisfied, comes back to change the position of chair, and books... While she is doing all this with eager nervousness, STANISLAUS quietly opens the door, and stands in the doorway watching her, amused, affectionate.)

AMELIA: Stan dear, you've come!... *(Goes to him quickly—kisses him.)*

STANISLAUS: Well, Amelia, and how are you?... *(Affectionately, hands on her shoulders.)* ...You look...just the same.

AMELIA: Do I, Stan? *(A happy little laugh.)* I suppose I do... I'm so glad to see you... But won't you sit down... *(Fluttering movements about him; about to draw out a chair for him, then not quite sure whether he wants to sit down.)* That's if you like...

STANISLAUS: Yes. Did you not get my letter?

AMELIA: I did, Stan.

STANISLAUS: —Because Katie didn't know.

AMELIA: I forgot to tell her. Wasn't that stupid of me?

STANISLAUS: No matter. Only I wondered...

AMELIA: I don't know how I forgot... Wasn't it very stupid.

STANISLAUS: Sit down, Amelia,— sit down... Nothing stupid about it. Now I won't have tea...not till we're all having it...

AMELIA: No, I remembered. I remembered you wouldn't... *(Triumphant.)* but if you'd like to change your mind— *(He shakes his head.)* —no trouble at all...

STANISLAUS: Now you want to know why I've come.

AMELIA: No, no, dear. I don't. I'm pleased. I'm always very pleased.

STANISLAUS: Yes, I suppose so, but if you want to know why—

AMELIA: —Not at all, I don't... You've come: that's enough for me. *(Draws her chair near him, looks lovingly at him.)*

STANISLAUS: Amelia— *(Abrupt.)* —haven't you sometimes regretted this?

AMELIA: This?

STANISLAUS: Your life and all that...

AMELIA: Oh, Stan, I know I have much to regret. My dear, when I think of God's goodness, and all the grace and help—

STANISLAUS: Dear, dear... I mean this— *(Gesture including all the room.)*

AMELIA: *(Perplexed.)* I'm fond of my little house, Stan.

STANISLAUS: Are you? I see. I see... *(Pause.)* I thought you might have regrets... *(Pause.)* I think you've lived here always?

AMELIA: I have, dear...

STANISLAUS: Yes, you were born here.

AMELIA: I was.

STANISLAUS: Yes. I remember my mother speaking of that hot summer when you were born... *(Pause.)* You've grown old—well on,— if I may say so—in the house where you were once young... *(Looks slowly about the room.)* Of course why wouldn't you, if that's what you like... *(Smiles at her.)* You've always been kind. I must say you've always been kind.

AMELIA: What is it, Stan? *(Quietly, watching him.)*

STANISLAUS: Why do you say, "What is it"?

AMELIA: You're troubled, I think.

STANISLAUS: Do I look troubled?... Has my face a troubled look?

AMELIA: You seem troubled, my dear...

STANISLAUS: *(Offended.)* I'm sorry to hear that. Of course I know my face isn't the same as it used to be... *(Smoothes his face.)* I was hoping that wasn't very noticeable... Troubled... *(But she just keeps looking at him quietly. After a moment he changes, says simply:)* You're quite right—I am,— a little bit troubled...

AMELIA: Yes?

STANISLAUS: Yes. I was lying in bed this morning, and I said to myself, "It's terrible." ...Fact is, I've a lot of expense...

AMELIA: You have, dear; oh, you must have... And I know how good you've been to me always, to Margaret and me... You have a heart of gold...

STANISLAUS: *(Absent.)* Yes, yes—but you see it's pretty expensive,— this house and my rooms...

AMELIA: I suppose it is.

STANISLAUS: Amelia, things can't go on much longer.

AMELIA: Can't they, dear? No, I suppose they can't... *(So unruffled, that he grows desperate.)*

STANISLAUS: —Then where'll you be? I'm your brother, Margaret's your sister—but *where'll you be? (Fiercely. AMELIA shakes her head.)* ...Of course, you're perfectly entitled to do what you like...*perfectly entitled*—please keep on thinking of that. My own opinion is you should do something...

AMELIA: Perhaps I should. What do you think I should do?

STANISLAUS: *(Swift.)* Wouldn't it be nice for you to get married?

AMELIA: Married! Me!...Stan...me married?

STANISLAUS: It sounds silly,— but it needn't be... People often marry when they're not...well, when they're not quite so young... I met Frank Lawlor. I *reminded him.*

AMELIA: Frank!...Mr. Lawlor... Oh, Stan, what did you remind him of?

STANISLAUS: Don't be frightened. There's nothing to be frightened about.

AMELIA: But...what did you say to Mr. Lawlor?

STANISLAUS: I spoke of old times.

AMELIA: Oh dear, oh dear.

STANISLAUS: He said he'd come see you.

AMELIA: Come and see me! Oh, what have you done?

STANISLAUS: You'd think you were fifteen... There, Amelia,— you'd have liked it long ago—why not now?...

AMELIA: Not now, oh no.

STANISLAUS: Very well: just say that,— though it's a pity. He likes you! I know that. I won't say more: it wouldn't be fair...

AMELIA: But what did you say to him, Stan? You didn't say that I like him?

STANISLAUS: Not at all. He knows that. Forget it now, since you've no wish.

AMELIA: And if Mr. Lawlor comes here you'll see him,— won't you, Stan? I won't, I couldn't...

STANISLAUS: Very well, very well. *(Sorely tried.)* Whatever you like...

AMELIA: —And you'll tell him it was all a mistake...whatever you said. That you made a mistake...

STANISLAUS: That I made a mistake. Try to have sense.

AMELIA: Oh, I know I'm foolish.

STANISLAUS: Doesn't matter: you *can't* help it... Though it *is* a pity... *(Pause—then suddenly.)* Would you like me to come and live with you?

AMELIA: Oh, Stan—wouldn't that be very nice?

STANISLAUS: But—would you mind very much if there was a wife too?

AMELIA: *(After a moment.)* Now wouldn't that be very nice? *(Bravely.)*

STANISLAUS: Thanks Amelia, thanks very much. *(Sits back, relieved.)* You're very...obliging. I'd like it myself.

AMELIA: And why wouldn't you, Stan? Why wouldn't every man want a wife? Yes, and children too. Quite right.

STANISLAUS: You're...very kind.

AMELIA: But—Stan, I'd like somebody nice for you.

STANISLAUS: Yes, yes. So would I. *(Absent now.)*

AMELIA: I mean, somebody suitable, somebody really nice.

STANISLAUS: Yes, somebody suitable...

(Door is pushed open, KATIE comes in, radiant.)

KATIE: Wait now a minute. *(To someone outside. Shuts the door, turns to AMELIA.)* That's two of the boys of the dance committee, and what they want—would you give a lend of the bench for the supper tonight?

STANISLAUS: "Give a lend"...

KATIE: I know, I know, but an odd time I forget. *(Turns to AMELIA.)* And if you would they'd take it now.

AMELIA: Yes, yes. I suppose they may have it. I think I promised.

KATIE: You did indeed.

AMELIA: I suppose they won't break it?

KATIE: *(Opening the door.)* Come in, Michael. Come in, Jo. *(MICHAEL MAGUIRE comes in, followed by JO MAHONY—another youth of the village.)* If Miss Gregg will loan you the bench, will you bring it back safe? —if she'll be so kind as to loan it? *(Superior: pleased with her way of dealing with this.)*

JO: We will, we will indeed. *(Low, eager tone.)*

KATIE: Will you both swear on your honor that nothing'll happen?

MICHAEL: Keep out of my way. *(Steps forward, turns to AMELIA.)* I'm sorry, Miss Gregg,— what brought us up was the bench for tonight... If you'd leave us take it now, Jo'd give me a hand.

AMELIA: Oh yes, certainly. Yes, I remember I promised.

MICHAEL: You did so. You'll have it back in the morning. We're short for the supper.

AMELIA: *(To KATIE.)* It's in the kitchen, I think.

KATIE: *(Goes to the door, stops, turns to AMELIA.)* Give me a minute. It's loaded with delft. I was dusting the dresser when Mr. Gregg came. He put everything else out of my head. *(Goes.)*

AMELIA: It won't be broken, I suppose?

MICHAEL: It will not, Miss Gregg. We wouldn't trouble you at all but for the girls to sit down.

JO: We'll stand around ourselves, but the team-boys will be tired.

AMELIA: Oh, you're welcome to have it, very welcome indeed.

JO: *(To STANISLAUS.)* How we're short this time is that at the last meeting they broke up two of the benches.

STANISLAUS: I see. *(To AMELIA, a little grim.)* They're short this time because at the last meeting they broke up two of the benches *(Slowly.)*

MICHAEL: *(Quickly.)* That was the Coolbeg crowd: they're a rough lot,— not the fellows that'll be here tonight though. *(Turns to JO.)* Couldn't you give her a hand.

(JO goes out to the kitchen, MICHAEL also moves towards the door, hesitates, appears to have something on his mind.)

STANISLAUS: I hope the regatta was very successful.

MICHAEL: Fair, only fair. The Coolbeg team walked away with it.

STANISLAUS: Dear...dear,— stronger men?

MICHAEL: Ah, they have more time for practice, and a better part of the river. *(Turns to AMELIA.)* But the dance tonight—that'll be good.

AMELIA: Yes, I'm sure it will be very good.

MICHAEL: 'Twill be very select.

STANISLAUS: I suppose there'll be a big crowd.

MICHAEL: The crowd that's coming— they're very select. *(Emphasis.)* Some of the committee from Dublin will be there. 'Twill be a better-class dance than is usually held.

STANISLAUS: And I believe Mrs. Riley has a very good hall.

MICHAEL: Would you leave her come? *(To AMELIA suddenly.)*

AMELIA: Come?

MICHAEL: Tonight... over to Riley's... 'twill be very select.

AMELIA: You mean Katie?

MICHAEL: If you'd leave her come I'd keep an eye to her. I'd send her home before it got rough.

AMELIA: Oh, dear... I'm afraid I couldn't let Katie out at that hour.

MICHAEL: The whole town will be in it: she'd like it very much.

AMELIA: Not to a dance, no, no. I couldn't... I don't think so.

MICHAEL: Very well, Miss Gregg... Though 'twill go hard on her to stop here the night, an' we dancing beyond... She'd come to no harm.

AMELIA: But,— I don't think I ought to let her... to a thing like that. I wouldn't like to, though I do like Katie to enjoy herself. *(Laughter from the kitchen; sound of something falling.)* Oh, she's very giddy.

MICHAEL: Giddy for sure: you'd have to mind yourself when you're with her.

(More laughter.)

AMELIA: Oh, I'd better see...

(Goes out to the kitchen. MICHAEL is about to follow; STANISLAUS stops him.)

STANISLAUS: Excuse me. *(Turns; shuts the door.)* Would you mind telling me— though I know it's not usual—are you very friendly with Katie?

MICHAEL: *(Guarded.)* Come-and-go. I can pass her.

STANISLAUS: I see. *(Pause.)* I thought perhaps you were very friendly. *(Nervous.)* She's a very nice girl.

MICHAEL: Oh—she's a nice girl, I'll grant you.

STANISLAUS: Yes, very nice... *(Increasingly nervous.)* I had some idea you were very friendly because I remember meeting you often—just the two of you—walking along down by the river... Of course, why wouldn't you?... I hope you don't mind.

MICHAEL: *(Stolid.)* That's all we do... to walk along... Often I bring the paper with me.

STANISLAUS: I see... I had thought you might be fond of her.

MICHAEL: Fond of her, is it? 'Tis that she was mad to be at this dance.

STANISLAUS: As a matter of fact I'm fond of Katie myself.

MICHAEL: *(After a moment's silence.)* Oh, she can be very nice.

STANISLAUS: Yes,— very nice.

MICHAEL: *(With great detachment.)* When she takes the fancy she has a sweet way.

STANISLAUS: A very sweet way.

MICHAEL: And she's that quick-hearted.

STANISLAUS: Very quick-hearted.

MICHAEL: *(Suddenly swift.)* 'Tis a pity about her...

STANISLAUS: A pity—?

MICHAEL: What chance has she? Sure there's no one round here would think of her—for want of a name. *(Silence.)* ...And look at some of them—what good is their name?

STANISLAUS: Not very much, I suppose...

MICHAEL: *(Snorts contempt.)* And yet—... *(Slowly.)* —you wouldn't like it yourself—the way 'tis about her. *(Silence.)* ...My mother would die if I were to bring her in the door.

STANISLAUS: That would be a great pity! And how is your mother?

MICHAEL: *(In a flash.)* I don't know, Mr. Gregg, how she is!

(KATIE and JO come in, carrying the bench; both are full of merriment. AMELIA follows.)

KATIE: Do you know what Jo said? ...He said— *(Overcome with laughter.)* —tell them...tell them you...

(JO laughs a little self-consciously. MICHAEL looks disapproval.)

MICHAEL: *(Severe.)* You can't come to the dance. You'll have to stop here. Miss Gregg won't leave you: I asked her now.

KATIE: *(Looks at him, draws herself up.)* You made a mistake, Michael Maguire. You stepped out of your place—to mention my name. *(They look at one another, hostile.)* You and your dance!

MICHAEL: Oh you have a great notion! ...You wanted that dance, you said it yourself...

KATIE: Early this morning... *(Far from that now.)*

MICHAEL: *(Turns aside, takes one end of the bench.)* You couldn't please a girl. Come on, Jo.

JO: The chair from the kitchen. *(Goes hurriedly to the kitchen.)*

STANISLAUS: *(To KATIE.)* I think you might say thanks to Michael.

MICHAEL: I wouldn't care whether she was in it or no. 'Twas that she had me pestered.

KATIE: *(To STANISLAUS.)* And what would I say "Thank you" for?... *(Suddenly flies out.)* Oh, he's a double beauty... a great floundering gander that thinks he knows all, and comes spattering—

STANISLAUS: Katie! *(Thundered.)*

KATIE: Oh! *(Turns aside trying to keep back tears.)*

STANISLAUS: Not very much dignity.

(JO reappears with a chair, puts it on top of the bench. MICHAEL takes one end of the bench, JO the other.)

MICHAEL: We're very much obliged to you, Miss Gregg.

STANISLAUS: Excuse me. *(To MICHAEL, stopping him. Turns to KATIE.)* We must ask you to apologise.

MICHAEL: Ah, leave her alone. 'Tis losin' the dance. She was mad to go; I know her well.

AMELIA: *(To KATIE.)* Perhaps...if you get the tea.

STANISLAUS: Wait a moment, please. *(Turns to MICHAEL.)* I'll ask you to wait too, if Jo doesn't mind... Michael will be down in a few minutes *(To JO.)*

JO: *(To MICHAEL.)* I'll leave you the chair. *(Takes the bench.)*

STANISLAUS: Thanks... I hope you don't mind. *(Opens the door for him.)*

JO: That's all right, Mr. Gregg. *(Goes.)*

STANISLAUS: *(Shuts the door, turns to the others.)* Excuse me a moment... *(Nervous.)* ...Certain things have been said here this evening that make it imperative for me to say others... Not perhaps exactly imperative, but I decided it was better to speak... *(Looks towards KATIE.)* If you're finished crying, please turn round.

(KATIE wipes away her tears, partly turns, listens with interest. STANISLAUS turns to MICHAEL.) You're both young people. I'm not very young. I know that well. I want to be fair... *(Pause.)* ...Fact is—a long time ago I made up my mind that I'd marry Katie: I mean that I'd try .*(Bows towards her.)* I didn't know her then: I was living abroad, and when I came home I found she hadn't been properly educated—

AMELIA: That wasn't your fault, Stan, you thought that she—

STANISLAUS: Excuse me—*excuse me one moment*... You don't speak well. *(To KATIE.)* I was disappointed: I went away... But afterwards I came again and I found she was what I wanted. Her heart and her mind were what I wanted. I've asked her now, and she's thinking about it... *(Bows to KATIE. A moment's silence.)*

AMELIA: Stan, I think you're fine... I think—

STANISLAUS: Yes. Wait a moment. *(Looks at KATIE.)*

AMELIA: My dear, you have a heart of gold...

STANISLAUS: Yes, yes, perhaps. *(Looks at KATIE.)*

KATIE: *(Turns to MICHAEL.)* Are you going home now?... He don't care what you'll think. He's not afraid to belittle himself...

STANISLAUS: I'm sorry you're behaving like this. *(Stern.)*

KATIE: *(Flaming.)* My heart and my mind! A queer way to love!... Taking a body to pieces!

STANISLAUS: Very well, whatever you like... *(Takes this as refusal, moves a little away.)* At any rate, I wouldn't have let you go to this dance.

KATIE: It wouldn't be grand enough for you? *(Thrilled.)*

STANISLAUS: It wouldn't be grand enough. *(Pause: looks at her.)* Perhaps I should have told you, my desire to get married was partly because that might benefit my work. But I'd have liked it very much. I know that was true. *(As one who fears to say a word more than he feels.)*

KATIE: *(Goes to him.)* Is it me to be the woman behind you? A help at your work? Is that what you want? *(Eager.)*

STANISLAUS: You might indeed: you very well might. *(So condescending that she is repulsed.)*

KATIE: I might!

AMELIA: Oh, dear...shall I get the tea?

STANISLAUS: Do Amelia, do please.

AMELIA: I will... The kettle must be boiled away.

(Goes. STANISLAUS delays, expecting MICHAEL to go. MICHAEL watches him. After a moment STANISLAUS goes.)

MICHAEL: He's a little bit cracked. *(Silence.)* The Greggs are nice people but they're all a little bit queer... Ah, you'd know he had no regular work...only drawing plans for houses... *(Silence, MICHAEL takes the chair, goes to the door, puts the chair down, turns to KATIE.)* It would be yourself with me, Kate.

KATIE: Isn't he the grand man!

MICHAEL: He might be grand right enough, but he's not for you. What we're born to—that's what we'll be. *(Moves nearer, lowers his tone.)* Everyone here knows about you...an' they don't hold it agen you till you'll be putting on "side"... So you'd like to be grand...ho! Katie Roche. *(Pause.)* Ah, come on now, don't mind about him. Let us be like we were, and in a couple of years I'll make you a home you can take that from me. I won't let you down.

KATIE: Jo is waiting for you...

MICHAEL *(Takes up the chair.)* So 'tis good-bye to you and me?

(Silence. He goes, KATIE sighs, sits down. She is deep in thought when AMELIA comes to the door.)

AMELIA: Katie, Mr. Gregg said to tell you, I mean Stan said to tell you—

KATIE: What? *(Apprehensive.)*

AMELIA: He's in the little room, if you care to go to him.

KATIE: *(Rises, alarmed.)* Must I go now?

AMELIA: Do whatever you wish dear. He said not to try to influence you. Do whatever you wish. *(Withdraws.)*

KATIE: Oh— *(In turmoil.)* —who knows what they wish! *(Clasps her hands—then, seeking strength.)* "One false step and you're over the precipice, one bad link and the chain goes snap, one wrong act and a life is ruined, one small...one small...one...one" *(Trying to concentrate.)* *—ach!— (Turns to run from the room, meets STANISLAUS coming in. He opens his arms, takes her.)* Oh-h...Oh-h... *(In ecstasy.)*

STANISLAUS: I couldn't wait. *(Kisses her.)*

KATIE: Oh! *(Overcome. Then frees herself; stands back from him.)* Yes, I'll give you my hand.

STANISLAUS: That's right. That's a good girl. Now don't be nervy. Don't be upset. It's only the strain. *(Pats her shoulder reassuringly. KATIE stiffens.)* Why—even I felt it. We'll be sensible. We'll get married very soon. My sister will live with us—if you don't mind. She'll go away sometimes. *(KATIE looks at him now with the anger of a child at a clumsy companion. AMELIA comes in with the tea things. STANISLAUS turns to her.)* We're going to be married. I hope you don't mind.

AMELIA: Oh, Stan dear, why should I mind? Katie, dear. *(Kisses her.)* I'm pleased. I'm so very pleased. I hope you'll both be very happy.

STANISLAUS: I hope we will.

AMELIA: I'm sure you will, Stan... I think you know one another well. I think we'll be a very happy little household.

STANISLAUS: I hope so.

AMELIA: Well, come now, and we'll have tea.

(AMELIA and STANISLAUS go to the table, and sit down: KATIE does not move.)

STANISLAUS: We'll live here. I'll go on with my work. You and Katie will look after the house... And sometimes— *(A smile over at KATIE.)* —she'll come to Dublin with me.

AMELIA: Oh, won't that be nice! Katie, won't that be very nice?...Come now, your tea.

(KATIE comes slowly to the table, and sits down.)

(Curtain.)

ACT II

A December evening—shortly after six. The furniture in the room is unchanged, but the whole room now has an air of life and warmth. There are gaily colored prints on the wall. Two or three cushions have vivid covers. The lamp on the table is lighted, the curtains are drawn and the fire is bright.

STANISLAUS and KATIE sit in front of the fire, side by side. They bend eagerly over some papers which STANISLAUS holds. KATIE's arm is thrown across his shoulder. In her eagerness, bending forward, reading, she comes in the way of his view. He moves a little from her: she moves closer to him, drawing him down toward the papers. STANISLAUS quickly frees himself, sits back. After a moment KATIE sits back too, sighs contentedly.

KATIE: I am the proud woman this night. I know now for sure you're great.

STANISLAUS: I think it is good—so far. *(Anxious.)* I think it is a fine plan.

KATIE: Fine. It is like what would come out of the head of a prince. *(He laughs.)* I think that it is. *(Takes a letter from him, reads:)* "The Commissioners are very pleased—" So well they might. You have taken the breath out of their body.

STANISLAUS: And my little wife's very pleased too.

KATIE: 'Tis what I was hoping when we stood at the altar... Those plans you have here there are few could think of.

STANISLAUS: They're not finished yet.

KATIE: No,— let you go on with them now.

STANISLAUS: Yes...yes, I must show them to Amelia.

KATIE: *(Springs up.)* She'll be back any minute—I have nothing ready. *(Takes the tea cloth from the drawer, about to spread it on the table, then leaves it, and goes over to STANISLAUS.)* Was it I made you do this?

STANISLAUS: Made me do it?

KATIE: Wasn't it like because of our love?

STANISLAUS: Because of our love?...

KATIE: Or what made you do it?

STANISLAUS: *(Judicial, as always afraid of saying a word more than he feels.)* I think, Katie, I did this chiefly for love of the work...and of course to get on.

KATIE: Were you thinking of me, and you working at it?

STANISLAUS: Well, my mind was mostly on my work but I do think of you very often, very often indeed.

KATIE: What good is "often" that should be "always"? *(She looks again at the plans.)* No matter—a prince. *(From outside—the sound of a concertina. They listen. She laughs.)* Michael...himself and Jo must have something on foot. *(Music comes nearer; they listen.)* He's very fond of that thing... "I dreamt that I dwelt in Marble Halls."... So well he might. So well they all might. *(They listen.)*

STANISLAUS: Very nice...very nice indeed.

(The music passes. The door is opened. AMELIA comes in, a little breathless.)

AMELIA: I hope I'm not late. I delayed making the stations...

STANISLAUS: We were looking at these. Some of my plans...as far as I've gone. *(Holds out the papers to her.)*

AMELIA: Oh, Stan isn't that very nice.

STANISLAUS: I think it good.

AMELIA: I'm sure it is—though I don't understand it.

KATIE: Show me those papers. *(Takes the papers. Goes to the table, spreads them on it.*

Turns to AMELIA, glowing, excited.) Look at this now. Isn't that a grand thing? Here is the ground floor, and the entrance hall, there two pillars…and a portico…and—see that— *(Pointing.)* Can you see it all now like it was built there before you? The spire—can you see it? With maybe the sun shining on it?

AMELIA: Won't it be lovely? Isn't it very well done?

KATIE: Well done! 'Tis the work of a genius. *(Excited.)*

AMELIA: My dear, aren't we happy!

KATIE: Happy all right. He's going to finish it now.

AMELIA: *(To STANISLAUS.)* Oh—are you going to finish it now?

KATIE: He is so. Why not?

AMELIA: *(To STANISLAUS.)* Only that you promised you'd call down to see Margaret.

KATIE: He can't now; he's too busy.

AMELIA: *(Hesitant.)* You see it's her birthday… *(To STANISLAUS.)* You promised you'd go. Just for a minute.

KATIE: I'll run down and tell her you have no time.

STANISLAUS: No, I'll go myself. I remember I promised.

AMELIA: She'll be very pleased.

KATIE: Is that the care you have for your work?

AMELIA: Katie, she won't keep him.

KATIE: She might as well—if he goes at all. *(STANISLAUS looks at her.)* To run here and run there—will that do your work?

STANISLAUS: *(To AMELIA.)* I'll go.

AMELIA: You're very good: she was hoping you might… After all, it is her birthday, you know. *(To KATIE. Turns to STANISLAUS.)* You'll be able to finish it later?

STANISLAUS: Yes,— it's practically done.

KATIE: I doubt will he ever finish! *(In a blaze.)* I doubt is he any good at all!

(Silence.)

STANISLAUS: *(After a moment.)* Margaret might come up with me. They might both come. I'll ask them. I forgot 'twas her birthday.

AMELIA: Oh, that would be nice! Wouldn't it, Katie? We'd have a little party… *(Coaxing.)* And we'd all be talking about Stan's work.

KATIE: I could never hold with a pat on the back.

AMELIA: But it's nice being all together in times of happiness, isn't it? Now, we'll prepare for a party, you and I. We'll get everything ready while he's down there. I'll take off my things. *(Goes.)*

(STANISLAUS gathers his papers together, puts them into his case.)

KATIE: *(After a moment.)* How well that Frank Lawlor never married Amelia.

(Silence. STANISLAUS sorts his papers.)

STANISLAUS: After all, Margaret is my sister.

KATIE: So I believe.

STANISLAUS: And though we don't care much for Hubert, well, after all, he's her husband…

KATIE: I understand that he is. *(Very distant.)*

STANISLAUS: Yes, yes; and though we do sometimes see too much of them—well, just for this evening it won't matter.

KATIE: Just for this evening...just this once... *(Low, scornful.)*

STANISLAUS: *(Gets his hat and overcoat, holds out a scarf that has been left with his coat.)* I never wear this. Where's the other?

KATIE: You might find it upstairs.

STANISLAUS: I might find it upstairs! I want it now.

(Silence. KATIE does not move.)

KATIE: Yourself left it upstairs.

(After a moment STANISLAUS goes, KATIE, relieved, nods triumphantly at herself in the mirror: then stands looking into the fire. From outside comes the sound of the concertina—faintly heard. It dies away. STANISLAUS comes back, scarf in hand: comes over to KATIE.)

STANISLAUS: It's pleasant, you know, telling people when you have good news. *(Gentle.)*

KATIE: I suppose that it is. *(Silence—then.)* I was thinking in my mind about them plans. *(Pause: he watches her.)* Maybe they're not so perfect good as we thought.

STANISLAUS: Not so good?

KATIE: It might be we were too easy pleased.

STANISLAUS: We may have been. *(Quiet.)*

KATIE: Wouldn't it be a grand thing now if you could improve them? *(Silence.)* Wouldn't this be the best ever—to sit down and write the Commissioners them plans were rotten bad, an' if they'd give you time you'd do something better?

STANISLAUS: "Rotten bad," "them plans"...

KATIE: And then to put them in the fire, and work out a new thing, the like was never heard.

STANISLAUS: I won't be long. *(Turns to the door.)*

KATIE: Is that the heed you'd give what I say? I dunno do you put a right value on me at all of late? Three months now since we stood at the altar, and three times you drew from me.

STANISLAUS: *(Putting her aside.)* I can't delay. There's a good child.

KATIE: Child! I am your wife that you married.

STANISLAUS: Then do what you're told! Keep out!

KATIE: *(Springs back—stands aside, stiff.)* Is that what I'm for?

STANISLAUS: *(Goes out, looks back at her.)* If they're out I'll be back in a minute.

(Shuts the door; goes. KATIE comes to the fire, stands looking into it. The concertina is heard again—faintly.)

AMELIA: *(Opens the door right, looks in.)* I think I'll make scones for tea... He might be pleased.

KATIE: He might.

AMELIA: I think I'd have time—before he comes back.

KATIE: Why wouldn't you? And plenty of time.

AMELIA: Because I don't suppose he'll come back at once...

KATIE: What would bring him back?

AMELIA: No,— because Hubert might want to see the plans, and Margaret might want to talk about them.

KATIE: —And himself will talk too,— so go make the scones, let you.

AMELIA: Yes...yes, I think I will... And we won't take very long to set the table.

KATIE: Sure we won't. *(AMELIA goes, KATIE swiftly crosses the room, turns the key in the door, comes back, puts the key on the mantelpiece—and gazes into the fire again. Music comes nearer. KATIE moves, hesitates—then:)* I will... I will. "Great deeds were never done by little hearts." *(Goes to the front door, opens it, goes a little way out. Her hair and skirt are blown by the wind. She looks to the left, waves, comes back into the room, holding the door. MICHAEL MAGUIRE appears.)* Come in, Michael...won't you come in?... *(Nervous.)*

MICHAEL: Why so would I come in? *(But he steps in.)*

KATIE: Shut the door, Michael.

(Goes to the fire, inviting him. He shuts the door.)

MICHAEL: Do you want something of me?

KATIE: What a great stranger you are.

MICHAEL: What call have I to be anything else?

KATIE: Come and sit down.

MICHAEL: Why would I so? I'm out for a walk. I'm going down now to meet Jo Mahony. He and myself—along with some others—are walking over the hill of Knock. To the music we're walking... 'Tis waiting around for them I was.

KATIE: Let Jo wait a few minutes. *(Nervous. MICHAEL watches her.)* Walking over the hill of Knock... I'd like to be out there, walking with you.

MICHAEL: What's on you tonight? *(Pause.)* I thought you were very well pleased with yourself. I'm watching you often since you went and got married... Are you alone in the house tonight?

KATIE: Miss Gregg is inside.

MICHAEL: *(Puts his concertina on the table, comes nearer the fire.)* Was that Mr. Gregg I seen come out now and go down the way? *(KATIE nods. MICHAEL laughs suddenly, mocking.)* So he went out, and you're to stop here, and you're in a tantrum. Is that what's on you? *(Silence. Then, more kindly.)* Sure I knew very well that man was too old, but you've done the harm now.

KATIE: It isn't he is too old for me, but I am too young. I'm a child always to him... Whatever I'd say is only a joke.

MICHAEL: There's no cure for that now—you've made your choice.

KATIE: There'll be a cure soon.

MICHAEL: How so?

KATIE: I'll cure it tonight.

MICHAEL: *(Laughs again.)* You're in a wax right enough.

KATIE: *(Pokes the fire, looks round at him, smiles suddenly.)* Michael, what's on you? Out on a night like this with only a thin coat around you! Let me give you a muffler against the wind on your chest.

MICHAEL: I'm in need of no muffler—

KATIE: Wait now a minute. *(Goes to the rack, takes STANISLAUS's muffler, brings it over to MICHAEL.)* Take a loan of this now—

MICHAEL: Is it mad you are? What would I want with the like of that?

KATIE: You can give it back to me later. *(Puts it round his neck.)*

MICHAEL: There's great comfort in it.

KATIE: What harm would it do it to be round your neck? *(Ties it about his neck.)* And the wind that will be tearing over the hill of Knock.

MICHAEL: What a great fool you were, Kate.

KATIE: *(Steps back from him.)* Michael Maguire, do you think I regret the thing I done?

MICHAEL: So what made you call me to come in an' I passing? Did I ask to come in? And when I did come, it wasn't dancing with joy I found you.

(Silence. KATIE fingers his concertina.)

KATIE: I had ever a great love for your music.

MICHAEL: Oh 'tis grand to be free...to wander around with that wherever you'd like. To be at no one's bidding, but to please yourself. I wouldn't change my lot now for a king's ransom. *(Pause. KATIE fingers the concertina.)* Often we're breaking our heart for a thing, and when we don't get it we're very glad after.

KATIE: You could play me a tune now while I'm getting the glasses.

MICHAEL: The glasses!

(KATIE crosses to the press: takes two glasses and a small tray, puts them on the table, then takes out a whisky decanter and soda water siphon. MICHAEL watches—astonished, curious.)

KATIE: Wouldn't you like some of this?

MICHAEL: Whisky and soda...so that's what he takes. Do you have a glass too? *(Laughs.)*

KATIE: A half glass of beer might do you better. *(To MICHAEL's astonishment she puts a bottle of beer on the table.)* That'll set you up for the cold walk before you. Let you play me a tune first. I'll get the biscuits. *(Goes to the press, takes a box of biscuits from it, comes to the table, opens the box.)* Won't you play something for me?

MICHAEL: *(Slowly.)* I wouldn't like to be playing in this house... It would be making very free,— with Miss Gregg inside.

KATIE: *(Laughs, pours beer into a glass.)* Is it getting shy you are now? Take a little of that.

MICHAEL: I will not. I don't think I will. How do you know—what would he say? *(She laughs.)* I don't like the humor is on you tonight.

(They look at each other.)

KATIE: Here's to you, Michael! *(Puts the glass to her lips, swallows a little, makes a face.)* You're better without it.

MICHAEL: *(Takes the glass, drinks, puts the glass on the table again.)* Since 'twas put before me.

KATIE: Are you afraid to sit down?

MICHAEL: What would make me afraid? *(Sits down.)* But I won't delay, Jo Mahony'll be waiting.

KATIE: Can't you take something more.

MICHAEL: *(Drinks a little more, pushes his glass aside.)* Kitty Phelan will be out with us tonight, and a couple of others. *(Laughs.)* For a bet they're doing it. Oh, we'll have a great time... She's a terror, is Kitty. Jo's gone about her, and I like her myself... Ah, 'twas a pity about you,— and all that you're missing... You made a mistake that night in the summer, when you gave up the dance.

KATIE: Will you have any more?

MICHAEL: Are you sorry now?

KATIE: Will you have any more?

(Sound of footsteps outside.)

MICHAEL: I'd better be going.

KATIE: Yes— *(Slowly, listening.)* —you'd better be going… *(Before MICHAEL knows what is happening she is on his knee, her arms about his neck.)* But come again—some time he's out. *(Very distinctly—over MICHAEL'S shoulder, towards the door, MICHAEL starts up, tries to push her off: she clings to him.)* Come again, Michael…

(REUBEN comes in. Stands for a moment, looking at them. Turns, shuts the door, turns again to KATIE.)

REUBEN: I heard what you said.

MICHAEL: 'Tis a trap she laid! I never asked to come near her once. She put her arms round me, she wouldn't let go.

KATIE: Oh—the poor leanav, what great harm did I do you?

REUBEN: You'd better go now.

MICHAEL: I've done no wrong, Reuben.

REUBEN: Go on now, and don't come to this house again.

MICHAEL: She called me to come in. I was passing the door. I didn't ask her arms round me—nor this old muffler! *(Pulls off the scarf, throws it on the floor.)*

KATIE: Isn't he the grand fellow! Now if you were Mr. Gregg—

MICHAEL: *(Furious.)* And if I were I'd teach you something!

(REUBEN holds up a warning hand.)

KATIE: There's the real "rough." You should hear Mr. Gregg…oh, he's high up above you. He'd think little of himself to let slip a sharp word. You should hear the talk is between us… It is "please" and "thank you" and standing back at the door… 'Tis in looking at him you'd learn how to live… Oh, go your way!

(MICHAEL looks angrily at her, turns to go, meets STANISLAUS coming in.)

STANISLAUS: Good evening…

MICHAEL: Good evening, Mr. Gregg.

STANISLAUS: *(To KATIE.)* I met Margaret outside.

KATIE: I thought you were coming a minute before.

STANISLAUS: *(To REUBEN.)* Good evening. Wild evening.

REUBEN: It is wild. *(Dry.)* It's the month of December.

MICHAEL: *(To REUBEN, in low tone.)* I'd swear to it—what I said was true.

KATIE: *(To STANISLAUS.)* I was sure 'twas yourself, and then Reuben came in: I got the drop of my life.

(MICHAEL looks angrily at her, goes.)

STANISLAUS: *(To REUBEN.)* Sit down and rest for a while. Have you come from Dublin?

REUBEN: Yes: from Dublin. I'd like a word with the woman.

STANISLAUS: Certainly… *(Turns to KATIE.)* Tell Amelia she's wanted.

REUBEN: This woman… If you've no objection.

STANISLAUS: Oh, Katie…yes. Very well. I don't mind at all. *(Crosses the room—sees his scarf on the floor—looks at KATIE.)* What's this?

KATIE: *(Calm.)* 'Tis Michael threw it down: a great temper came on him.

STANISLAUS: *(Looks at her, at the glasses on the table.)* You offered refreshments to Michael?

KATIE: He only took a half glass.

STANISLAUS: *(Goes to the door at the right, finds it locked.)* This door is fastened.

KATIE: Myself that locked it. The key's up there, I didn't want Amelia, and her scones.

(STANISLAUS looks again at her, then takes the key, unlocks the door, and goes.)

REUBEN: You're a nice saint. You could hurt that man badly—he's fond of you.

KATIE: *(Slowly.)* So you'd put that before me—not to hurt the man I'd love. And whoever done a great thing if they must be guarded from hurt?

REUBEN: I'd put this before you—you'll hurt yourself worse.

KATIE: Is it snug as the turnips you'd have us live? *(Scornful. Laughs, turns from him, takes a few steps. REUBEN, with surprising vigor, raises his stick, hits her across the shoulders. KATIE collapses onto a chair. Groans. Silence. Then:)* Now I'll say this—'tis a mistake for a body to be too meddlesome. If you had broken my shoulder you could be put in the court... You've no more right over me than a man on the road...

REUBEN: I'll have your promise now, or I'll warn your husband.

KATIE: *(Looks at him, turns her head towards the door where STANISLAUS has gone.)* Stanislaus, are you there? *(Silence.)* Are you there, Stanislaus? *(Silence: she looks at REUBEN, laughs scornfully.)* So you thought to frighten me! Do you forget I come of grand people?

REUBEN: You come of vile people.

KATIE: Oh!

REUBEN: What's more—they wouldn't own you... Get all that "grandness" out of your mind. You've no claim on earth but what he gave you.

KATIE: A man off the road to talk like that!

REUBEN: *(Gentle.)* Yes,— I'm a man off the road—and your father.

KATIE: Could such a thing happen!... *(Stares at him—rises, excited.)* You weren't drowned?...

REUBEN: So you see... "Grand people"!

KATIE: Well, what was I born for?... A great thing, surely... *(Then gazing at him, grows tender.)* ...Reuben...my father...you that were grand and now like this... You have trampled the world under your feet!

REUBEN: I've told you—as a warning... Remember now—

KATIE: Oh—you're a great man!... You're a saint!—

REUBEN: Be good now. Be a good wife.

KATIE: Good is it? *(Laughs, wildly excited.)* I'll be a great woman. I'll make my own goodness. *(He turns from her.)* Don't go from me without a word!

REUBEN: I have nothing to give you.

KATIE: And you a saint of God!

REUBEN: You're playing with danger—that's why I hit you.

KATIE: I'll get over that— *(As accepting apology.)* —for all you could know I might have deserved it...

REUBEN: You did deserve it. Do you care for that fellow?

KATIE: Michael is it? You know well I don't…

REUBEN: Only wanting excitement? *(Stern.)*

KATIE: Oh, you don't understand me. *(Injured.)*

REUBEN: I'm going to watch you: I'll come here again, and if you haven't been good I won't spare you… Mind now, if I find him here again I'll—flog you.

KATIE: *(Impersonal.)* I don't think you'd be able…and Stanislaus wouldn't leave you… Won't you stop on here now along with us? If you'd like you'd be welcome… I'll ask Stanislaus…

REUBEN: No. Say nothing about me. I've no claim on you,— nor you on me. Remember that. Remember too—

(A sound in the house. REUBEN turns abruptly to the door.)

KATIE: That's only Amelia making scones!

REUBEN: I must get back to my poor people…

KATIE: Reuben— *(Close to him.)* —there's no one knows this but you and me?

REUBEN: The name is known to a few people. They believe him dead. Better so. *(Going.)*

KATIE: There's no hurry…

REUBEN: You don't need me. I'm going down now to a sick woman,— Mrs. Maguire.

KATIE: *(Eager.)* I'll be outside Maguires' when you'll come out. Let us have a word then. Let me go a step of the way with you.

(He nods agreement: goes. AMELIA comes in with the tea tray, followed by STANISLAUS. KATIE stands gazing at the door through which REUBEN has gone.)

AMELIA: *(Puts the tray on the table.)* Now, Katie—

(KATIE turns.)

STANISLAUS: Your friend has gone… *(Not quite approving.)*

KATIE: Reuben, is it? He couldn't delay. The poor and the sick—they're clamoring for him.

AMELIA: I believe he does wonders. So they tell me. Katie, I'm watching my scones, will you set the table?

KATIE: I will to be sure. *(AMELIA goes, KATIE gets the tea cloth, moves about settling cups, etc. STANISLAUS watches.)* 'Tis no trouble to me to set the table. *(She is full of power and joy, delighted with her own way of doing everything. Turns to STANISLAUS, glowing, excited.)* There was a thing told me now—'twould make your heart burn.

STANISLAUS: *(Looks across the room, at the glasses.)* Very unnecessary—offering drink to Michael.

KATIE: *(Looks at him for a moment then laughs, excited—wanting now to rouse him—full of thought that she is "different.")* He had no wish for it—but he was ashamed when I drank it.

STANISLAUS: Did you take some of that?

KATIE: Only my lips to his glass—like all true lovers.

STANISLAUS: I see. Very romantic. You're not taking part in theatricals now. *(Pause.)* Margaret was pleased about the plans, very pleased.

KATIE: What plans were those? *(An utter stranger to him.)*

STANISLAUS: Very much interested. *(Pause.)* What brought Michael here?

KATIE: To see me he came—for old love's sake.

STANISLAUS: He wasn't here long.

KATIE: It didn't seem long to me.

STANISLAUS: Don't give him drink here again.

KATIE: *(Turns to him.)* 'Tis a terrible thing for a woman to marry an' she not very sure in her mind... And then the man she didn't marry to come in and sit down, and she by herself.

STANISLAUS: *(After a moment.)* Margaret said she'd come up, if Hubert didn't mind. He might come too.

KATIE: Michael wasn't here long... *(Putting the glasses fondly aside.)* It didn't seem long to me... When you'd be alone with the man you love...

STANISLAUS: Yes. I know very well who's the man you love. You're alone with him now.

KATIE: Oh I—oh! *(Outraged.)*

STANISLAUS: —But they may be here soon. We've had enough nonsense. Better have the table ready.

KATIE: I won't be here when they'll come. I'm going out. *(Silence. Then determined to rouse him.)* Reuben gave me a blow with his stick.

STANISLAUS: I don't believe that!

KATIE: You don't believe it! Great anger came on him to find Michael and myself alone here now—the way he found us.

STANISLAUS: Is that a lie?

KATIE: I've told you no lies since we stood at the altar.

(Silence for a moment. AMELIA comes in with a plate of scones.)

AMELIA: Now I hope these are nice... I think they are.

KATIE: Oh, look at those! *(With false enthusiasm.)* Don't they look very nice?

AMELIA: I do hope they are... *(Anxious.)*

STANISLAUS: *(Goes to the door at the right, looks back.)* Katie, when you're ready I want you in here.

KATIE: Will you look at those scones. *(In ecstasy.)*

(STANISLAUS goes out. KATIE relaxes, glows, as one who congratulates herself.)

AMELIA: I hope he'll like them... I hope they'll all like them.

KATIE: You may be very sure. I'm going out now. *(Takes her hat and coat from rack near the door.)*

AMELIA: Out?... But Katie...didn't Stanislaus say—?

KATIE: Tell him 'tis very important.

AMELIA: —But he said—

KATIE: —Ah, what about that?

AMELIA: And Margaret is coming... And I thought we were going to have tea...

KATIE: *(Puts on her hat, settles her hair, etc., at the mirror.)* If he asks where—off in the direction that Michael went, towards the hill of Knock, and I'm taking this... *(Takes STANISLAUS's scarf. Opens the door. Steps back. JO MAHONY is seen in the doorway.)* What do you want?

JO: 'Tis for Michael I'm looking. They said he was here.

KATIE: I thought you were off over the hill of Knock.

JO: Michael never turned up. I went below to his mother now. She said 'tis on your account he's very upset.

KATIE: Did you hear that? *(To AMELIA, glowing.)* Michael is upset on account of me.

AMELIA: Good evening, Jo.

JO: Good evening, Miss Gregg… 'Tis how I thought Michael was here, or I wouldn't come up.

KATIE: Go in there now. *(Points to door at right.)* The room on your right. Mr. Gregg is inside. *(Urgent.)* Tell him Michael is upset on account of me,— and I'm gone out,— like I said I'd go.

AMELIA: But Katie—

(KATIE disappears: shuts the door.)

JO: Well, she'd beat all. Sure how could I go in on Mr. Gregg?… I wouldn't come at all but I thought Michael was here…

AMELIA: Yes. I think Michael was here, but I don't think he's here now. *(Looks about helplessly.)*

JO: Sure he's not. Thank you, Miss Gregg. *(Listens.)* There's someone outside. *(Goes to the door, opens it suddenly. A woman draws back from the door, has obviously been listening. JO turns to AMELIA.)* 'Tis your sister… 'Tis Mrs. Drybone.

(MARGARET DRYBONE comes in: she is small and pinched—about forty—with an air of suspicious, brooding intensity.)

AMELIA: Oh, Margaret, you've come!

MARGARET: Yes, Amelia—and why shouldn't I? Stan's my brother as well as yours…

AMELIA: Of course he is, dear…

MARGARET: So why did you say "you've come"? —Why shouldn't I come? *(Turns to JO.)* Good evening *(Frigid.)*

JO: Good evening, Mrs. Drybone.

MARGARET: Excuse me. Your friend, Michael Maguire. I think he was here?

JO: 'Tis that brought me up.

MARGARET: Where has he gone?

JO: I don't know, Mrs. Drybone.

MARGARET: I see. I was wondering. *(Suspicious.)* Of course why wouldn't he go wherever he liked… but all the same…

AMELIA: Michael was only here a few minutes.

MARGARET: *(To JO.)* I thought perhaps he was going over the hill of Knock.

JO: He was too. He promised, but he didn't turn up. You couldn't count on Michael. Three times now we had it planned, and 'tis on him we were counting for the music,— and he never turned up.

MARGARET: *(Dry.)* Perhaps something upset him…

JO: He's easy upset. He was ever the same. *(Moves towards the door.)*

MARGARET: Wait a moment.

JO: They're all outside. They're mad with him. The girls are saying they won't come anymore. They asked would I find out was it here he was.

MARGARET: Are you sure he hasn't gone?

AMELIA: He was waiting for you. He was waiting round here. I met him when I was coming back from the chapel.

JO: *(His voice rising in desperation.)* Sure that's him all over!… 'Twas the same long ago an' we over beyond with the Christian Brothers… Ready and waiting, and if a straw blew up against his face he'd go off in a sulk. *(Turns to door.)* They won't come anymore.

MARGARET: One moment—who are "they"?

JO: A party of us that had planned to go.

MARGARET: I was wondering. Thank you. *(JO goes. MARGARET looks to see that he has shut the door, turns to AMELIA.)* There's something very queer about this.

AMELIA: Do you think there is, Margaret? *(Troubled.)*

MARGARET: Has something happened?

AMELIA: I…I don't know.

MARGARET: Oh, there's something very queer about it… Of course I always knew this was bound to happen…

AMELIA: But— I don't think there's anything wrong.

MARGARET: Don't you, Amelia? *(Crushing.)* Stan said, "Come and have tea; we'd be very pleased"… I met Katie outside: she seemed excited. "Have the tea, let you. Tell him I'm gone out with Michael towards the hill of Knock." *(KATIE's tone.)*

AMELIA: Margaret!—

MARGARET: This was bound to happen.

AMELIA: Oh dear, oh dear!

MARGARET: A girl like that. My brother, your brother—and a girl like that… I said it often to Hubert. He said, "Don't interfere."

AMELIA: But I don't believe—

MARGARET: No, I said "Amelia won't believe—"

AMELIA: I mean, I never thought, I never dreamed—

MARGARET: I said that often to Hubert! *(Triumphant.)* "Amelia would never think or dream—she'd never see." I'm not surprised… I saw it coming.

AMELIA: What did you see? *(With spirit.)* They're fond of each other—I know they are…

MARGARET: And how do you know it?

AMELIA: They're happy too—I'm sure they are! *(Suddenly breaks.)* Oh dear, oh dear…she shouldn't have gone… Now what will happen?

MARGARET: That remains to be seen… They should never have married… I wasn't consulted… I didn't mind… Hubert said to me, "They seem happy, I wonder how long it will last." I said, "I don't suppose it will last very long"… —How could it, Amelia?… Now she's gone out to Michael Maguire.

AMELIA: Mind, he's coming…

STANISLAUS: *(Looking in.)* Katie—

MARGARET: I met her outside.

STANISLAUS: Outside?

AMELIA: *(Distressed.)* Yes, she went out. I don't know why. I said weren't we having tea…but she went out.

MARGARET: She said something about the hill of Knock.

AMELIA: Yes, she said that to me. And—Stan—Jo Mahony was here. He said Michael Maguire was very much upset.

STANISLAUS: Poor Michael. *(Quietly sardonic.)* …Well, Amelia, are we not going to have tea?

MARGARET: I can't delay. I came up to say that.

AMELIA: Oh, can't you, Margaret? What a pity!…

MARGARET: It's not very easy—when you're married… Some people don't mind. I try to do my duty by Hubert... He didn't want to come this evening... He said he was busy. I wouldn't leave my husband alone.

AMELIA: Isn't that a great pity!

STANISLAUS: *(Quiet.)* In that case, Amelia, perhaps you'd like to go down with Margaret and stay there for tea...

AMELIA: *(After a moment.)* Now, wouldn't that be very nice?... And you won't mind?

STANISLAUS: No, I won't mind at all.

AMELIA: Won't that be nice, Margaret?

MARGARET: It might be the best plan—considering all...

AMELIA: You won't mind having me?

MARGARET: You're quite welcome. Hubert never objects. I don't have people to whom he objects. I don't think a wife should.

AMELIA: I'll get my things. *(Goes hurriedly.)*

MARGARET: *(Clears her throat.)* I won't interfere. I don't think people should. All the same I'm sorry—very sorry.

STANISLAUS: What do you mean?

MARGARET: I'm not saying much. I'm not doing anything. People don't like it—when they're troubled. I quite understand.

STANISLAUS: What do you mean?

MARGARET: Hubert often says, "Nobody is so terribly happy." Very often it's our own fault. Sometimes people are wishing to help. We won't let them. *(Cough.)* Other people have troubles too.

STANISLAUS: I've letters to write. *(Moves towards door.)*

MARGARET: *(Stops him.)* Just a moment. We could make things better by being better tempered... *(He moves to go.)* ...and by listening to people...when we make mistakes... People could tell us things beforehand but we won't listen... Then later on we think too much of our own troubles—

AMELIA: *(Coming in.)* Stan, are you sure you don't—

STANISLAUS: I don't mind at all...

AMELIA: But...about your tea?

STANISLAUS: I'll have it with Katie. I'm not ready yet. She won't be long.

MARGARET: I hope she won't *(Doubtful.)* Would you come with us?

STANISLAUS: No, thanks. She won't be long. Don't let me keep you.

(Moves towards the door, anxious for their departure. The door is opened; KATIE comes in. She is in a softened mood, happy, glowing. Smiles round at them all, takes off her hat and coat, crosses to the fire, and sits down.)

MARGARET: *(Coughs.)* It's cold.

(KATIE smiles, and nods to her.)

AMELIA: Yes, isn't it very cold... It was cold all day today. *(Moves to go.)*

MARGARET: *(Delaying.)* I think it's like rain.

AMELIA: Yes, perhaps it is... *(Silence.)* Yes, I think it's like rain.

STANISLAUS: Wild too...it's very wild.

KATIE: *(Smiles at him.)* 'Tis so, but it is a grand wind.

(STANISLAUS goes to the door, holds it open for MARGARET and AMELIA.)

MARGARET: Well, good-bye. When we make a mistake we must make the best of it, then.

AMELIA: *(To KATIE.)* The little kettle is on the boil, and Stan is waiting for his tea.

KATIE: We'll have it now. Let you go on.

(They go. STANISLAUS shuts the door, comes over to KATIE.)

STANISLAUS: Well?

KATIE: *(Looks up at him, glowing.)* I had a grand talk with Reuben; it would lift your heart. I'll tell you about it. *(He does not respond.)* Would you like better I'd get the tea? *(Stands up.)* You're famished for it. *(Hurrying out, stops, looks back at him.)* Oh, I've a lot to tell you: you'll be very surprised.

(STANISLAUS stands for a moment looking after her. A knock. He opens the door. MICHAEL MAGUIRE is seen.)

MICHAEL: Could I come in for a minute?

STANISLAUS: Come in.

MICHAEL: *(Steps in, looks quickly round the room.)* If I could see you alone.

STANISLAUS: You can see me now.

MICHAEL: Would it be all right to talk here?

STANISLAUS: What do you want?

MICHAEL: 'Tis my mother sent me up... *(Pause.)* I wouldn't come myself, but she said it was better for me to be on the safe side. *(Silence.)* ...She said if you'd hear it first from me that's how you'd believe me... And if I'd tell you the truth no one could blame me... I didn't know myself what would be right, or what way you might hear it... *(Looks nervously towards the kitchen.)*

STANISLAUS: What did you come for?

MICHAEL: 'Tis about Katie I came.

STANISLAUS: You mean Mrs. Gregg.

MICHAEL: *(With a flash.)* She threw her arms round me. She held onto me tight. *(Silence.)* I wouldn't tell you at all, but my mother said it is better always to be on the safe side. *(Silence.)* I have nothing against her. I don't wish her harm... All the same— *(With another flash.)* —it wasn't a fair thing... And Reuben to come in, and find me like that.

STANISLAUS: You'd better go now. *(Opens the door.)*

MICHAEL: That's all very well for you, Mr. Gregg!... but if she were to start telling lies about me... And me so great not very long gone.

STANISLAUS: Yes, go on now. *(Showing him out.)*

MICHAEL: Oh, she has you twisted round her little finger! I declare it's a fright when a man can't speak honest about a woman...

STANISLAUS: I'm quite sure you're honest. I have no doubt.

MICHAEL: Let you give the weight of your mind to her so. 'Tis she is to blame. The world knows I never went near her since that night in the summer when she turned me down... Only she was put out about yourself.

STANISLAUS: That's enough now.

MICHAEL: I didn't think you'd treat me like this, Mr. Gregg.

(Goes out. STANISLAUS shuts the door, stands for a moment in thought, turns to leave the room, meets KATIE carrying in the tray. Stands aside for her to pass. Goes.

KATIE puts the things on the table; moves about table, settling cups, cuts some bread, etc., singing very softly. STANISLAUS reappears with a small suitcase.)

KATIE: *(Over her shoulder.)* I'm glad they went off and left the two of us. It is what I like always. *(Turns, sees the case.)* What is that for?

STANISLAUS: A few books from here. I'll take it upstairs then for the rest of my things. I'm going away.

(KATIE stares at him, fear starting up. STANISLAUS turns aside to the bookshelf. After a moment she goes to him.)

KATIE: I asked too much of you. I shouldn't have said to burn them plans.

STANISLAUS: "Them plans"? *(Stern.)*

KATIE: We can only be great in our own way. You and myself couldn't ever be like two other people… *(Pause.)* Is it in anger you're going?

STANISLAUS: It certainly is.

KATIE: Because I went out? Well, I made my choice for this tonight, I won't cry now. *(Then in low tone.)* "Is it snug as the turnips you'd have us live?" All the same— *(She breaks.)* —I didn't think you'd go off from me in such a great hurry. *(Silence. Struggles for composure, looks towards the table; says in lighter tone:)* You had a right not to tell me till after the tea. Now 'twill be spoiled…and your bit of sausage.

STANISLAUS: Take your tea.

KATIE: *(Hesitates, goes to the table, sits down, pours out her own tea.)* Won't you have any?

STANISLAUS: No, not now.

KATIE: *(Sighs, sips her tea; then, after a moment.)* 'Tis to Reuben I went that time, not to Michael. *(Silence.)* I only made up about the hill of Knock. *(Silence. Thinks again—then.)* It is you I love best. I never changed in my heart at all. *(Silence.)* Ah, take a bit before you'll go. That would be good sense. I'll be that brave you can go off jaunty. I'd like you'd enjoy yourself wherever you'd be. *(Silence. Frightened now.)* Will you come back ever?

STANISLAUS: Yes, I'll come back.

KATIE: I dunno where are you going? *(An attempt at being casual—jaunty. Silence. She goes on with her tea.)* Won't you take any at all?

STANISLAUS: When you've finished.

KATIE: Oh!—oh-h! *(Wounded. Turns to him with a beseeching gesture.)*

STANISLAUS: Go on with your tea!

(She tries to: only pretence now. STANISLAUS gets books together, puts them in his case: crossing for more books he passes near KATIE. She turns to him.)

KATIE: I don't think I could bear this… I…don't think I could… *(Glides from her chair to the floor.)*

STANISLAUS: *(Furious.)* Get up off the floor!

KATIE: *(Gets up slowly, sits down.)* Wasn't I foolish?… Ah, here now, look at Amelia's scones… Well, sure I won't take any more, and that'll finish me, and let you have yours. *(About to leave the table.)*

STANISLAUS: *(Stopping her.)* Finish your tea. I'll take up my case. *(Goes to the door.)* I'm in no hurry. I'll get the seven-ten.

KATIE: It would be better for you, and for me, that you'd stop where you are. *(Sadly. He goes. KATIE sips her tea, dejected. After a moment she rouses herself, turns towards the open door, and calls:)* Stanislaus, will you stop very much beyond a week? *(Pause.)* I don't think you will! *(This last angrily, but in the silence that follows she grows frightened again.)*

(Curtain.)

ACT III

August—late afternoon. The sun streams in through the window and open door. There are flowers in a bowl on the table. Some religious pictures hang on the walls.

JO MAHONY stands at the house door, outside—a telegram in his hand. Someone is heard shouting, "Up at the bend!" "Connolly's field!"... JO turns from the door—calls, "I'll be up in a jiff." Knocks impatiently. FRANK LAWLOR, a big man of about fifty-six or so, comes to the door, also outside.

FRANK: Is there anyone here?

JO: You could rise the dead and get no answer. I'm knocking this half hour. *(Comes in, knocks with his knuckles on the door at the right side of the room.)* You wouldn't mind but the race'll be starting... 'Tis this darned wire. There might be an answer.

FRANK: I thought I'd find Mr. Gregg.

JO: Very seldom you'd find him here. 'Tis to his sister the house belongs.

FRANK: But he's married now,— and living here?

JO: The wife lives here with his sister: he comes an odd time. *(Sound of running, and shouts from outside, JO looks out.)* There's time enough yet... From Ballyhack you came?

FRANK: From Ballyhack.

JO: Mr. Lawlor—Mr. Frank Lawlor? *(The other nods.)* A good crowd came over for the regatta.

FRANK: I clean forgot about the regatta, or I wouldn't come today.

JO: 'Tis well worth seeing.

FRANK: *(Comes a little way in, looks about the room, at the pictures on the wall—looks at JO.)* They've the wall well decorated.

JO: *(Laughs.)* The wife put them up,— after the last time he was here.

FRANK: Is she very religious?

JO: Ah, she's very... very vegarious...

FRANK: Vegarious?

JO: That's it.

FRANK: I see. *(Obviously he does not.)*

JO: She varies off and on.

FRANK: Ah, yes. Yes.

(Sound of a rocket let off.)

JO: They're off! *(Leaves the telegram on the mantelpiece; runs out. At the door he turns.)* You'd get a pretty good view from the field above—if you'd stand on the ditch.

FRANK: I won't stand on the ditch; that day is over.

(JO is gone, FRANK delays, looks slowly around the room, goes to the window, stands there looking out. More sounds from outside. Someone calls, "Hurry up, Jo." After a moment frank goes out—turns off in the direction opposite to that taken by JO. The door at the right opens. KATIE comes in with a book in her hand. She has an air of exasperation; crosses the room swiftly, shuts the door, draws the curtains across the window, sits down at the table, and, elbows on table, fingers in ears, studies her book. A

cheer from outside. KATIE jerks her chair closer to the table, bends over her book. AMELIA comes in.)

AMELIA: I wonder was there somebody here? *(No answer.)* I wonder was somebody knocking?

KATIE: I don't know, Amelia. *(Finger marking the word she has stopped at.)*

AMELIA: I was out at the back. I thought I heard something.

KATIE: I heard a terrible racket. It is better to keep our mind off these things. *(Lofty.)*

AMELIA: I thought perhaps something was happening... I saw a crowd down the road.

KATIE: Sometimes you'd think something was happening, and when you'd look in the paper that night there wouldn't be anything! *(Bends over her hook again. AMELIA has opened the door. They hear whistles, calls, sound of hurrying steps.)* 'Tis only the fellows running up for the race. The crowd gathering in Connolly's field.

AMELIA: Look, Katie—

KATIE *(Groans.)* Surely to goodness I have virtue! *(Appealing to the pictures on the wall.)*

AMELIA: But my dear, you might—

KATIE: I must be steady. That's what he said. I must read sensible books. *(AMELIA shuts the door.)* It was you had told him about the Coolbeg dance...

AMELIA: I thought Stan should know that you were there.

KATIE: Well, he knows now. I'm not to stop out in the night. I'm not to ask the boys to the house.

AMELIA: Katie, he'd come back if you said you'd like that.

KATIE: And doesn't he come? Wasn't he here last Friday week?

AMELIA: But...but I mean, to stay...to live here, if you asked.

KATIE: *(Looks at her in scorn—then at the pictures.)* I must have patience!

AMELIA: *(Turns aside, sees the telegram on the mantelpiece.)* A wire! When did it come? *(KATIE springs up, seizes the telegram eagerly.)* I suppose it's from Stan...

KATIE: It might be, and it might not... *(Turns the telegram over.)*

AMELIA: Open it!

KATIE: Mightn't it be a good thing for the two of us to wait a while? *(Exasperating, cool, puts it back on mantelpiece.)*

AMELIA: Ah—Katie, open it now!

KATIE: Would you like that I would? Well, myself would like it. *(Opens the telegram.)* He's coming. You're right.

AMELIA: He might be here any minute! The five-fifteen. Isn't that lovely? They were very slow.

KATIE: Likely Jo Mahony stopped on the way, if there was a race on.

AMELIA: Oh, Katie won't it be very nice?

KATIE: *(Gives a sudden laugh.)* What possessed him? Today of all days!... And the regatta on...and the boys...the boys will be coming up for the bench... Oh, Amelia...and he might— *(Cannot finish—with laughter.)*

AMELIA: My dear! What's wrong?

KATIE: Wrong? Is it? *(Controlled, defensive. Stands up.)* I must have his room ready—like a good wife. *(Goes to the door—laughs again, this time more happily.)* They'll be coming like...like last year. *(Goes.)*

AMELIA: *(Troubled.)* But, Katie... *(KATIE is gone.)* Oh dear... Oh dear...

(A knock at the door; AMELIA opens it. FRANK LAWLOR is seen.)

FRANK: Good evening.

AMELIA: Oh, Frank. Mr. Lawlor, good evening.

FRANK: May I come in?

AMELIA: Oh yes...won't you come in.

(He comes in. She shuts the door.)

FRANK: How are you, Amelia?

AMELIA: I'm very well, thanks.

FRANK: I'm glad to see you.

AMELIA: Oh yes. I'm very glad to see you. I'm very pleased... Won't you sit down?

(He sits down, she flutters about, indecisive.)

FRANK: Stan isn't here?

AMELIA: No... I mean he isn't here now...but he'll be here very soon. We've had a wire.

FRANK. Yes?

AMELIA: Yes. He might be here at any moment.

FRANK: Queer genius.

AMELIA: I beg your pardon...

FRANK: Queer genius. Your brother.

AMELIA: I don't know what you mean.

FRANK: Sit down for the Lord's sake. Let's have a chat.

AMELIA: But wouldn't you like a cup of tea?

FRANK. I'd like a talk with you. *(She sits down.)* A long time since we've had a talk.

AMELIA: Yes—a very long time.

FRANK: Often I think of coming over...

AMELIA: But you don't come...

FRANK: One thing and another turns up. I'm meaning this long time to come and see you. *(Pause.)* Did Stan tell you I met him a few times lately in Dublin?

AMELIA: Yes, yes; he told me, when he was down...

FRANK: Did he tell you to expect me ever?

AMELIA: He said you might come... *(More nervous.)* Frank,— Mr. Lawlor, let me get you some tea.

FRANK: What did he say to make you like this?

AMELIA: Oh dear... I don't think he said anything.

FRANK: I bet he did. I know what he said—

AMELIA: *(Rises, desperate.)* I must get the tea.

FRANK: You must sit down.

AMELIA: Oh dear, oh dear...

FRANK: Queer fish.

AMELIA: I suppose I am. *(Humble.)*

FRANK: Not you... Your brother. Clever! We must take his brains on faith.

AMELIA: I don't know what you mean.

FRANK: Did he say I was coming to ask you to marry me?

AMELIA: Oh no... I mean—

FRANK: Well, he shouldn't have, but since he did—

AMELIA: Please, Mr. Lawlor—

FRANK: Since he did—he's all wrong. I wouldn't. I've too much respect for you.

AMELIA: Oh!

FRANK: Far too much. *(Pause.)* Is that all right?

AMELIA: Yes, thanks. You... you're very kind.

FRANK: Not at all. Is that all right now?

AMELIA: That's all right.

FRANK: And you're satisfied? *(Pause, AMELIA cannot speak.)* Now we can talk.

AMELIA: Yes, now we can talk. *(Pause.)* What shall we talk about?

FRANK: About Stan. I'm angry with him, Amelia, I'm very angry...

AMELIA: *(Timid.)* On account of me?

FRANK: Not at all. On account of his wife. He treats her badly.

AMELIA: *(In arms.)* Stanislaus doesn't treat anyone badly. He's awfully good. He has a heart of gold.

FRANK: Pretty hard stuff. What did he mean, marrying that child? And then going off...

AMELIA: At present he's working in Dublin, but—

FRANK. Bah! Most unfair...

AMELIA: Stan couldn't be unfair! He's wonderful... He's kind... he thinks of everyone—

FRANK: Except his wife.

AMELIA: Oh, that's not fair. It isn't true. You don't know. You have no right. *(Then frigid.)* I think this is a matter for Stanislaus himself.

FRANK: I love you, Amelia—be my wife.

AMELIA: Oh!

FRANK: There, I didn't mean it. Honest I didn't. Never meant to. Felt too damned nervous myself. Rotten feel. *(Pause.)* You'd better think about it.

AMELIA: No, Frank; no, I couldn't...

FRANK: You couldn't?... Won't even think of it?

AMELIA: I... I'm not young enough...

FRANK: Neither am I. I wish we both were...

AMELIA: Frank, you must marry somebody young.

FRANK: Good Lord,— not if you paid me! I thought we were fond of one another.

AMELIA: But... I'm too old.

FRANK: Nonsense, woman. Do you think I want children. I want you. I've been a fool. Don't know why I didn't come before.

AMELIA: *(Shakes her head sadly.)* I couldn't... now...

FRANK: Stanislaus would be very pleased...

AMELIA: You think he would?

FRANK: *(Laughs.)* That settles it. You'll marry me for Stanislaus' sake... *(An arm about her.)*

AMELIA: *(Shrinking.)* I couldn't change now...

FRANK: *(Gentle.)* I wouldn't ask you to change at all. Come over and live with me. We'll get married quietly, some morning very early.

AMELIA: Oh dear... give me time to think about it...

FRANK: We've had too much time for thinking...

(STANISLAUS is seen in the doorway; he comes in.)

AMELIA: Oh, Stan, you've come...

STANISLAUS: Amelia...Lawlor...grand weather.

FRANK: Fine.

STANISLAUS: Yes, Amelia, I've come...

AMELIA: Very good of you...

STANISLAUS: Got my wire?

AMELIA: Yes, Stan, but only just now...

STANISLAUS: Katie here?

AMELIA: Yes, I mean she's not here now,— but I'll call her.

(STANISLAUS goes towards the door but AMELIA, eager to make her escape, slips out before him. Silence. STANISLAUS puts his case near the door, hangs up his hat, goes to the window, then turns to FRANK.)

STANISLAUS: Amelia looks well.

FRANK: *(Hostile.)* I have seen her look worse. *(Silence.)* How is—your wife?

STANISLAUS: We'll see that in a minute. She was well last week.

FRANK: Poor little thing.

STANISLAUS: Excuse me—?

FRANK: I said, "Poor little thing." *(Pause. STANISLAUS looks angrily at him. Then,— very deliberate.)* Not much of a life—supposed to be married.

STANISLAUS: *(Low.)* Who are you speaking of?

(They face one another.)

FRANK: Mary's daughter... Mary Halnan's...

STANISLAUS: I see. *(Pause—then in a blaze.)* Few enough thought of that when I was abroad, and Katie was sent to Mrs. Roche.

(The door opens. KATIE comes in: she carries a small stepladder. Puts the ladder down when she sees STANISLAUS, leans on it. AMELIA follows in.)

KATIE: So you're here, Stanislaus!

STANISLAUS: Yes, I'm here. How are you?

KATIE: I'm very well.

STANISLAUS: *(Looks towards FRANK.)* Mr. Lawlor...

KATIE: I met you that night of the Coolbeg dance.

FRANK: Yes... I remember. *(They shake hands. FRANK turns to AMELIA.)* Well, I'll be off now. Good-bye...for the present.

AMELIA: But...won't you stay for tea?

FRANK: No, I've a call to make... I can't delay.

KATIE: Let you have a cup of tea first.

FRANK: Not this evening, thanks. Some other time. *(Turns again to AMELIA.)* You'll think it over...

AMELIA: *(Nervous.)* I will... I will...

(They go to the door.)

STANISLAUS: *(To KATIE.)* I don't like these. *(The pictures on the wall.)*

KATIE: I was thinking you wouldn't... *(Long-suffering.)* I was taking them down. There's not very much wish for the things of God.

STANISLAUS: I like the place properly furnished.

KATIE: Oh, we are all inclined unto evil.

(Lofty; tolerant. She draws the ladder across the room. AMELIA and FRANK shake hands at the door.)

STANISLAUS: *(To FRANK.)* A word with you. *(To KATIE.)* I'll be back.

(Goes out quickly after FRANK. KATIE mounts the ladder.)

AMELIA: I'm going up to the chapel.

KATIE: You couldn't do better.

AMELIA: I'll get my things. *(Stops, seeing someone outside.)* Oh, they're coming, Michael and Jo—I suppose for the bench.

KATIE: That's a good thing. They might be gone before he'll be back *(A little nervous.)* Let you go on. *(AMELIA goes. MICHAEL MAGUIRE and JO MAHONY are seen in the doorway. They are laughing, breathless, shouldering one another aside.)* Is that Michael Maguire?

MICHAEL: Would you like that it was? *(Comes in.)*

JO: *(Following in.)* We won the race! Our fellows walked away with it.

KATIE: *(Very prim.)* That's good news. I am pleased to hear that.

MICHAEL: The Coolbeg team are flattened out.

KATIE: That's very pleasant news.

JO: They got the sell of their lives.

KATIE: I'm sure you're pleased.

JO: It was a grand race.

KATIE: I'm very glad to hear that the local team was victorious.

MICHAEL: *(Abrupt.)* About the bench we came.

KATIE: You can have the bench. 'Tis in the kitchen. Better take it out by the back.

MICHAEL: We're not taking it now. Only to know could we count on it. *(Turns to JO.)* Let you go up to Riley's about the band.

JO: I will so. *(Turns to go.)* You should have been there *(To KATIE.)*

KATIE: *(Condescending.)* I used to like it long ago.

(JO goes, MICHAEL comes over to the ladder. KATIE sits on the top step.)

MICHAEL: 'Tis a pity about you. The way you're gone lately. I liked you "long ago." *(Imitating her tone. Laughs. Silence.)* Will you come to the dance with me tonight?

KATIE: No, Michael, I won't.

MICHAEL: You'd be afraid. *(Pause.)* He wouldn't know a word about it. He'd never come back as soon as a week.

KATIE: Let me down now till I'll move the ladder.

MICHAEL: *(Not moving out of the way.)* He has you done for. When he went away first we had some fun. I thought there was more spirit in you… Two years we were at the regatta together.

KATIE: I wasn't at the regatta last year.

MICHAEL: Did I say you were? *(KATIE listens for a sound outside.)* What is it?

KATIE: I thought I heard someone.

MICHAEL: Two years now. The year before last you came with me. You were on holidays out of this from Miss Gregg. *(Pause.)* There's no holiday for you out of it now. You were better off before. *(Pause.)* I wouldn't be blowing any old trumpet if you'd give in you're sorry now.

KATIE: I'll tell no lie. I'm very glad. *(Comes off the ladder, moves it to another picture.)* I won't keep you now. You'll be back for the bench.

MICHAEL: *(Resentful, watching her.)* Anyway he gives you plenty of money. You were never dressed like that. You never looked better…

KATIE: I won't ask you to wait. *(Gets up on ladder again.)*

MICHAEL: But you had a blue muslin one day last summer. Do you remember that day? *(Silence.)* Do you remember that day in the meadow, with the long grass around us?

KATIE: Yes, I think I remember.

MICHAEL: You think you remember! *(Catches her.)*

KATIE: Michael, let go! You'll knock me off.

(MICHAEL draws back. KATIE comes down; she listens for a sound outside.)

MICHAEL: What is it at all?

KATIE: I was wondering did I hear someone.

MICHAEL: *(Close to her.)* That day in the meadow… *(Catches her so that she cannot move.)* I kissed you that day… I will again.

KATIE: *(Frightened.)* Hurry on so.

MICHAEL: *(Releases her.)* I should tell Father Power: you're married now.

KATIE: There's the grand lover! *(Laughing, roused.)*

MICHAEL: Lover, is it! 'Tisn't love or liking! But I'll do what I want with you! The way you treated me there in the winter! Himself holding the door for me to walk out! Wouldn't hear a word agen you.

KATIE: Wait now a minute. When was that? Why didn't you tell me?

MICHAEL: You're daft about that old man. He was sick to death of you in three months… Sure he only took you on like a servant girl.

KATIE: *(After a moment, very quiet.)* 'Twould be a pity for the two of us to fall out.

MICHAEL: Why would it so? I see no pity.

KATIE: Suppose I was below with your mother some day, and you to come in,— wouldn't it be well we could talk like any two people?

MICHAEL: She'll have you in the house now; she wouldn't before. *(Then, on rising note.)* And she was the one to ruin my chance, with her talk against you. Like a fool I listened to her bitter tongue. Sometimes at night I'm near out of my mind… To think of the heed I gave her talk…and how Mr. Gregg came…oh, I'll go out of my mind.

KATIE: We don't so easy go out of our minds. *(A silence.)* 'Twas grand our fellows won the race. *(Gentle.)*

MICHAEL: Wasn't it, though! We never had a better crew. They got a great cheer.

KATIE: I was listening to it. *(Pause.)* Well, you'll be back.

(MICHAEL turns to go. JO MAHONY runs in, excited.)

JO: Here's the fellows! They're coming down… They're going over to Fleming's hotel!

(MICHAEL runs to the window. KATIE jumps onto the ladder, and looks out over his shoulder. Sound of shouts, footsteps… a few cheers.)

MICHAEL: *(Laughing.)* Did you see that?

JO: Trying to shoulder Bill Murphy… The cheer they gave him down below!

MICHAEL: They have him up!

(Laughter and cheers.)

KATIE: *(Laughing, delighted.)* They're out of themselves—after winning the race! And so well they might!

JO: He'll have a bad time! They'll pull him to pieces.

KATIE: Oh—it is a grand day!

JO: The best regatta for twenty years!… Come on, Michael! *(He runs out.)*

MICHAEL: Come on, Kate!

KATIE: No, I couldn't…I couldn't go now, but isn't it grand?

MICHAEL: Grand it is! *(He whirls her off the ladder and puts her down near the door. They laugh.)* Come on with me! *(Suddenly he stops, staring out.)* Mr. Gregg! You knew he was here!

KATIE: Michael!

(They draw back from the door, gazing at one another, dismayed.)

MICHAEL: Anyway, he didn't see. I'll walk out. I'll say "good evening" to him.

KATIE: Do not.

MICHAEL: I'll go the back way.

KATIE: Don't cross the room. Stand in there for a minute. *(Pushes him towards the heavy curtain which hangs at one side of the window.)*

MICHAEL: Is it to hide you want me? I will not!

KATIE: *(Beseeching.)* He'll go upstairs. He always does. He'll bring up his things. He'll make no delay. You can slip away then.

(MICHAEL, unwilling, is pushed behind the curtain. KATIE hurriedly mounts the ladder. Then, frightened, flurried, decides to go out of the room. She is hurrying out when STANISLAUS comes in. He comes over to her, gentle, affectionate.)

STANISLAUS: Last time I was here I'm afraid I wasn't very…

KATIE: —I'm changing the pictures. I must get more from above.

STANISLAUS: *(Stops her.)* Last time we didn't part very good friends.

KATIE: Didn't we now? No, I believe we did not. Let you come too.

STANISLAUS: There's no hurry.

KATIE: Won't you take up your things?

STANISLAUS: Yes—when I'm ready. *(Draws her to him.)* Katie, I'd like you to know—

KATIE: Ah, look at this! You were never like this! Can't you take up your case.

STANISLAUS: What's the matter?

KATIE: There's nothing the matter,—but let us talk after.

STANISLAUS: If there's nothing the matter, why not talk now?

KATIE: Ah no, Stanislaus,— I'm in the middle of changing the pictures.

STANISLAUS: Is this done on purpose? To show you don't care? *(Then, quietly.)* I've come home, and I want to talk to you. *(KATIE stands before him, meek now: when he looks away she glances towards the curtain.)* I think we might find something to say to one another… *(Sits, draws her down on his knee.)* What do you think?

KATIE: I suppose that we might... *(Miserable.)*

STANISLAUS: Yes. I think we should. *(Pause.)* Katie, coming up now I was thinking of one night long ago when I was at College... I woke up in the night. We slept in a dormitory. All around, close to me, fellows were asleep... Queer feel—the first time you find yourself awake in the night with people around you fast asleep... I felt—

KATIE: —Lonely, I suppose.

STANISLAUS: Lonely?... perhaps. Magnificent. I knew then, that night, that we must be lonely before we can be anything... So how can a person expect understanding? Or complain about it?

KATIE: I suppose they cannot. Will you come up and give me a hand with the pictures? *(Stands up.)*

STANISLAUS: *(Looks at her for a moment.)* What does this mean? *(From outside comes the sound of cheering. STANISLAUS turns towards the window. MICHAEL is just slipping out of the room. At the door he stumbles, and disappears.)* Who was that? *(Silence.)* I asked—who was that?

KATIE: Michael Maguire. *(Low. STANISLAUS gazes at her for a moment, turns away: takes his hat.)* Will you go away now? *(Whispered. He goes towards the door. KATIE watches, then springs after him, stops him.)* So you'd like I'd be broken-hearted while you're away! The world don't stop still around any one man! And—

(She falters... gazes at him terrified—shrinks back. He goes out. KATIE stands motionless. Door at right opens. AMELIA comes in, her hat and coat on.)

AMELIA: Well, I'm going now, but I won't be long... My dear—what's the matter?

KATIE: He's terribly angry... *(Whispered.)*

AMELIA: Oh... Is he? Stan,— angry? Isn't that too bad... Oh, Katie, isn't that a great pity?

KATIE: Something terrible is going to happen...

AMELIA: Do you think it is, Katie? Oh dear! Oh dear!

KATIE: Am I a bad Christian?

AMELIA: No, I don't think so. *(Then, as she sees KATIE'S distress.)* My dear, I often think how good you are.

KATIE: Well, I must think now what will I do. *(Goes slowly out through door at right.)*

AMELIA: *(Looks after her, troubled.)* But...what?...

(MARGARET appears outside, comes in.)

MARGARET: I believe Stan has come.

AMELIA: He has. He came now.

MARGARET: I hope he'll stay.

AMELIA: That would be very nice...

MARGARET: *(Looks sharply at her.)* Has something happened?

AMELIA: Oh no,— I mean I don't know...

MARGARET: Is he going to stay?...

AMELIA: I...I don't know... I hope he will...

MARGARET: I hope so too; where is he now?

AMELIA: He's just gone out.

MARGARET: And where is she?...

AMELIA: She...she's just gone in there...

MARGARET: Amelia, I think you might tell me... I'm sure something has happened... Why did he come?

AMELIA: I suppose to see Katie… I don't know… Margaret, I don't think we should know… It's for Stan and Katie… She said now he was angry,— but I don't know why…

MARGARET: Angry… That might be a good thing… Oh, there's something very queer about this… Was it Stan who brought Reuben?…

AMELIA: Reuben?

MARGARET: That man they call Reuben…he's down the road…

AMELIA: —But I expect he walked from Dublin… That has nothing at all to do with Stan…

MARGARET: I see. I was wondering… You'd never know… *(Moving off.)* I'll look in again…not that he wants me—but still, he's my brother…

AMELIA: Of course he is, dear…

MARGARET: *(Delaying.)* I hope he'll do something. I'll come back—just in case…

(Door opens. KATIE peers in, miserable.)

KATIE: If you're going, Amelia—

AMELIA: Yes, I'm going now.

KATIE: You might see Reuben. They said he was here. Maybe he'd help me.

AMELIA: I'm sure he will. *(Turns to MARGARET.)* I was going up to the chapel.

MARGARET: I'll come with you. We'll take the short cut. *(To KATIE.)* I'm glad Stan has come.

KATIE: *(Miserable.)* Isn't it lovely!

AMELIA: You'll be here, Katie?

KATIE: I'll be here till himself comes. I don't know where I'll be then. *(MARGARET and AMELIA go out. KATIE mounts the ladder, begins to take down the pictures; hears someone outside.)* Is that you, Reuben? *(STANISLAUS comes in; she turns again to the pictures, talking nervously—and too much.)* I was taking these down. 'Twas a mistake having them here. I'm not like them. They're not like me… —I thought in my mind—wouldn't God like what we like ourselves…

STANISLAUS: Go and pack your things. You're leaving here!

KATIE: *(Turns round, sits on ladder, holding to it.)* Where am I going?

STANISLAUS: You're going away…

KATIE: Stanislaus, where am I going? *(Beseeching.)*

STANISLAUS: You're coming to Dublin…with me.

KATIE: Oh, what matter if we'll be together.

STANISLAUS: Go and get ready. We're going at once. We're not coming back… Get all your things…

KATIE: Is it…for always? *(Silence, STANISLAUS goes to the window, stands with his back to her.)* I'd like to come back. *(Pause.)* I'd like to live my life here. *(Silence.)* I'd like the two of us to live here… I think we're meant for this place.

STANISLAUS: I'll give you ten minutes. I've ordered the car.

KATIE: *(Comes off the ladder, goes to him.)* I did no great wrong. *(He wheels round furiously: she falls back a step or so. REUBEN is seen in the doorway.)* Oh, Reuben, come in! …I want you badly…

STANISLAUS: Get your things.

KATIE: But—can't I talk to Reuben?

STANISLAUS: No! Not now. *(Turns to REUBEN, who hesitates in the doorway.)* Please come in.

(REUBEN comes in.)

KATIE: But he won't stay...

(Beseeching. STANISLAUS looks at her; she turns to REUBEN: he gives one swift look then lowers his eyes. KATIE turns away. Goes out. A moment's silence.)

REUBEN: I met Miss Gregg. She said I was wanted.

STANISLAUS: I expect Katie asked her. Please sit down... Katie hasn't time now, because we're going away. She didn't know: she has to get ready...else we'd miss the train. *(Crosses to sideboard: pours water into a glass, brings it to REUBEN.)* I believe you take only this...

REUBEN: Yes. Thank you... *(Drinks. STANISLAUS watches him.)*

STANISLAUS: You've walked from Dublin?

REUBEN: Part of the way. Some people took me in their car. *(Pause.)*

STANISLAUS: Will you have something to eat?

REUBEN: Not now, thank you. *(He waits quietly—knowing the other wants to speak to him.)*

STANISLAUS: You remember that night last winter when you were here?

REUBEN: Yes, I remember... *(Silence.)*

STANISLAUS: I went to Dublin that evening... I didn't intend to remain away... *(Pause—then:)* ...I went off that evening purposely to frighten Katie: I wanted to show her that I wouldn't put up with any nonsense... *(Pause.)* I was amazed at the relief. *(Silence.)* I'm fond of her—but the relief was—amazing.

REUBEN: So you stayed away?

STANISLAUS: I came back in a month. She appeared quite indifferent... I thought she was only playing a part...

REUBEN: So you let her keep up the game? *(Dry.)*

STANISLAUS: By that time I was interested in some work. It went better in Dublin... But now it's finished... I never believed—

KATIE: *(Opening the door, tearful.)* I'm packing my things. But that's the boys for the bench. I won't be here, so what'll I say?

STANISLAUS: Amelia'll be here. They can have the bench.

KATIE *(Comes in.)* Take it, Jo. Take it out by the back. *(Said over her shoulder, in a light tone. Then she shuts the door; turns to STANISLAUS.)* They won the race. They're awfully glad. Everyone's happy. Couldn't you let us be happy too? *(Silence.)* 'Twas the best regatta for twenty years. *(Pleading.)*

STANISLAUS: *(Catches her, pushes her towards REUBEN.)* Stand over there!

KATIE: Well, what is this for?

STANISLAUS: *(To REUBEN.)* I came back this evening—

KATIE: Ah, please now! Please don't! *(Beseeching.)* I wanted to tell it to you myself. *(To REUBEN.)*

STANISLAUS: Katie was up there on the ladder—pretending to do some work—

KATIE: Ah, please!

STANISLAUS: *(Harsh.)* I spoke to her. She seemed ill at ease. *(With passion.)* She tried to get me out of the room. I turned round and saw a fellow sneaking away. She had hidden him—behind that curtain—when she saw me coming…

KATIE: Oh-h!

(Silence.)

STANISLAUS: What does a man feel, finding that? *(Silence.)* What would you do?

KATIE: *(Sighs.)* I thought you'd go upstairs in a minute. Then he could slip out!

STANISLAUS: What do you think of her?

(Silence. REUBEN bends forward, his head drooping.)

KATIE: 'Twas very foolish, but that's all it was. There was no harm between us.

STANISLAUS: Why did he hide?

KATIE: We were only having a junk of fun! When I seen you coming fear made me stupid.

STANISLAUS: Why?…

KATIE: Don't I know you don't like them?

STANISLAUS: What have I ever done to make you afraid?

KATIE: *(Plaintive.)* You said I'm too friendly! 'Tis because of the harsh way you have… I pushed him in. I said, "Wait there a minute." He had no wish.

STANISLAUS: But you were afraid!

KATIE: Oh, 'tis easy be grand, but when you're fond of a person—

STANISLAUS: —You don't try to deceive them.

KATIE: Oh, you have a very harsh way.

STANISLAUS: *(After a moment, unexpectedly.)* Yes…yes…perhaps I have.

KATIE: *(Quickly gaining confidence.)* You have indeed. That's a great fault on a man: when you can't get him to listen to reason! We were only joking and laughing over the race.

STANISLAUS: Why didn't you tell me?

KATIE: Is it tell you that and you in a roaring temper! *(Sure of herself. Turns to REUBEN for sympathy. Meets his angry look.)*

REUBEN: *(Turns to STANISLAUS.)* I'd give her a flogging.

KATIE: Oh!

REUBEN: She knew you didn't like them, that she was "too friendly." But she'll amuse herself,— like that night in the winter. She'll make her own goodness. What does that mean? She won't be punished. She'll play tit-for-tat.

KATIE: Oh, look at that now! I'm not bad at all.

REUBEN: What did you promise me out there in the winter?— that you'd be good. Is that the way to keep your promise?

KATIE: I was only trying to keep up my heart. *(Pause.)* I would like that God would be pleased with me—I've tried for that.

REUBEN: —But you'll please yourself! She'll serve God—when she's ready! She'll be a saint—in a way she likes! Full of false pride! *(Turns to STANISLAUS.)* She's not to be depended on. What she needs is humiliation,— if she was thoroughly humbled she might begin to learn.

(Stops abruptly: STANISLAUS is looking at him in surprise.)

KATIE: *(Turns to STANISLAUS, pleading.)* 'Twas a hard thing surely—saying to myself for so long, "He'll come tonight"... and again, "I don't mind," and that a lie. And all because I once tried to put my strength against you.

(Silence.)

REUBEN: *(Having watched STANISLAUS for a moment, turns to KATIE.)* I want him alone! *(Authoritative: a gesture towards door—for her to go.)*

KATIE: Oh!

(Laughter from the kitchen. MICHAEL'S voice: "Ask her yourself. I'm not opening that door." More laughter. Voices. Shuffling. Door opens: JO MAHONY is seen.)

JO: Mrs. Gregg *(Very deferential.)*—if you wouldn't mind for a minute.

KATIE: I can't go now. What do you want?

STANISLAUS: See what they want...

KATIE: *(Hesitating.)* When Reuben is gone...

STANISLAUS: See what they want.

(She goes, followed by JO. A moment's silence.)

REUBEN: She's in great danger. *(Quiet.)*

STANISLAUS: Danger?

REUBEN: *(Flashing.)* You know that well— She doesn't know how wild she is... A girl with such a parentage...

STANISLAUS: I think we'll leave that alone.

REUBEN: You can't leave it alone!... You must face it!... A man of your age...to marry that girl...and leave her here, among young people!...— *(Lowers his voice.)*—and that wild blood in her veins.

STANISLAUS: *(Gazes at him.)* What right have you to talk like this? Who are you?

REUBEN: Fitzsimon of Kylebeg. *(Quietly.)*

STANISLAUS: *(After a long silence.)* I see. *(He sits down, arms on table, head bowed.)*

REUBEN: *(Crosses to the door, hesitates.)* Take care of her.

STANISLAUS: Does Katie know? *(Low.)*

REUBEN: Yes.

AMELIA: *(Coming in.)* Oh, Reuben... you've come. I hope you saw Katie.

REUBEN: Yes, I saw her. Good evening, Miss Gregg...

AMELIA: But—won't you stay?... *(REUBEN shakes his head, goes quietly. AMELIA looks at STANISLAUS, concerned.)* I came back, Stan... I was going up to the chapel, but I came back... Stan, is there something wrong?

STANISLAUS: No— *(Without moving.)* —there's nothing wrong... *(Pause.)* We're going away—Katie and I.

AMELIA: Oh, won't that be nice!

STANISLAUS: Yes, very nice. We're going to Dublin.

AMELIA: Oh, that will be very nice.

STANISLAUS: Yes. We're going now. She's packing her things. Perhaps you'd help her.

AMELIA: Yes...yes, dear. I will help her. *(Hesitates.)* Stan, Katie is very good.

STANISLAUS: Thank you, Amelia.

AMELIA: No,— but I mean, she does her best. She's a brave little soul. I think you're not quite fair to her, Stan! I came back to say that.

(Puts her hands on STANISLAUS' shoulders. He does not move. She withdraws. KATIE comes in: looks swiftly round.)

KATIE: If we go away now, Amelia'll be lonely! *(No response, no movement from STANISLAUS.)* She'll be very lonely...

AMELIA: No...no, dear Katie. I won't mind... I can get someone—

KATIE: Or if she goes and gets married the place might be sold. That'd be a great pity.

AMELIA: But Katie... I'm not going to get married...not at once... Perhaps I could help with your things. *(Goes.)*

STANISLAUS: *(To KATIE.)* Come here. Sit down. *(Looks at her fixedly.)*

KATIE: *(Nervous.)* I thought we had finished. *(Pause.)* So Reuben is gone. Will we see him again? *(Trying to be jaunty.)*

STANISLAUS: I don't think so...

KATIE: He's a bit of a crank. He was nicer before. *(Silence.)* ...I took note that you and himself have got very friendly.

STANISLAUS: We met a few times in Dublin.

KATIE: Stanislaus... I...I come from grand people.

STANISLAUS: I know all about you! *(Fierce.)*

KATIE: Oh-h!

STANISLAUS: Have you anything else to say to me?

KATIE: I'd like to stop here. I don't want to go. *(Pleading.)* What would I do away from here?

STANISLAUS: We'll be together *(Cold, watching her.)*

KATIE: What would I do away from this place—I that have lived all my life here—when you'd go off and leave me?

STANISLAUS: I won't go off and leave you.

KATIE: Oh, I think you will often... And I wouldn't know when the trees would be changing, or what way was the river... I'd be in a strange place.

STANISLAUS: We'll be together.

(Silence. In the house something falls.)

KATIE: Amelia—trying to pack my case! *(Suddenly she shakes with laughter.)*

STANISLAUS: *(Angered.)* You and Michael—have you done wrong?

KATIE: *(Amazed, sobered.)* How could I do wrong on you?

STANISLAUS: *(After a moment.)* I see. I'm sorry, Katie, I wasn't quite sure.

KATIE: The world is a very flat place *(Bitterly.)* It takes everything out of what it gives. *(Stands up.)*

STANISLAUS: *(Draws her to him.)* When I went away, when I stayed away a long time, that wasn't...want of love. It was that I had to be on my own. *(Pause.)* I didn't know, when we married, how used I had got to being on my own... Being with you was too...too vital. Sometimes it was a strain...because you were so eager.

KATIE: Maybe I won't now.

STANISLAUS: Ah, do!

KATIE: And we can stop here?

STANISLAUS: We're going away... *(Determined.)* ...We're beginning again... I may seem old to you; I'm not an old man. We're going to start fresh together...

KATIE: I don't think we can start fresh. I don't think anyone can. Won't we bring ourselves with us? *(Tearful.)*

STANISLAUS: Get your hat. *(She crosses the room, takes her hat from the rack near the door; STANISLAUS watching. Suddenly, moved almost to roughness he goes over to her, takes her in his arms.)* You don't know what you mean to me. *(Kisses her passionately.)*

KATIE: Oh, that's very nice, Stanislaus,— but if you'd do what I ask.

(A light tap on the door; it is opened: MARGARET comes in.)

MARGARET: I heard you had come. *(To STANISLAUS.)*

STANISLAUS: Yes—I'm not staying...

MARGARET: Oh—I see... *(Great air of suspicion; pause.)* Perhaps I'm in the way?

STANISLAUS: Not at all,— but we haven't much time. We're going now.

MARGARET: Oh—are you *both* going?

STANISLAUS: Yes, at once.

MARGARET: That would seem wise...rather sudden...

KATIE *(In a flash.)* 'Tis all because Michael stood in behind the curtain...

MARGARET: Behind the curtain...very queer. *(Dry.)*

STANISLAUS: *(To KATIE, furious.)* Get your case.

(She turns to go. AMELIA comes in.)

KATIE: We're going away! He says we must—this very minute—though I want to stop here!...

AMELIA: This very minute...oh dear... Won't you stay for tea?

STANISLAUS: We must get the seven-ten. I've ordered the car.

KATIE: *(With a cry.)* And I'll never be here in my life again! *(Covers her face with her hands, sobs.)*

AMELIA: Oh dear...oh dear... Katie, don't cry.

STANISLAUS: Hurry on, now.

(She goes out, sobbing.)

MARGARET: She's not very pleased... Are you going to live in Dublin?

STANISLAUS: No,— we'll probably go abroad...

MARGARET: Oh— I see...

STANISLAUS: *(Aggravated.)* I've always wanted to live abroad.

AMELIA: But, Stan—won't that be a great change, I mean for Katie?

STANISLAUS: *(Turns to her.)* Katie should never have been left here. It wasn't fair. She's not coming back...

AMELIA: Not coming back!... Oh, Stan!

STANISLAUS: I'll come next week. I'll come for the rest of her things. We'll talk then, Amelia...

KATIE *(Reappearing with her case.)* I see no call for this hurry.

STANISLAUS: There's the car. *(Takes up his suitcase, takes KATIE's from her.)* Good-bye, Margaret, Good-bye, Amelia...see you soon. Come, Katie... *(Goes out hurriedly.)*

KATIE: *(Looks round sorrowfully.)* 'Tis that I made too free with the boys... *(Looks at pictures on the wall, shakes her head as at something that has failed her.)* He won't let me come back.

AMELIA: You'll be together,— won't that be nice!

KATIE: I'd like we were together here. Good-bye, Margaret. *(Holds her face to be kissed.)*

MARGARET: *(Softened.)* I hope you've learned a lesson.

KATIE: Let you say that to him! *(Angry, resentful.)*

MARGARET: Yes, perhaps I will. *(Follows STANISLAUS out.)*

KATIE: Good-bye, Amelia; don't be *very* lonely.

(Lets AMELIA kiss her: looks slowly round the room again. Goes to the door. In the doorway she turns, comes back and throws her arms round AMELIA.)

AMELIA: My dear!

KATIE: I suppose Michael and Jo will have a great night. *(Full of self-pity.)*

AMELIA: Katie, you must be brave.

KATIE: Brave is it? *(Bitter.)* There's no grandeur in this! Taken away…my own fault. *(Covers her face with her hands.)*

AMELIA: …If you're brave, you can make it grand. My dear, you must!

KATIE: *(Gazes at her for a moment, then:)* I think you're right!… *(Pause.)* I'm a great beauty…after all my talk—crying now… *(Grows exultant.)* I *will* be brave!

(They catch hands.)

AMELIA: We both will!

KATIE: *(Gentle now and suddenly perceptive.)* I think *you* were, always… 'Tis a promise between us—whatever'll come, good or bad.

AMELIA: A promise, my dear.

KATIE: I was looking for something great to do—sure now I have it.

STANISLAUS: *(From outside.)* Katie—!

KATIE: I'm coming! *(Looks at AMELIA, smiles.)* I won't forget. I'll keep my word… Tell Michael and Jo I hope they'll have a good night.

(Almost gaily this time: goes. AMELIA stands at the door, looking after her.)

(Curtain.)

WIFE TO JAMES WHELAN

INTRODUCTION

Jonathan Bank

In March 1942, an item appeared in the "Four Corner Survey" section of the *Irish Times* reporting that "Miss Teresa Deevy, one of the most remarkable playwrights of Ireland, has completed a new play which, under the title *Wife to James Whelan* will be produced by the Abbey Theatre." This gossipy column goes on to report that "*Katie Roche* is, I hear, awaiting presentation in London. Bronson Albery has signed the contract."

That spring must have been full of disappointment for poor Tessa Deevy, as neither item turned out to be true. She had indeed finished a new play, but the Abbey's new managing director, Ernest Blythe, rejected it, breaking Teresa's heart (but not her spirit.)

"I felt the play was good and was confident of it," she wrote to her friend Florence Hackett.

> Blythe's letter when returning it showed clearly that he had no use for my work—never asked to see any more. Said the characters were too like Katie Roche. No one else could see this resemblance... The subject matter is quite different. I suppose every play by an author has a certain resemblance—the author's viewpoint, but that is all.

Deevy, always a meticulous writer, had labored long and hard on *Wife*. Earlier that year, writing to her friend, she grumbled: "For ages now a play which will neither get finished or left alone has held me back."

> I don't know what length of time I've wasted on it (if it is waste) and I still love the thing and long to finish it... Last week it was (I thought) almost finished: and then I read it over and discovered it was hopeless, had gone flat. I decided to put the thing away and turn to something else. I felt desperate. No sooner do I try to concentrate on some new subject than I fancy I can just work out the old one.

Apparently Teresa continued to labor over *Wife to James Whelan* even after the Abbey rejection. In 1944, a few disaffected members of the company broke ranks and formed the Players Theatre. Deevy held out hope that they might produce her work: "I am sending my 'rejected Abbey' one, hoping they may like it. I have been working hard, re-writing it," she told Hackett. It's interesting to see Deevy referring to the play by its rejection, revealing the wound she still felt. The Players Theatre did indeed like it—they awarded it a prize of £50 in the summer of 1945 (under the title of *All on a Sunny Day*). Unfortunately, the company didn't last and never produced the work.

There's no way to know how closely the play submitted to the Players resembled the one that Blythe had rejected. Nor can we be sure how long she had been working on it. Her last produced play had been *The Wild Goose*, which premiered at the Abbey in November 1936.

An abridged version of *Wife* was broadcast on Radio Éireann in 1946. It was another ten years before the play was produced on the stage, at the Studio Theatre Club on Upper Mount Street in Dublin, under the direction of Madame Bannard Cogley. It ran for three weeks. On the eve of *Wife*'s opening, the *Irish Times* ran a warmly worded item under the heading "New Deevy Play":

> Teresa Deevy has held a unique position of respect and affection among discriminating Irish playgoers for many years, and they will welcome the news of the stage premiere of her newest full-length play... Miss Deevy's first major work since *Katie Roche*...

No mention was made of the Abbey rejection, here or elsewhere.

Cogley's production of *Wife* was well received, with critics from all of the major publications attending. The *Irish Times* called it "a play of tragic proportion," language echoed by the *Irish Tatler and Sketch*, which described the play as

> a remarkably successful attempt to present in local terms a tragic situation cast in the classical mold... The hero and heroine with their twisted and conflicting passions ending in their mutual destruction belong to the world of Sophocles and Hardy.

In pointing out the complexities of Whelan himself, the critic for the *Irish Independent* suggests that "his compelling motive is never quite clear—even, it seems, to the author, who is content to present him in all his contradictions." Not only content, but determined to do so. The contradictions between what people want and how they behave provides the central conflict in this haunting and enigmatic play. Deevy artfully mines the gap between what is felt and what is said. The text is riddled with ellipses, pauses, and silences, all carefully measured, and the play's most powerful moments are silent—vibrating with the tension of unresolved, unexpressed feelings. It is tempting to speculate that, as a deaf woman, Deevy might have learned to read silence even more effectively than she was able to read lips.

There is an ironic footnote to the story of this play, which took so long to reach the stage. Long after the brief run in Dublin and twenty years after Teresa died in 1963, an effort was made to find a copy of *Wife to James Whelan*. The play had never been published and there seemed to be no trace of it anywhere. Sean Dunne, a Cork poet, placed an ad in the *Irish Times* in 1984 seeking the text, but with no luck. (Dunne was responsible for the first publication of *Temporal Powers* in the *Journal of Irish Literature* in May 1985.) It was another ten years before Jack Deevy, Teresa's nephew who had been living with his family at Landscape, the Deevy home in Waterford, found an envelope containing the only surviving copy of the play. It had been loaned to a writer and historian in Kilkenny in 1966 and promptly returned, but apparently the envelope had been misfiled. The play was published in 1995 by the *Irish University Review*. Fifteen years later, the play was finally produced again, this time by the Mint Theater. The *New York Times* wrote that "the Mint Theater is certainly making an elegant case that the Abbey Theatre in Dublin missed an opportunity almost 70 years ago when it declined to produce *Wife to James Whelan*, a drama by Teresa Deevy (1894–1963), whose six previous plays had been staged to some acclaim there."

Jonathan Bank has been the Artistic Director of Mint since 1996 where he has unearthed and produced dozens of lost or neglected plays, many of which he has also directed. He is also the editor of three additional volumes in the Reclaimed *series (Harley Granville Barker, St. John Hankin, and Arthur Schnitzler) as well as* Worthy But Neglected: Plays of the Mint Theater Company.

Mint Theater Company's production of *Wife to James Whelan,* written by Teresa Deevy, began performances on July 29, 2010, at the Mint Theater, 311 West 43rd Street, New York City, with the following cast and credits:

Tom Carey .... Aidan Redmond
Bill McGafferty .... Jeremy S. Holm
Nan Bowers .... Janie Brookshire
Kate Moran .... Rosie Benton
James Whelan .... Shawn Fagan
Jack McClinsey .... Thomas Matthew Kelley
Apollo Moran .... Jon Fletcher
Nora Keane .... Liv Rooth

Directed by: Jonathan Bank
Set Design by: Vicki R. Davis
Costume Design by: Martha Hally
Lighting Design by: Nicole Pearce
Sound Design: Jane Shaw
Props Design: Deb Gaouette
Production Stage Manager: April Ann Kline, Samone Weissman
Assistant Stage Manager: Lauren McArthur
Dialect and Dramaturgy: Amy Stoller
Press Representative: David Gersten & Associates

CHARACTERS

TOM CAREY	BILL McGAFFERTY
NAN BOWERS	KATE MORAN
JAMES WHELAN	JACK McCLINSEY
APOLLO MORAN	NORA KEANE

SETTING

Act I: A Sunny, sheltered spot on the outskirts of an Irish town—Kilbeggan. Early summer.

Act II: The office of The Silver Wings Motor Services. Early summer. Seven years later.

Act III: Same as Act II. Six months later.

ACT I

"The South of France"—a sunny, sheltered spot on the outskirts of the town of Kilbeggan.

At the back—a wall, with trees beyond showing a young green. On the right side—portion of a shed serves as protection against wind, and helps to make "The South of France" a favourite leisure-hour gathering place. There is a space between the shed and the wall that runs at the back, so that on the right side, there are two entrances—back and front of the shed. To the left stands an old pump; two cart wheels rest against the wall. Further left, the wall gets gradually lower, showing more trees at the back. Nearly offstage, left, the beginning of a footpath can be seen, suggesting that the town is at this side.

TOM CAREY, a small wiry man of about thirty-two, shabbily dressed, sits on a bench which is against the wall at the back. TOM is reading a newspaper and smoking. His hat is beside him on the bench. After a moment he folds the paper—folds it carefully—and puts it into his pocket, and just sits there, obviously enjoying the sun and his pipe.

BILL McGAFFERTY comes on from the right. BILL is twenty-seven or so—dark and saturnine-looking. He wears dungarees, no collar, shirt open at the throat. He crosses the stage and examines one of the cart wheels, then leaves the wheel against the wall and comes back towards the bench where TOM sits.

BILL: You're the man for the sun, Tom—the rest cure on a sunny day.

TOM: What do we have the half-day for? Don't the bees themselves rest?

BILL: Do they have the half-day? I didn't know that. *(Lights a cigarette.)*

TOM: By the same token, I'm moving off from here this very minute… *(Gets up.)* The fellows now—they "must get on"… Huh… I tell you they have no time to live. Does the sun shine warmer on the rich man's skin?

BILL: You bet it does.

TOM: Give me Kilbeggan life here, and this place to sit in.

BILL: "The South of France"—you'd ask no better? Well, as a fellow worker

I wouldn't be the whole way with you, but a part.

TOM: So the officials were down from Dublin: I'll be bound they've picked a man from Tobin's?

BILL: Aye, we were all interviewed—and sized up—during the morning.

TOM: And who has got it?

BILL: We'll know that in a few minutes. Whelan most likely.

TOM: And right he would. You were going for it too, I think?

BILL: I "also ran."

TOM: And Tim Davitt?

BILL: Tim as well.

TOM: Whelan is better than either of you—a better man.

BILL: Don't mention it. You're very obliging. Anyway, I'm finished at Tobin's. If I haven't got the job in Dublin I'm going to my uncle's place beyond in Croom.

TOM: Crissing and crossing and moving around—the curse of unsettlement on the world...with the dread ever that someone else is doing better... *(Pause.)* I'm staying settled... There's some reason in Whelan wanting a move on since he has it in him.

BILL: A cocky young buffer—he's damn certain he has pulled this off.

TOM: You said he has got it.

BILL: I said very likely... —He was called back a second time. There are some that get things a bit too easy...not that I have it against Whelan—he'll be all right when the stuffing has been knocked out of him.

TOM: And you'll do that?

BILL: I'm not saying who'll do it.

(NAN BOWERS comes on. She is twenty-one, bright hair, clear face, carefree bearing. She wears an old pullover, a tweed shirt, heavy shoes, and no stockings. TOM, who has been moving off, delays to watch her.)

BILL: Did you come to meet someone?

NAN: Is it settled? Who's going to Dublin? *(Quietly.)*

BILL: Your friend James Whelan—seems he has carried off the laurels.

NAN: Is that so? Has he got it? *(Earnest, but not excited.)*

BILL: Very likely.

TOM: Some people will be lonely in a day or two, with him going off to Dublin.

NAN: But *is* it so? Is he going?

BILL: And I'm taking myself to Croom next week.

NAN: *(To TOM.)* Is it James they have chosen?

TOM: Sure you might know it. Who else would they have, with the bright group that are here at present... But keep up cheery.

NAN: It won't break my heart to see him go. *(Sits down, stretches her legs to the sun: puts her arms up behind her head.)*

BILL: I think she'll console herself,—won't you, Nan,— with someone else.

NAN: Mind your own business.

TOM: Myself might be that someone else. *(Jokingly.)*

NAN: You might, Tom.

BILL: *(To TOM.)* You're not leaving the sun?

TOM: I'll be back to her shortly. She's the lady of my desire. *(Goes.)*

(BILL delays about, crushes out cigarette, comes over and sits beside NAN. She gives him an unwelcoming look.)

BILL: Oh, I beg your pardon. I didn't hear you say you were waiting for someone... Am I being asked to make more room?

NAN: You're being asked nothing. *(Leans back, hands clasped at back of head.)*

BILL: *(Gets up, bows.)* Anything to oblige a lady. *(Moves off: stops, comes back to her, and speaks in urgent manner.)* I'm going to my uncle's place in Croom: I'm going next week. You know his shop: he has a good business. He's likely to have me always with him from now on.

NAN: They tell me that shop is doing nothing this long time past. *(But she laughs and looks up at BILL.)*

BILL: —and besides the business, he runs the bus between Croom and Cloornagh.

NAN: And will you go drive that old bus for him?

BILL: I'm mentioning it only to you now.

NAN: That's all right, Bill.

BILL: Supposing you and James Whelan didn't clench up... A difficult fellow... A red-hot blaze without any warning. Hardly what would go to make a person happy.

NAN: That's all right.

BILL: There's no harm at all in what I'm saying... Supposing now when he went to Dublin—

(NAN turns away, out of patience. KATE MORAN comes on. KATE is twenty-five or twenty-six, round and comfortable; a manager in every movement: good-natured.)

KATE: *(As she comes.)* Have you the word, Nan? Who has got it?

NAN: No one has told me.

BILL: We'll be saying good-bye to young Whelan—

KATE: Ah! Ah! If that is so—good luck to him! It is his gain, but our great loss!

BILL: Our loss, is it? *(Cynical.)*

NAN: Don't mind him, Kate,— nothing is settled.

KATE: Well, if he were the one to go I'd be losing the best of neighbours... my mother too, and all the children. We'd be lost without him. But I met Tim Davitt now, and he told me there'll be a telephone message from Dublin about it.

NAN: I don't believe that... Do you think they'd bother. We are not that much importance.

KATE: What had James to say about it?

NAN: I don't know.

KATE: You didn't see him with the interview over?

NAN: No, I didn't.

KATE: *(Gazing at her.)* I'd thought you'd be the first to have word... *(Pause.)* Most likely he went to tell his mother—

BILL: —Mother's darling—

KATE: No doubt he would go straight to her, seeing she was anxious...

NAN: I think he went up for his dinner. *(Dry.)*

(BILL laughs. KATE looks indignantly at him, turns again to NAN.)

KATE: Would you say 'tis likely he'll be going? *(NAN nods.)* ...We'll miss him very much from above. In and out like one of ourselves, and often doing an odd job for my mother,— to lift in the potatoes, or sweep the shed. I don't know what we'll do without him. *(BILL looks at her in disdain—moves off a little from them.)* ...Often of a Sunday, after Mass, James—sure you know it—how he goes, nearly every Sunday across to Croom, with the greyhounds. But would any other, at his age, let our two young lads go with him,—Dick and Willie— *(Laughs.)* ..."Apollo" James calls him—he's that good looking... Ah, they have great laughing always between them... Those two, they'd black the boots for him.

NAN: They're not the only ones I think.

KATE: You needn't mind me. He has no thought of me at all. I know that well. *(A little bitterly.)*

NAN: I wouldn't care.

KATE: Too old I am—older than I should be by right, but if you had your hand on the young ones always... *(Stands up.)* I'd better go on... They'll be asking what kept me... There's no reason for me to be dangling around... whatever about other people...

(She goes. NAN leans back once more, hands behind head: she is serious: clearly something is pressing on her all the time.)

BILL: *(Moving over.)* That is a good riddance—

NAN: I was hoping to be left alone. *(But she sits up and looks eagerly beyond BILL.)* Here's Jack McClinsey...

(JACK McCLINSEY comes on: he is unobtrusive, delicate-looking, twenty-six or so, shabbily dressed: looks hot and dust-covered, socks pulled up over trouser ends, to do duty for bicycle clips. NAN turns to him, warmed and gentle.)

BILL: Apparently he's very welcome.

NAN: Jack,— so you rode over all the way from Cloornagh.

JACK: I rode over. They're taking me on for work at Tobin's— *(Suppressed excitement.)* ...like you said they might... if I was on the spot at the right moment...

NAN: Oh, are they?

BILL: I think I'll be moving... will I, Nan?...

NAN: *(To JACK.)* When do you start?

JACK: I'm to start on Monday morning. *(Turns to BILL.)* Why need you be going? Isn't it the half-day here?

BILL: I can see well enough when I'm not wanted... *(As he goes.)*

NAN: Yes, that's right. *(After him.)*

JACK: *(Eagerly.)* Wasn't it well you had told me, Nan? —the likelihood of this job going...

NAN: All the same you needn't have said it. *(But she smiles at him.)*

JACK: Did I do wrong—to say it out before him... that you had told me?

NAN: It makes no difference: he's forever tormenting me, but I don't mind him.

JACK: *(Sitting beside her.)* And now we'll see one another often.

NAN: Yes, that's likely...

JACK: —When I'm working at Tobin's... I lost no time, I have everything settled... I'm to sleep above at Mrs. Moran's...

NAN: You were mighty quick about it...

JACK: I wanted that; I wanted to be near you... Nan. *(Gently.)* you'll be a bit sorry after James Whelan... I know that well...

NAN: He mightn't be going... It isn't yet settled,— though likely now when they're having you...

JACK: They told me for certain,— and if it is he goes, you'll be sorry... You'll be bound to miss him. Why wouldn't you and the two of you so well suited.

NAN: Not so well as we used to be. I told you that. *(Then, half angrily.)* Didn't I tell *you* to be at Tobin's? Do you doubt me?...

JACK: Not that, no, I could never doubt your goodness... But it would be nearly beyond what I could expect... that you'd... that you'd...

NAN: Leave it so. *(Testily.)* Why must there be always too much talk? I think we're crazy—that we can't let things come and go, without forever twisting and wondering,— and I'm the worst at that myself.

JACK: Nan,— will you tell him about it?

NAN: About *what? (A silence.)* Well, no matter what... But look now, I am making you no promise.

JACK: I wouldn't like to act badly by any person.

NAN: Jack you are gentle. You are different from anyone I ever knew before...

JACK: He is stronger.

NAN: In what way do you mean? I think you have the strength of gentle people... Bill,— coming back this way—would you doubt him?

JACK: I got that said. It was on my mind to say it.

NAN: —He's spying on us,— what about him!—a low-down lounger...

JACK: Your hand—he can't see now. Will you tell James about me—before he'll go? It mightn't be right if we didn't... Whatever you like. I'll leave it to you... But I wouldn't have my joy, if I could help it, at cost of another.

NAN: *(Colder.)* James is not that kind at all... And isn't there, most times, someone that must pay?...

BILL: *(Coming on.)* Is that your bike McClinsey,— down in the ditch below?

JACK: That's where I left it.

BILL: Very likely it will be "missing"... if you're on for throwing it around.

JACK: I'll push it up so... and get my bag that I brought, hoping I'd want it... *(Goes.)*

NAN: We don't go nabbing bikes around here,— nor any other person's belongings... you needn't pretend it.

BILL: Too bad to be disturbing you, but if he'd lose the machine he mightn't think,— or maybe he would think,— the conversation was worth it.

(NAN looks at him—makes no reply. At this moment they hear a whistle, and look round to the back. JAMES WHELAN appears, behind the low wall.)

JAMES: Nan, I'm a winner! *(He jumps over the wall and comes forward eagerly to her. He is strongly built—about twenty-five—flushed with triumph.)* Hear that—I've been chosen.

NAN: Did they tell you?

JAMES: Yes, I'm for Dublin. Wish me luck.

NAN: Oh,— you'll find it. I think you'll find it always.

BILL: So you'll be leaving... isn't that now very lucky— *(A side look at NAN.)* ...at the right moment...

JAMES: *(With a touch of condescension.)* They'll be taking on some others later.

BILL: I must tell that to the fellows,— to build up their hearts for them... *(Moves off: stops.)* Even Jack McClinsey might, later on, be getting promoted…maybe at another right moment… With all the changing you'd never know…

NAN: *(Flaming.)* What do you want, Bill? What do you want here with me?

BILL: Don't you see that I'm going?… Many a time we put in together— *(With passion.)* —but the wind changed, for I know I'm not wanted…though I don't know for certain *who is* wanted. *(Goes.)*

JAMES: Gas-bag…gas-bag! *(Seizes NAN's hands.)* Twelve went in, and I was the only one they chose. Picked at once.

NAN: There'll be no standing you at all. But what matter—we're finished with you here it seems.

JAMES: For the present.

NAN: What was wrong with the job you have at Tobin's? You had the air and the freedom, and me in the evenings.

JAMES: I'll have you in the evenings another time.

NAN: I wonder will you! *(A flash.)*

JAMES: So that's it now—she wants petting. *(An arm about her.)*

NAN: Ah—go off.

JAMES: Well, and I'm not that kind either, but I thought you wanted it.

NAN: A lot it matters what I want.

JAMES: *(After a moment.)* He asked my age, and when I told him. "Twenty-five—the weight of years is on your shoulders." *(Laughs a little.)* A nice old topper.

NAN: Was that funny?

JAMES: Ah, Nan, give over!

NAN: Like an old cap thrown in a corner—that's what I am—to be picked up whenever it suits you, and left forgotten when you like.

(JAMES throws back his head and laughs delightedly, taking her resentment as a compliment.)

NAN: Well, I mean it.

JAMES: Yes, that's what you are—an old cap—nothing better.

NAN: Couldn't content yourself as we were.

JAMES: Only a fool is content when he could have better. I know what I want. I know the difference 'twould make to have power and money.

NAN: Go off so—after your power and money.

JAMES: A lot of good if I stopped here. Yes,— I'll go off, but I'll come back.

NAN: A lot of good your coming back.

JAMES: *(Out of patience.)* I'll do what I think well about my work: I won't be bossed. I'll go the way I want to go. You may as well know that from the beginning.

NAN: It's well to know the kind you are.

JAMES: Yes, it's better.

NAN: So's we can part before it is too late.

JAMES: We won't part. *(Gentle now.)*

NAN: You're very sure.

JAMES: You'd wait for me ten years, and more. *(Tenderly: in a teasing way.)*

NAN: Make it fifty.

JAMES: —But I won't keep you waiting long—I'll be back soon—with better to offer. *(Silence.)* Everyone else had a good word for the winner.

(Silence. After a moment he takes a newspaper from his pocket and opens it.)

NAN: *(Standing up.)* If you want to read the paper—

JAMES: You won't talk—

NAN: You wouldn't tell me anything.

JAMES: *(Stands up too.)* What didn't I tell you?

NAN: When you're going, and what's the payment, and whether it's for six months or twelve. *(He laughs—happy again.)* Well, what's funny?

JAMES: *(Quickly, growing serious.)* I start work in Dublin on Monday morning, bound for six months only. I'll come back here when I have more money—and then—we might be able to get married.

NAN: I'll make no promise. I never did.

JAMES: I never asked you. But I will ask you, and then you'll promise.

NAN: And if I said now, "I'll have you if you'll stop here," you wouldn't do it.

JAMES: What a fool I'd be! And you'd be a fool, too, if you'd have a fellow of that making.

NAN: You never cared for me at all.

JAMES: Did I not? *(Tenderly.)*

NAN: Only to have me. Yourself—that's all that ever mattered... You'd never give in. You'd never think of another person. I might go off with someone else. *(Watching him.)*

JAMES: Off with you so.

(They sit down together again, but silently.)

NAN: *(After a moment.)* We won't have time to finish the book.

JAMES: No,— I was thinking you'd better keep it.

NAN: I wouldn't be bothered with it now.

JAMES: I'd like you'd keep it and finish the story. *(A silence.)* ...The man that asked me all the questions was surprised I had the answers so quick. He said, "I think this fellow will go far."

NAN: *(Groans.)* Oh, you're a wonder! I think I will take up with another.

JAMES: *(Throws back his head and laughs happily.)* Go on, let you.

NAN: Yes, but I mean it.

JAMES: I'm sure you do.

(Throws an arm across her shoulder. Her hand goes up and catches his hand: they sit silent.)

NAN: James, you're childlike... I... I wish you weren't...

JAMES: That'll get less as the years go by. You won't know me when I come back.

NAN: I will have forgotten. Maybe you'd get a weekend sometimes.

JAMES: I don't know. I might be too busy—or if you had taken up with someone, what would I want coming back?

NAN: Ah—that's true.

JAMES: *(After a moment.)* Although I would—to see my mother, and because it's here I'll be in the end always.

NAN: Here—is it?

JAMES: I'll come back to Kilbeggan to do something.

NAN: What will you do?

JAMES: I'll start some sort of a business. I'll give employment here in Kilbeggan.

NAN: Take your hand from my shoulder—Kate is coming.

JAMES: Well—what matter? *(But he takes away his hand.)* Yes, I'll give employment. I'll do something to better the people.

NAN: Bill McGafferty is gong off next week to join his uncle. I think it's to drive the old bus he's going.

JAMES: That's a thing I thought of sometimes—a chain of buses—a proper bus service. But, 'twould take money. I'd have to save a lot and get them built. Once started, I'd make a great success of it.

NAN: *(Looks at him.)* I think you would.

JAMES: It would be exciting—it's a thing might grow to something big.

NAN: They wouldn't let you. Likely the railways would take them over, or in some way you'd be hampered. It is no use trying anything. *(Careless: content that this should be the case.)*

JAMES: Don't speak of it.

NAN: I won't even remember.

JAMES: Nan, I'm going this evening.

NAN: You said Monday morning.

JAMES: To start work on Monday. I'm going today on the 3:15.

NAN: *(After a moment.)* It's a wonder you thought of mentioning that.

JAMES: You took it so badly.

NAN: I think you're mad with delight at the thought of going.

JAMES: I'm very glad.

NAN: So much for your feeling.

JAMES: *(Bends over her.)* You won't get anything out of me that way. You needn't think it.

NAN: And I don't want to.

JAMES: I want one promise—you won't take up with anyone while I'm away.

NAN: You're downright selfish! You want the best of it all round.

JAMES: *(Gentle.)* I want you to wait a little while. I'll miss you a good bit, though I'm glad going.

NAN: You can miss away—I'll make no promise.

(Gets up, turns to go. JAMES catches her arm.)

JAMES: I must put a few things together, and talk to my mother. Will you come to the train to see me off?

NAN: I'd look well.

JAMES: I think you'll come.

NAN: *(Enraged by his assurance.)* I'll tell you now. Jack McClinsey will likely be at Tobin's in place of you. He's friendly towards me. I like him well.

JAMES: And I'm to be very frightened about it? *(A smile, half tender.)*

NAN: I don't mind what way you are.

(TOM and BILL saunter on, from right front, talking.)

BILL: Nothing will do them but to play it out.

TOM: They should bide their time: it is too hot for the hurling now—nearly into the month of June.

(From some distance away to the right a whistle is heard: then a few distant shouts.)

BILL: Off with them.

TOM: Out of season. Out of season.

BILL: A lot they care about the season—those chaps from Croom—and do you think our fellows would leave them the victory until the autumn? *(Looking away to the right.)*

(TOM looks to the right also. JAMES and NAN are a little to the left now—just standing there.)

TOM: What harm would it do them taking defeat for a while? All must wait till the right time comes.

(KATE comes in quickly, from the left—comes quickly to JAMES.)

KATE: I thought I'd be one of the first to hear this.

JAMES: You're not far off.

KATE: A wonder but you'd look in to me, and you next door.

JAMES: I looked in. You weren't there.

KATE: How could I be, when you wouldn't come at the right time? You never want to talk to me. You never tell me anything. *(JAMES groans. She suddenly changes, beams on him.)* Right proud I am! And your mother—she's divided in two even pieces. *(The others all laugh.)* Yes, one minute she crying, and the next she's up in the sky in Heaven… Crying, you know, because he's going away so sudden.

BILL: Aye—going to set fire to Dublin City.

JAMES: *(To BILL.)* I hear you're for Croom. I'd like that better. I've no wish for the City.

(Comes over to BILL; produces two cigarettes—one for himself, one for BILL. TOM is smoking his pipe.)

KATE: Don't say that James! This is a great step on for you, and on your own merit.

NAN: He knows that well.

BILL: *(To JAMES.)* I'm joining my uncle.

KATE: Well, when you join him tell him at once—

BILL: *(Stops her.)* I'm not the man for your advice.

(The others laugh.)

JAMES: Had I your uncle—in your place—I'd no more go to Dublin.

NAN: You'd go to Croom?

JAMES: *(To BILL.)* That business could be worked up to something good. You have the place: it is established: it only wants new blood in it, and proper running. When you have a place you have half the battle. *(Full of interest: his ambition is always kindled at possibilities of achievement.)*

BILL: Aye—but, you have the old man too—and his temper.

JAMES: You could get over that.

BILL: I could do wonders.

KATE: *(In a managing tone.)* James, when you go to Dublin—

JAMES: What must I do?

(The others all laugh.)

KATE: I won't open my mouth again. I'm only a nuisance, and a laughingstock.

JAMES: *(Turns to her.)* One of those fellows who were asking us questions—when I walked into the room he said at once—"He's too young." He soon sat up. Before I had given many answers they were looking at one another.

NAN: *(Groaning.)* Oh, the World's Wonder.

KATE: I'm sure they were.

NAN: "Twelve they had and him they chose." *(Chanting.)*

KATE: And why wouldn't they? Is it fools they are? Who, in this place, could be put before him?

TOM: True for you, I wasn't trying. *(Laughter.)*

KATE: A lot of difference you'd make, Tom Carey. *(Good-natured bantering.)*

NAN: Now you'll hear all about it—what a great fellow they thought him and said he'd go miles high up.

KATE: You've an edge on your tongue today.

JAMES: Ah, don't mind her—she's very lonely.

(They laugh at NAN now, and she joins good-humouredly.)

NAN: I never knew so uppish a fellow. *(With a toss.)*

TOM: And so would I be uppish, too, had I his parts. *(Getting up.)* You're a prize man, James. Give us the hand. Good luck to you.

JAMES: She doesn't know a good man when she sees one.

NAN: *(Also moving to go.)* That's not for the want of being told. *(But this jibe is a friendly one.)*

JAMES: *(Moves over to her.)* Am I to say good-bye to you now?

NAN: No, you're not.

(The others laugh.)

KATE: *(Quickly.)* We'll all go down to the train and see you off.

JAMES: Good for you, Kate...

NAN: That's what he'd love—Kilbeggan's hero!

JAMES: *(Stung.)* What's wrong with you? *(With sudden passion.)*

(There is a moment's silence.)

NAN: *(A little uncertain of herself now.)* Going off to better himself and everybody—whatever good there is in betterment.

BILL: I hear McClinsey is coming in your place... They promised as soon as they'd have it vacant.

JAMES: Who is he?

TOM: You know, that long, weedy fellow from over the River?

JAMES: I don't know him.

BILL: Do you, Nan? *(Sudden.)*

NAN: I know him well.

KATE: A mouse-coloured fellow—with curly hair. Comes on his bike to the late Mass on Sunday—you'd have seen him often of a Sunday.

BILL: That's if you were minding.

NAN: James wouldn't be minding. He'd be thinking of what he was going to do... Another would rest happy with the work he had—and not be forever pushing forward.

TOM: *(Nods.)* Rob a man of content and he has nothing.

KATE: I differ from you. Don't the best men spend themselves always with the strength of endeavour, eating their hearts out all the time?

JAMES: Contentment is the devil's own snare.

NAN: And so is pride and lordship too. *(Quickly.)*

BILL: We'll settle it all here, now—in Kilbeggan. *(Cynical.)*

JAMES: And why not Kilbeggan—as well as another place? *(Pause.)* What's wrong with Kilbeggan?

NAN: And you're the one to go away.

(A distant cheer.)

TOM: There's another goal for Croom.

(He is the only one interested: gets up and goes off, right: the others are silent for a moment. BILL looks after him.)

BILL: This now is McClinsey coming.

(JACK McCLINSEY comes in, carrying a suitcase, and with a raincoat thrown over his shoulder.)

KATE: So well to you.

JACK: So well yourself. *(Puts his case on the ground, puts his raincoat on the bench, pushes back his cap.)*

KATE: The room you're renting is at my mother's. I think you'll have comfort. It's a step from here only; if you'd like I'll show you.

JACK: I'm in no hurry. I rode hard. *(Seems tired, sits down beside JAMES.)*

KATE: She's renting that room this long time past, and never a complaint about it. You'll find no stint.

JAMES: Are you Jack McClinsey?

JACK: That's right, I am.

JAMES: I'm Whelan—you might know me.

JACK: I know you by sight a good while now.

JAMES: I had the job you're taking on—the job at Tobin's.

JACK: Yes, Nan told me. *(Smiles over at NAN.)*

JAMES: It's only now I knew I'd be going.

JACK: Yes, but she said it was likely.

JAMES: *(After a moment.)* You rode over?

JACK: The bike is there. *(Nods back to the right.)*

TOM: *(Reappearing.)* Were you watching the Hurley?

JACK: No, I came the short way over.

TOM: Are you stopping here the night?

JACK: No. Tomorrow. —I start at Tobin's on Monday morning.

TOM: The Cross fellows have two goals, to nil.

KATE: *(To JACK.)* I wouldn't think you'd need to make the double journey. Have you that much luggage?

JACK: Well, the way I thought *(Gentle, slow.)* to bring the bag this evening, and tomorrow—being Sunday—coming to Mass I'd strap the coat across the bars. I'll ride back before my tea this evening.

KATE: Couldn't you stop and have it with us and ride back later?

JACK: That's friendly of you. I will, so.

JAMES: The foreman at Tobin's—Dwyer is his name—he comes from near you, over at Croom.

JACK: Yes, Nan told me.

JAMES: You'll find him decent.

NAN: I told him that.

(A moment's silence: something electric in the air.)

TOM: Where will you be putting up?

KATE: Above at my mother's... He's renting the room.

TOM: You'll have comfort.

BILL: He'll have no lack of attention, if you ask my opinion. *(Cynical—a look at NAN.)*

(A silence.)

TOM: *(To JACK.)* The wind was against you?

JACK: Pretty strong, and great heat in the sun as well.

TOM: There's never much heat till May is out.

NAN: *(To JAMES.)* They say it's unlucky to make any change in the month of May. You had a right to wait till the month was over.

JAMES: Am I the only one to make a change?

KATE: *(To JACK.)* Let you come with me and see the place.

JACK: *(Not moving.)* Sure it's all right.

BILL: You'll be with us this evening giving Whelan the push off for Dublin.

JACK: Aye, I will.

JAMES: And I'm glad to be going.

NAN: *(Quickly.)* So everyone's pleased, and that's a great matter.

KATE: *(Uneasy—urging JACK.)* Come on, I'll show you.

(JACK gets up, takes his case, lifting it as if a great weight.)

JAMES: Shoulder it, man, if it's so heavy. *(Irritable.)*

JACK: I'll do it this way.

TOM: Heave it up, and you'll feel no weight.

(JACK hesitates: tries to pull the case up on his shoulder, but cannot do so.)

NAN: Let me help you. Those fellows are lazy. *(Jumps up and goes over to him.)*

JAMES: If I were you, I'd know first for certain where I was going.

JACK: *(Leaving it down.)* I think you're right.

JAMES: Only a fool goes dragging around a weight he needn't. *(With contempt.)*

NAN: You never would. *(Hostility.)*

JAMES: I fling everything from me—and start off free.

NAN: It's well to know it.

BILL: Aye—that's outspoken.

NAN: I'm coming, Kate, with Jack and you.

KATE: If you are there's no need for me. Show him the house: my mother is there.

(NAN and JACK go off.)

BILL: That's the new broom and no mistake! *(A laugh.)* I wouldn't take it from her, Whelan.

JAMES: Mind your own business.

KATE: Did I disturb you?

BILL: Nan Bowers is disturbing him very much.

JAMES: *(Springing up.)* What's that you say?

BILL: *(Also up.)* Ah, go easy. It's not the first time a woman was fickle.

JAMES: *(Striking him.)* That'll teach you!

BILL: So will that.

(Blows exchanged.)

TOM: Easy there...ease off now... I'm surprised at you, Whelan...

BILL: He's in terror that he'll lose his girl.

(With TOM between them now, JAMES makes another move towards BILL.)

KATE: I beg of you! Don't give him heed. Don't notice what he says at all.

TOM: Come on, Bill.

(TOM and BILL go off.)

JAMES: I'd like to give that fellow something.

KATE: And so would I.

JAMES: Himself and his sneering. I'm not afraid of losing her.

KATE: Of course you're not.

JAMES: *(After a moment.)* Did I show myself there in a foolish light?

KATE: Ah, what matter.

(A silence.)

JAMES: What made Bill turn that sneering way against me?

KATE: Didn't you win the job that he was after? *(Silence.)* I don't know how you'll get on in Dublin. You're too simple. You're as open with everyone as a child. A man should have more sense than that... A man should be on guard against people!

JAMES: *(Laughs.)* You're a gem!

KATE: *(Defensive.)* A man should be on guard always—that would be right.

JAMES: Right or wrong, that's not my way.

KATE: It would give you greater dignity: to think what people might say about you.

JAMES: I must remember!

KATE: You won't be said by me?

JAMES: I will not! *(But he turns impulsively and takes her hands.)* You're a jewel, Kate. We'll be friends always.

KATE: That's enough now. *(Low, trembling: greatly affected.)*

JAMES: *(Lets go her hands, sobered now, rebuked that he means so much to her. After a moment:)* See—would you give those marbles to young Jim— *(Taking them from his pocket.)* and the screw pencil is for Apollo.

KATE: They'll miss you, James.

JAMES: Miss! Not they! Chaps of that age!

KATE: You'd be surprised how children feel... And your mother'll be lonely; but I'll go in to her often.

JAMES: You will, will you? *(Gratitude.)* You'd think I was going to New Zealand—and Dublin but a few hours' journey.

KATE: Ah! But this is sudden going!

JAMES: Better sudden. *(Pause: she watches him.)* There's Jo Peters—he'll wonder that I don't look in to him.

KATE: You mean blind Jo?

JAMES: We used often have an hour or so in the evening. I used like to be with him,— hearing what was in his mind. We used be comparing thoughts. Tell him I had to go sudden.

KATE: *(Fumbles in her pocket and produces a small medal.)* Maybe you'll keep that in your pocket. *(Giving it to him.)*

JAMES: What is it! St. Joseph on one side. *(Examining.)*

KATE: Will you keep it?

JAMES: I won't, Kate. I don't care for those things at all. What?— *(For he sees her disappointment.)* Well, I will, so.

KATE: No, give it to me.

JAMES: I'm keeping it. I'm glad to have it. *(Pause.)* Wouldn't you think Nan might come and my time so short?

KATE: Look at this, James. If you want Nan, settle something with her before you go.

JAMES: What do you mean? *(Angrily.)*

KATE: I always say the wrong thing to you—and there's nothing I wouldn't do to please you.

JAMES: Nan is not flighty.

KATE: She's at liberty to make a change, you know.

JAMES: She won't make it.

KATE: How sure you are.

JAMES: Don't tell her I took much heed she didn't come now.

KATE: Look at this! You could say what you like! It would never go past me.

JAMES: Yes, I know. *(Gratitude.)*

KATE: Whatever at all was in your mind, and not a soul on earth would hear of it. *(Heavily sympathetic.)*

JAMES: I know that well.

KATE: If it would relieve you, say out now whatever you're feeling.

JAMES: *(Stands up.)* I don't think I'm feeling very much. *(Pause.)* ...Why wouldn't a man make a break for something better?

KATE: Why, indeed?

JAMES: Everything is a contradiction—you can't move or stay still but you're up against something.

(JACK and NAN come on.)

JACK: That place will suit me very well.

KATE: You'll stop, so, and have the tea with us before you ride back to Croom this evening?

JACK: I will, thanks. *(He takes up his suitcase.)*

JAMES: *(To JACK.)* I'll give you a hand with that.

(He helps to lift the case and goes out with JACK.)

NAN: *(To KATE.)* Very thick all of a sudden.

KATE: *(Earnest.)* Nan, don't let there be bad feeling at parting.

NAN: I don't think we'd ever agree. He's too much master. I couldn't brook him.

KATE: Were you born blind? Couldn't brook him! ...Some wouldn't mind what they'd put up with... *(Silence.)* He'd feel it now if you went off.

NAN: He'd get over it, wouldn't he—like another.

(JAMES reappears: KATE goes off after JACK.)

JAMES: Well, Nan?

NAN: You didn't go far. Was the case too heavy?

JAMES: Yes—for me. *(A smile.)* I never care to carry a burden.

NAN: You said you must go and put your things together.

JAMES: I didn't go.

NAN: So, to get rid of me was all you wanted.

JAMES: To get rid of you—that must be it. *(Tenderly. She turns and looks at him.)* What do you think? *(Restrained—passionate.)*

NAN: How would I know what to think? I don't understand you. *(She looks away.)*

(They stand together rather miserable.)

JAMES: *(After a moment.)* You never spoke of him to me.

NAN: If I did you wouldn't listen: you'd listen only to your own concerns. *(Speaking harshly: she is near tears.)*

JAMES: *(After a moment.)* If I was like that how did we ever come together? *(Silence. When she does not answer, JAMES turns away, takes his cap he has left on the wall, goes a little way to the left: looks back at her: stops.)* Come here to me. *(She comes to him—reluctant, yet drawn. He smiles, too readily triumphant that she has come: she stiffens.)* You know well it's to build for the two of us I'm going.

NAN: You needn't bother to build for me. *(A moment's silence.)*

JAMES: Mind what you're saying! *(Sharp, frightened.)*

NAN: I like Jack better.

JAMES: Nan, mind what you're saying. *(A cry this time.)*

NAN: It's better you'd know it: you're at will to go your own way now—and so am I. We have our freedom.

JAMES: Don't be foolish. *(Dull, stupefied.)*

NAN: So you won't go away now, will you, if it was for the two of us you were going?

JAMES: I will go. *(Dead, but holding onto what he has.)*

NAN: I knew well I never caused you too much thought.

(She turns from him, walks across to the right, and goes off at the right side. JAMES stands motionless, looking after her; then with a slow movement, his hands come up and cover his face. Next instant he hears someone coming, lowers his hands, and turns away to the left. TOM comes on from the right side, pulling the newspaper from his pocket as he comes; he sits down on the bench, glances towards JAMES's motionless figure.)

TOM: It was Manahan scored the goal for them.

(No response from JAMES. TOM watches him, keenly: BILL follows in, stands near TOM, looking off towards hurley players, but without much interest.)

JAMES: Kate! *(Low.)*

KATE: *(Appearing behind wall at left.)* Yes,— did you call me? *(Coming quickly over low part of wall.)*

JAMES: I'm having a send-off before I leave— *(Quiet, urgent.)* I'm having it here. Will you tell them?

KATE: Sure the boys will stand you a send-off, James.

JAMES: No, I want something different. I want it to be out here in the open. Let everyone see it. We'll lift over those planks and make a table.

KATE: But—what is the meaning? I thought you'd all be below at Brophy's...

BILL: Closing hour!

JAMES: I'm telling you now what I want done, Kate,— will you do it?

KATE: Oh, I'd better—

JAMES: It'll be a party. Let anyone who likes come to it.

BILL: *(Coming over.)* Don't you see he's giving a ladies' party. Scatter that.

KATE: *(To JAMES.)* Does Nan know? Will I tell her?

JAMES: Tell everyone. This is a public send-off: we'll have singing—why shouldn't I have it?

KATE: You can't start people singing unless they have the feeling for it… Only a foolish man forces what should come from nature.

JAMES: Yes,— but they will have the feeling when they see how jolly and glad I am to be leaving—

KATE: *(Close to him.)* James, you're lonely!

JAMES: Will you go on and tell them— *(Angrily.)* we haven't much time.

KATE: I'll do what I can…always I'll do my best for you. *(Goes.)*

BILL: Will I give hand with that plank, Whelan?

(They lift over the plank.)

JAMES: Will you go down to Brophy's, Bill—and get a dozen.

(Giving money to BILL. BILL takes it, amused and sardonic, and goes.)

TOM: *(Coming over, rubbing his hands.)* And I'll do anything to be obliging.

JAMES: See couldn't you borrow the glasses…

TOM: To be sure I will. Bill,— I'm coming.

JAMES: And get some lemonade for the girls…

(TOM hurries off after BILL. JAMES, left alone, stands motionless. Behind the wall, JACK McCLINSEY passes quietly. JAMES gazes after him.)

(Curtain.)

ACT II

Seven years later. The Office of The Silver Wings Motor Service—scantily furnished.

A writing table and a chair stand at the left side of the room, to the back. On the table a telephone, a directory, a railway guide, two or three timetables, some brightly coloured advertisement bills, a new ledger, pens, ink, blotting paper.

At the right side of the room a door leads to the outer office, near this door a second chair, and on the wall above the door a clock.

Except for this clock, the walls, which have been washed a light coffee colour, are quite bare. At the back, to the right, there is a good window, and through it we see part of the bus which stands in the yard outside. Beyond the bus there are trees, showing the same fresh greenness of seven years ago. The sun is shining, filling the yard outside with brightness, and coming a little way in through the open window. It is a lovely day—full of promise—one of the last days of May, shortly after noon.

APOLLO MORAN comes from the outer office with some letters. He is a thin, peevish-looking youth, but at this moment he *is very pleased with himself. Leaving the letters on the table, he crosses the room and puts up on the wall at the right side a gaudily painted advertisement for travel in Ireland—Irish jaunting car careering through a mountainous district. Having admired this, he proceeds to decorate the wall opposite with the same type of picture, then steps back and surveys his work, head sideways.*

While this is going on, a young woman, neatly dressed, with a dark shawl covering her head and shoulders, comes quietly into the room and sits down on the chair near the door. She is NAN McCLINSEY—NAN BOWERS of the previous act.*)*

APOLLO: *(With a glance over his shoulder.)* You shouldn't come in. You should wait in the outer office.

NAN: I want a word with Mr. Whelan.

APOLLO: I know. I'll tell him. Nan McClinsey. I know the name—Mrs. McClinsey. He hasn't come yet.

NAN: It is only work I want.

APOLLO: I know, I know. I don't see myself what work there could be unless that he'd make it. True enough he has a fancy for himself handing round jobs. What would you think of that now?—*(The picture.)*

NAN: It's a beautiful picture.

APOLLO: I'm improving the place. He has no regard for the look of appearance. Now, if I were to run a concern like this I wouldn't have the table stuck out there. I'd have it over in the corner. I'd have the whole place laid out better; I'd have a good big desk against the wall. And I'd have—well, I think I'd have—

NAN: Will he be long?

APOLLO: He will not. He's like a child about the clock. Clocks and timetables his head is full of.

NAN: Are you here all the time?

APOLLO: I'm never here. I'm in the outer office. I'm answering enquiries and checking the cash. He was very anxious to have me.

NAN: Are you Willie Moran?

APOLLO: Yes. "Apollo" they call me—on account of my looks.

NAN: I remember you and your brother as young lads, following James Whelan round the place, when you were children.

APOLLO: That's a far day. *(Suddenly turns to her and speaks in an altered tone.)* Isn't he the fellow that got on? *(Goes to the table, takes up a large green advertisement bill, opens it, spreads it on the table and reads.)* "The Silver Wings Motor Service... Sole Proprietor, James J. Whelan." Hm... Sole Proprietor... Mind you that. There's no denying but he got on.

NAN: He was set always to do well.

APOLLO: At the height of his glory now. *(Reads.)* "On and from Friday next, June 1st, The Silver Wings Motor Service will ply between the Square, Kilbeggan, and Croom Courthouse, leaving Kilbeggan at the following hours..." Hm...

NAN: I knew him long past—that's why I'm here.

APOLLO: Did you see him at all since you came back?

NAN: We met for a minute in the street. He stopped to shake hands.

APOLLO: He did! That was kind of him. He's a kind-hearted man... You were friendly with him before you got married?

NAN: I was, very friendly. *(Quiet, detached.)*

APOLLO: Well— *(Impressive.)* James Whelan is now a different man from what he was some years ago.

NAN: I wonder is he...

APOLLO: He's a much sought-after man. *(Bends towards her, very confidential.)* All the girls are going at him full tilt. That Nora Keane is set full sail for him.

NAN: Nora Keane? *(Though asking, she is not greatly interested.)*

APOLLO: Her father owns the boat, you know, that brings the coal up from the pier. They're well-off people.

NAN: I don't remember. I am like a stranger in this place, although it is but six years since I was married. *(Gentle complaint.)*

APOLLO: *(Gently.)* My sister was telling me all about you—my sister Kate—how McClinsey got that job over in Cheekpoint and lived but only for twelve months.

NAN: He lived for two years after we were married.

APOLLO: *(Bent on sympathy.)* Ah! Two years—what is that? And now you have a child to provide for, too. I'm very sorry.

NAN: That's a thing to be very glad about.

APOLLO: *(Determined.)* Kate told me it is a pitiful story, so I'm sorry to hear it.

NAN: You're very kind. *(Dry.)*

APOLLO: *(With sudden humour.)* She has me grinded in kindness. *(He laughs, and she laughs a little with him.)* She's a well-meaning woman... All the same you had a right to talk to her about this job.

NAN: And I did talk too.

APOLLO: You're all right so. She'll tell him to take you.

NAN: Is that the way?

APOLLO: You might say it is Kate runs this place.

NAN: Are they so thick?

APOLLO: Thick! Said he to her—"If we get married I'll be master." "Oh!" said she, "whoever I'd marry I should run him." *(Laughs.)* She told me herself. They shook hands when they parted.

NAN: But they did part? *(Though asking these questions she is all the time quite detached.)*

APOLLO: They parted on that question, but they shook hands I tell you. She's up here often.

NAN: What sort of a man is he to work for?

APOLLO: Come and go—as you take him. *(Then confidential again.)* One minute he's the lord and master, the next he's like myself and you.

(TOM CAREY comes in.)

TOM: Has James come yet?

APOLLO: *Mr. Whelan* will be here at any moment. *(Very dignified.)*

TOM: Are you here all the time?

APOLLO: *(Wearily.)* I'm never here. I'm in the outer office. I'm answering enquiries and checking the cash.

TOM: Does he want me to drive that bus, or does he not?

APOLLO: Weren't you engaged to drive the Silver Wings?

TOM: But when is she running?

APOLLO: *(Taking up the bill.)* "On and from Friday next, June 1st—"

TOM: *(Testily.)* We're all able to read... But they tell me he's driving her himself.

APOLLO: On Friday, for the maiden voyage, but he'll want you on Saturday, June 2nd.

TOM: "The maiden voyage"—from here to Croom!

APOLLO: Memento tickets for all who travel on that day. Bright green tickets.

(They all laugh.)

TOM: He's like a child about that bus. He'll have the whole town laughing at him.

NAN: I think he's not very much changed since I knew him.

TOM: *(Turning to her.)* And how are you, Nan?

NAN: I'm well, thank you, Mr. Carey.

TOM: Tom is my name, as you might remember. You look well. You look the same as ever. *(NAN accepts this with indifference.)* Tom, remember. I was never troubled with a Mr....

APOLLO: Nor with a Mrs. either, for that matter.

TOM: I suppose Whelan now will be finding a wife.

APOLLO: Who would you give him?

TOM: He'd want someone, oh, you know, someone, well...well, someone...

APOLLO: He would.

TOM: What of Nora Keane?

APOLLO: What? That one? *(Excited.)* Would you have her in here as wife to James Whelan?

TOM: He could do worse.

APOLLO: Shed walk on you, man. We'd have no life. I hope to Heaven he won't do that.

TOM: Would your sister, Kate, think of him at all?

APOLLO: She would not, she's gone far beyond marriage.

TOM: Well, there should be a good few willing. Whelan is a likeable man, beyond what he has. *(Looks towards NAN.)* I think I may say he was one time a rival to Jack McClinsey.

NAN: Ye leave all the gossip to the women.

(Smiling: the men laugh a little.)

TOM: That's right, we do. *(Goes over to her.)* You and me...we could get on. We were good friends always—before McClinsey came on the scene.

NAN: Is that so?

TOM: Not many a man could work with you, as I did then, and be unmoved. I often thought that you and myself might make a pair.

NAN: You did not, Tom, for you never thought of me at all. *(Quietly.)*

TOM: *(After a moment.)* I believe you're right. I'm only acting. You're very sharp.

NAN: I'm a wonder.

TOM: At what moment does a man cease to act? That's a point of interest.

NAN: A point of great interest. *(Dry.)*

TOM: I suppose I won't know till the moment comes. *(Turns to APOLLO.)* Well, I'll be back to find about the bus.

APOLLO: You needn't then. Haven't I told you?

TOM: I want a few words with James himself. *(Goes to the door; stops: looks back at NAN.)* Sure, I know well you'd never think of me. You'd say I wasn't young enough. *(Pause.)* Tom is younger than you'd think. *(Goes.)*

APOLLO: Did you hear what he said—Nora Keane!

NAN: What kind is she?

APOLLO: I couldn't tell you. I knew at one time—now she doesn't look in my direction. Do we want her in here? Will you tell me that! *(Fierce.)*

NAN: Apollo, don't be eating out your heart. *(Gentle.)*

APOLLO: Eating it! For Nora Keane! Me! Not likely! But if she comes in here as Mrs. Whelan, I'll walk out.

NAN: And is he taken with her now?

(Sound of voices from the outer office.)

APOLLO: You shouldn't be here. Likely he'll blaze up at once to find you here.

NAN: Is he so hot?

APOLLO: *(Listening to the voices outside.)* That's not Tom he's talking to. How could they have missed one another?

(JAMES WHELAN appears in the doorway, and comes in. He is now very much the self-made man—blunt in appearance and manner—keenly perceptive, and with surprising sensitiveness. He stands for a moment, taking in the situation, his attention focused on NAN. NAN has pulled her shawl more closely about her, and has turned away from the door. APOLLO is ostensibly settling the papers on the table.)

APOLLO: A woman here to see you, sir. I told her to wait in the outer office.

JAMES: There's a man outside, he's looking for the fellow who should be there.

APOLLO: I declare I only left in these papers.

JAMES: Is that all? You don't tell me! *(Looks pointedly at the pictures on the wall.)*

APOLLO: And stuck these up for the sake of appearance. The place was very bare without them.

JAMES: So you thought to improve it! Go on now, and attend to your business. I told that fellow I'd give you something for not being there.

APOLLO: That was a very queer thing to say, Mr. Whelan. *(Dignity outraged.)*

JAMES: Along with you now!

APOLLO: *(Goes as far as the door, stops, turns.)* Tom Carey called up. He was surprised to hear you weren't in yet. *(Trying to get his own back.)*

JAMES: I should be ashamed no doubt—not to be here, to oblige Tom Carey, Go on now! *(Good-humoured fury.)*

(APOLLO goes. JAMES crosses the room, takes down the picture that APOLLO has put up: crosses again and takes down the one on the wall opposite—his attitude contemptuous, amused. Then he comes to the table, sits down, looks at his letters—the few that are there. Finally he turns:)

JAMES: Well, Nan—and what is it? *(Trying to be casual—but a certain tenseness has crept in.)*

NAN: If you could give me work, Mr. Whelan.

JAMES: Pull over that chair, sit down, and we'll talk.

NAN: *(Pulls over the chair and sits down.)* It is only work I want.

JAMES: I was sorry the old man left you nothing.

NAN: He hadn't anything to leave. The pension died with him, you know.

JAMES: Three years a widow, and now you have nothing. *(Sympathetic—watching her.)*

NAN: That's the way it is with me.

JAMES: Well—we must do something about it. *(Pause.)* Did McClinsey get no health after you married?

NAN: He did for a short time—that was all.

JAMES: And you stayed on with the father, minding him.

NAN: What else could I do? The last thing Jack said was—"Don't let the old man go to the Workhouse."

JAMES: He had no right to saddle you with such a burden.

NAN: How could he do otherwise?

JAMES: You were foolish— *(Bitterly.)* How old is the child on you?

NAN: Nearly four.

JAMES: Foolish—foolish.

NAN: And I saw that too—I wanted to go out working when Jack died, but there was the old man; he was bed-ridden; I couldn't leave him. *(Pause.)* One day I took the child across to my sister; she'd mind him for me, but she wouldn't mind Grand-da, no one would; he had a bad temper. I left him in bed. I got work that day. When I came home in the evening Grand-da was lying on the floor with his two legs scalded. That was the end of work for me. *(All this quietly, speaking without any change of voice. Her manner throughout is that of one past feeling very much—one whose life is over.)*

(JAMES—watching her—is very much affected. When she has finished speaking, he turns away from her for a moment, pushes the papers about on his table, placing, then replacing his letters. NAN looks at him—surprised at his emotion. He turns to her.)

JAMES: See how badly you served yourself.

NAN: —If you would give me some work to do—

JAMES: —And see how you broke my heart on me—

NAN: Joking you are now, Mr. Whelan, I did not.

JAMES: You did at one time, but now I'm above you. Your chance with me is over and gone. *(Pause.)* You might get another man yet.

NAN: I'd be long sorry. Once married is enough for me.

JAMES: Ah! But if you could get someone to keep you in comfort.

NAN: I have the child to think about.

JAMES: Double reason... What work can you do?

NAN: I'd do anything, no matter what—sweeping or scrubbing.

(JAMES pushes back his chair, stands up disturbed, angry.)

NAN: So you can't find any work for me?

JAMES: *(Takes a turn about the room, comes back to her.)* Sweeping or scrubbing! Is it to make a drudge of yourself you would? What do you want with that shawl on you?

NAN: It is a good shawl. *(But she loosens it.)*

JAMES: Making you look old before your time! *(Another turn, and comes back to her.)* Nan, if you come in here you won't come with your life behind you... Hear me now?

NAN: I do, Mr. Whelan.

JAMES: Your hair scraped back, that used to be so soft about you... I'm telling you now—*you're a young woman.*

NAN: I suppose I am. You'll give me work?

JAMES: Yes, we must think about it. *(Pause; then suddenly:)* Remember the books we read long ago, together?

NAN: I remember you read a lot to me. *(Pause.)*

JAMES: Are you able to tot?

NAN: Tot?

JAMES: Can you add one figure to another?

NAN: I had always a good head for figures.

JAMES: Could you give right change for a person's money if I put you at the desk in the outer office?

NAN: I could… But, Apollo Moran?

JAMES: I'll be wanting him for the bus as well as Tom Carey. The Silver Wings is going to be a big thing, Nan. There'll be three or four buses pretty soon. *(Eager.)*

NAN: That's very good.

JAMES: It will be good, with the help of God. I'll be driving part of the time myself. I'll put Moran helping Tom—that's if he's able. *(Turns to the door.)* Moran! *(APOLLO appears.)* I'm wondering now what hand you'd make…

APOLLO: *(Stopping him.)* One moment, please. A young person called to see you.

JAMES: A young person?

APOLLO: Well—a lady. I told her she'd have to wait.

JAMES: Have to wait! Who was she?

APOLLO: Nora Keane.

JAMES: You told *Miss Keane* she'd *have to wait!*

APOLLO: She stepped outside, I think she's there.

JAMES: Go out at once and apologise! Ask her to be so kind as to come in. *(APOLLO goes. JAMES turns to NAN.)* I'll see you later.

NAN: *(Stands up.)* Am I to wait?

JAMES: Yes. Wait outside. I'll send when I'm ready.

NAN: I'd be grateful if you could do what you were saying.

JAMES: We'll see. We'll see.

(NORA KEANE appears at the door. She is young, fair, smartly dressed.)

JAMES: Ah, Miss Keane, good day to you. Please come in. I'm glad to see you. *(Going to greet her and scattering NAN, who is trying to slip out of the room.)* Sit down, won't you? Sit down, Miss Keane. *(Fussing.)* I'm afraid that fellow was very rude. You must excuse him. I'm glad you've come.

NORA: Why are you glad?

JAMES: Why! Haven't I eyes in my head? It isn't so often they get a treat.

NORA: Do you say that to everyone?

JAMES: Is that the sort you take me for?

NORA: How could I know what sort you are?

JAMES: I suppose you couldn't—

MORA: Though I do know quite a lot about you.

JAMES: Do you, Miss Keane?

NORA: Couldn't we drop that "Miss Keane"?— Call me Nora.

JAMES: Kind of you.

NORA: Shall I say "James"?

JAMES: If you like— *(A little taken aback: he is so old-fashioned.)*

NORA: But, do you like? This is hard on me. I'm doing all the rowing.

JAMES: *(He laughs then.)* I'm very pleased we have Christian names. *(A little primly, in spite of himself.)*

NORA: Well, Christians are people who are nice and friendly.

JAMES: *(Getting uneasy.)* You saw my bus as you came in?

NORA: Oh, no—I never saw it: I was just able to squeeze in by it.

JAMES: The Silver Wings, as I call her—she looks well, at least I think so.

NORA: I want a ticket for that bus on Friday.

JAMES: So you're coming. *(Pleased.)* I'll be driving her myself that day.

NORA: That's why I'm coming.

JAMES: I'm complimented.

NORA: I wouldn't miss it for the world.

JAMES: Moran is selling the tickets in the outer office, one and six, that's the fare.

NORA: But, you're giving me a present of it.

JAMES: I'm giving no presents at all of tickets.

NORA: Not to me?

JAMES: Not to you or anyone else, Miss Keane.

NORA: Miss Keane again! I was certain you'd give me a ticket.

JAMES: I'm a businessman.

NORA: And business before everything?

JAMES: Business first when I'm in my office.

NORA: I thought since we're old friends you wouldn't refuse me.

JAMES: And are we old friends?

NORA: Haven't we always known one another?

JAMES: I knew you long past as a slip of a girl—too grand for me then.

NORA: I was never too grand for you.

JAMES: I was working in your father's yard.

NORA: Yes, I know.

JAMES: And now you come here to talk to me. *(Simple: wondering.)*

NORA: *(After a moment.)* Who was that woman? When I came in?

JAMES: Nan McClinsey.

NORA: You're having her in here, are you?

JAMES: Not here with me. In the outer office... I want someone minding the books when I'm away.

NORA: I'll be that someone—minding the books. I'd like that. Let me do it instead of her.

JAMES: No, Miss Keane. *(Decisive.)*

NORA: You worked for my father; it would be fun now if I worked for you. *(Pleading, close to him.)* Wouldn't it? Wouldn't you like that?... I wonder would you be a hard master? *(Would-be seductive.)*

JAMES: *(Stands up.)* Girl dear, rid your head of that nonsense, it is no good.

NORA: Why? What's wrong? *(Indignantly.)*

JAMES: Spoiling yourself in that cheap way! Shame on you. *(Turns towards the door.)* Moran!

(NORA stands up, moves to go.)

JAMES: No—stay where you are. *(APOLLO appears at the door.)* This lady wants a ticket for Friday. Bring one in.

(APOLLO goes. NORA opens her bag, takes out the money, and puts it on the table. She does not look at him. She is upset.)

JAMES: Yes, that's right.

APOLLO: *(Coming in.)* There are but two tickets left; am I to keep one for my sister Kate?

JAMES: Did she ask?

APOLLO: Oh! Kate didn't *ask.*

JAMES: Well, wait till she does.

APOLLO: *(Giving the ticket to NORA.)* I hope the day will be very pleasant, and the passengers enjoy themselves. *(Very superior, very distant.)*

JAMES: *(Sharply: disapproving of APOLLO's manner.)* Where is that lodgement for me to check?

APOLLO: I left it for you in the box. *(Opens a small cashbox which is on the table, takes out some notes and silver, lays them on the table.)*

JAMES: How much is there?

APOLLO: Fifteen pounds, ten. *(Turns to go, looks again at NORA.)* Very pleasant, the passengers *all* have my good wishes.

JAMES: That's all, Moran! *(Glaring. APOLLO goes. NORA moves to go.)* Wait now a minute. *(Comes over close to her.)* I didn't mean you to take so hard what I said now. I know well I'm a man many a girl would be glad to have—and no blame to her—only not to spoil yourself... Look at me now... Look at me. *(But she will not.)* Sure we *are* old friends. Will I remind you of something? ...Something that happened when I was working for your father: one day on my way home to dinner children passed me coming from school. They were calling out names at one little girl. She was very different from the lot of them. Long fair curls and a dark blue coat. She had a new basket, and they were making fun of her. She ran, and they chased her, and she fell. The bottle of milk was broken on her... I sent them about their business. I wiped over the books, and brought her home... Yes, Miss Nora—she wasn't so very small a girl... After that we'd have a smile whenever we'd meet, until one day, she was with some grander people, so she stared in front of her... See, I remember... *(Now very tender: carried away by his own words.)*

NORA: *(Taking it badly.)* So you were thinking of me even then. Feeling cheated when I did not look.

JAMES: *(After a moment's surprise.)* Young men are always feeling cheated. At least when I was young—

NORA: And now you think I'm running after you—

JAMES: I think only what I see.

(The door opens and TOM CAREY comes in.)

TOM: Am I to come and drive that bus for you?

JAMES: Tom, there's an outer office where people wait when I'm occupied. *(In his grandest manner.)*

TOM: I didn't know you were occupied. That fellow Moran said—"Walk straight in."

JAMES: Moran! *(APOLLO appears.)* Walk straight in!

APOLLO: *(Nervous.)* Am I after making a mistake?

JAMES: What do you think? When I'm engaged in here with one person does it seem to you exactly right to tell another to come in?

APOLLO: I declare I can't keep the people away from you. *(At NORA.)*

JAMES: For Kate's sake alone I took you here.

APOLLO: Who now could solve this problem— If I say "You must wait" that's a bad thing, but "Walk in" is even worse.

JAMES: Go down and tell Kate you're more than any man could put up with.

TOM: I only want you for a moment. There's no need at all to be so fiery.

NORA: I was going in any case.

APOLLO: Who'll mind the office while I'm away?

JAMES: Who minds it when you're here?

(APOLLO turns to go. KATE MORAN appears in the doorway. She is a well set-up woman, of thirty-three, plainly dressed; comfortably attractive.)

KATE: Good morning, James.

JAMES: Good morrow, Kate. Come in if you like.

KATE: Of course, I do like, why wouldn't I like? *(Comes in smiling, nods to them all.)* Good morning, Miss Keane.

(NORA responds. The whole atmosphere is lightened by her entry; her good humour. Everyone relaxes. NORA sits down again.)

JAMES: *(To APOLLO.)* A chair for your sister.

KATE: *(To NORA.)* I see we're all drawn in the one direction...like a magnet...

JAMES: Kate, what is the sense of saying that? *(Annoyed.)*

KATE: The whole town is talking of you this morning. Look at me. I came up for a ticket.

JAMES: Ticket? You're not coming on Friday?

KATE: I am so. I must be in your maiden voyage.

(She laughs a little at herself, at the idea. The others join in her laughter.)

JAMES: I think you're all laughing at me. *(Affably.)*

TOM: It wouldn't be the first time, James, and it doesn't do you much harm either. We laughed long ago—the day you got that job in Dublin, and said you'd come back here to give employment. The joke is on your side now.

KATE: If I laughed that day, I think I cried a bit as well, to see him go.

JAMES: Kate, you were always a lovely girl!

KATE: Ah, go off—as if you didn't know it well.

TOM: She wasn't the only one to cry, I think. You had always a way with the women.

JAMES: *(Turning to APOLLO.)* See have you a ticket left for Kate. *(Brusque.)*

APOLLO: We have just one. *(Goes out to get it.)*

KATE: And how is Apollo getting on?

JAMES: Oh, very well!

KATE: I was thinking he'd be a help to you.

JAMES: Oh, a great help!

(TOM and NORA exchange looks.)

KATE: I knew well you'd be glad to have him.

(NORA stands up—turns to go.)

JAMES: Good-bye, Miss Nora. *(Offers his hand.)* Are we friends now?

NORA: I suppose so.

JAMES: Then, we are. I'll come outside with you. *(They move towards the door.)* I hope you'll call in and see me soon again.

TOM: *(Suddenly.)* You know what Bill McGafferty is saying?

(JAMES and NORA stop. APOLLO, bringing in the ticket for KATE, also stops. NAN appears in doorway.)

JAMES: What is that?

TOM: McGafferty is telling the world you have no call to start this bus: he was on the roads before you: he holds the right of Freeman's Lane.

JAMES: The Silver Wings won't touch that lane.

TOM: No, but you'll take all his halfway people—they walk now as far as the Cross.

JAMES: So, no one must stir a foot for fear Bill would lose a penny.

TOM: I'm giving you a friendly warning.

JAMES: Bill McGafferty is the man to warn.

TOM: You did bad to start so near to him…

JAMES: Did I, Tom?

NAN: *(Unexpectedly from the door.)* Where is the harm in a jaunt to Croom?

(All look at her, surprised.)

JAMES: That's right, Nan. There is not—no harm at all. *(Turns to TOM.)* Bill will have to face a rival. What's wrong with you? Where do you stand?

TOM: I stand with you, man; that's plain as day.

JAMES: Then what the hell are you driving at?

KATE: Well, you're a very hasty man.

TOM: Indeed, he is. *(Then to JAMES.)* You might know I had your good at heart.

KATE: Of course you had.

TOM: I was well within my rights with you.

KATE: He was so. James, you must learn to listen to people.

JAMES: *(Flaring.)* Listen to people! Fellows that haven't it in them to make a move, coming in here with talk like that.

TOM: "Haven't it in them to make a move." *(Hurt.)* Conceit spoke then. I thought we were friendly and confidential: I was speaking in open confidence here.

JAMES: I keep my confidence for myself. What I say to you—you can shout across the street.

KATE: Well, that's very unfriendly.

JAMES: Your opinion wasn't asked for, Kate. *(Turns to NAN.)* I thought I told you to wait outside. *(NAN withdraws.)* So you're going on, Miss Keane?

NORA: Yes, I'm going— *(At the door.)*

APOLLO: Here now is your ticket. *(To KATE.)*

NORA: One and six—he doesn't give presents! *(A laugh: she goes.)*

KATE: I'm quite willing to pay for my ticket. *(She gives the money to APOLLO.*

APOLLO goes.) I'm to be sent away now, I suppose.

JAMES: You are not. *(Quietened, as always, by her.)*

TOM: *(Steps up close to him.)* Bill could be easily settled. A small sum of money and he'd leave the roads wide before you.

JAMES: I'll win the roads—

TOM: High and mighty! The shop in Croom would suit Bill well. He made no hand of the bus at all. *(Pause.)* A small bit of money to keep the shop going, and then—maybe he and Nan McClinsey would get married.

JAMES: Did you come here to tell me this? *(Blazing.)*

TOM: Oh, high and mighty once again!

JAMES: Settling how I'll spend my money.

TOM: *(Having looked at JAMES silently for a moment.)* I tell you, you have a lot to learn. *(Silence.)* Am I to come here on the 2nd?

JAMES: As we settled.

(TOM goes. JAMES walks about, to and fro. Then comes back and stands beside KATE.)

KATE: There's a very foolish man.

JAMES: You mean, I'm foolish? *(Defensive.)*

KATE: No, but Tom Carey: coming out with a thing at the wrong time.

JAMES: *(Sits down beside her.)* You're a great one, Kate. I thought it was myself you meant. *(A smile between them.)* I wouldn't doubt you—saying the comfortable thing to please me... Did I show myself now in a foolish manner?

KATE: Well, a bit—but what matter?

JAMES: Was there truth—would you think—in what Tom said about Nan McClinsey and that fellow?

KATE: I couldn't tell you. *(Pause—then suddenly.)* Look at this James—you *must* get married.

JAMES: And whose fault is it that I'm not married long ago? *(Smiling at her.)*

KATE: Ah, go on. Was there ever a woman you didn't speak soft to?

JAMES: Are you pretending you don't believe me?

KATE: You *were* fond of me at one time, no doubt.

JAMES: You're very sure it's the past tense, are you?

KATE: Don't torment me... I'd like to see you settled now.

JAMES: Who would you give me?

KATE: Nora Keane.

JAMES: I think she's foolish.

KATE: You could put a check on her foolishness. She comes of a good family, James.

JAMES: *(Repeats slowly.)* I think she's foolish. I never speak for long with Nora, but that I feel myself disappointed.

KATE: Ah, what does disappointment matter? You're like a child! A man should think of other things—

JAMES: You'd like her for me?

KATE: There's only one other I'd like better.

JAMES: And who is that? *(Suddenly tense.)*

KATE: *(After a moment.)* If you and myself were a bit different...

JAMES: *(Plainly disappointed.)* Ah—yes—but we'd have to be different—you often said it.

KATE: I'm sure I did. *(Pause—then bravely.)* Better have Nora. Go to her father. Don't delay. Say to him—"I'm desirous of having your daughter."

JAMES: And what must he say?

KATE: Oh, I'd better leave it to yourselves.

JAMES: It might be better... *(Dry: pause.)*

KATE: Look at this, James—about the bus. Don't fall out with Bill McGafferty.

JAMES: I will not.

KATE: No: it would be a great mistake. Tell him you have no wish to do him harm. Say to him that you are to be friendly rivals. Say "Every man must meet a rival, you and I will not fall out." Tell him, "There should be room for both of us." Say, "I knew your father and your mother, too, so why should I wish to harm you now?"

JAMES: Are those the words I am to say?

KATE: I'm at it again! Well, I'm a fright!

JAMES: You *are* a fright. Why must you go and spoil yourself?

KATE: Am I the only one that spoils myself?

JAMES: You and me—we'd have to be different. *(Stands up.)*

KATE: We would, indeed. You'd never bear a word from me.

JAMES: You'd never give me any peace.

KATE: No, I couldn't leave you alone at all. *(Regretfully: a pause.)* James, about Nan McClinsey?

JAMES: Well, what of her? *(Tense again.)*

KATE: You must give her work in here. That woman is very badly off.

JAMES: I think she is.

KATE: Sometimes she hadn't enough to eat.

JAMES: Nan?... And she dressed decent!

KATE: She must dress decent. That is the only chance she has... That woman went through a very hard time.

JAMES: Whatever she went through, it didn't leave much mark on her... She has the same softness she had always... *(Then with sudden fire.)* Kate, there's not a woman round here to compare with her.

KATE: That's a queer thing to say! And to another woman!

JAMES: I never meant to hurt you, Kate! I never dreamt you'd mind at all. *(Distressed.)*

KATE: You're welcome to admire whoever you wish, but we all have our feelings.

JAMES: I wouldn't hurt you for the world... Sure you're the one I can talk to best.

KATE: So, I'm your Aunt Sally.

JAMES: I don't know who you are. I can be myself with you. *(A silence.)* Tell me, how do you like this place?

KATE: I like it well. And it will get more tone as you go on.

JAMES: Tone?

KATE: It will get the look of being lived in, James. It will lose the great bareness.

JAMES: Your brother thought to give it more "tone" this morning, putting these up. *(The advertisements.)* I took them down. That isn't the tone I want. Did you look at the bus outside at all?

KATE: Didn't I tell you before how well I liked it.

JAMES: Yes, but it hadn't the upholstering then.

KATE: Well, I'll look at that as I go out. *(Plainly humouring him.)*

JAMES: I have no sense, that's what you're thinking.

KATE: Not very much.

JAMES: I tell you this is a great excitement... I got Father O'Connor to bless the bus.

KATE: Is that so?

JAMES: Am I an old woman?

KATE: You are not!

JAMES: I don't know, I'd have laughed at that not so long past.

KATE: So, a man can't pray?

JAMES: I was taunting myself with the thought of old Peter. You remember old Peter muttering his prayers long ago in the Friary, and we as children laughing at him.

KATE: I remember that time. *(She stands up.)* Nora Keane has a lot to commend her.

JAMES: She's very light-minded.

KATE: What great thoughts has Nan McClinsey?

JAMES: I don't know—she has the same soft look she always had.

KATE: Soft looks don't get us anywhere. *(A tap at the door.)*

NAN: *(Opening the door.)* I beg your pardon, Mr. Whelan, but I must get back, the child will want me, so if you could tell me now—am I to come?

JAMES: Very well, Nan, I'll take you on, come in tomorrow morning.

NAN: I'm grateful to you—very grateful.

KATE: What will she do? *(JAMES does not answer.)* Couldn't she start this evening without waiting for tomorrow morning?

JAMES: Is this my office?

KATE: Oh, I beg your pardon!

JAMES: *(Calling.)* Moran! *(APOLLO appears.)* Are you able to drive a bus?

APOLLO: I often thought I'd be well able.

JAMES: *(Fierce.)* Have you a driver's license?

APOLLO: License! The fellow they give a license to! *(With fine scorn.)*

JAMES: Go down to Jim Fitzgerald this evening. Say I sent you. Let him see what hand he can make of you.

KATE: Do you mean for Apollo to drive the bus?

JAMES: I'm thinking of trusting him with the Silver Wings.

KATE: But he has never driven a bus at all!

APOLLO: *(Thrilled.)* Can't I begin? *(Then to JAMES.)* You won't regret it.

KATE: But, you don't know...

APOLLO: A man can learn what he wants.

JAMES: That's right, Moran. *(Turns to NAN.)* Nan, you can have his job, minding the books, he'll show you the work, a child could do it. Or, no, I'll show you myself, so's you'll learn it right. *(Turns to APOLLO.)* Bring in the ledger. *(APOLLO goes.)*

KATE: *(Going towards the door.)* I'll say Good morning. *(Stiff.)*

JAMES: *(Quickly.)* Are you not pleased? This will be a great thing for him.

KATE: I should be pleased, if that is so.

JAMES: The fellow is dancing with delight.

KATE: No doubt he is. I would have liked a word of warning.

JAMES: I couldn't tell you—you were talking.

KATE: Then I'm the one at fault, no doubt.

(She goes. APOLLO comes in with the ledger.)

JAMES: *(To APOLLO.)* Tell Kate I'll be with her if she'll wait a minute. *(APOLLO goes. Turns to NAN.)* Now, I'll show you. *(He opens the ledger, showing it to her. NAN bends in over the book, letting her shawl slip back.)* See, you enter there the amount taken, and there you put down the number of tickets... There's the charge for carriage on all parcels... Now, take that pen and write your name, not in the book—on this paper.

NAN: What for, Mr. Whelan?

JAMES: I want to be sure you won't spoil my book. *(He puts a loose sheet in front of her.)*

NAN: *(Having written rather laboriously.)* My hands are cold or it would be better.

JAMES: That will do. There are the expenses, paper and printing. *(Pointing.)* Advertisements too—mind you, it is of great interest.

NAN: I'm sure it is.

JAMES: You'll get to like it.

NAN: What will you pay me, Mr. Whelan?

JAMES: I don't know. We'll see later... This concern is very dear to me.

NAN: It will be dear to me, as well.

JAMES: And why so?... For your bread and butter?

NAN: Why so? Didn't I come in here thinking maybe you'd let me scrub—and you give me this. *(Gesture.)*

JAMES: See that you're worth it! *(Abrupt.)*

NAN: Indeed I will.

JAMES: That's what they call "Carried Forward."

NAN: Yes, I see.

(They bend together over the page.)

JAMES: I don't know why I'm doing this. *(Watching her—tender now, noting the signs of hardship in her face.)*

NAN: I'm sure I don't either. *(Looks up at him: grateful.)*

JAMES: You must dress better. *(Abrupt again.)*

NAN: Then you must give me the money, Mr. Whelan.

JAMES: I'll give you one pound straight off now. *(Takes a pound note from the money on the table and gives it to her.)* You'll be earning one pound a week.

NAN: Thank you, sir.

JAMES: I'll take it off later for your payment.

NAN: Yes, very well.

JAMES: It is wages given in advance.

NAN: Yes, I see.

JAMES: Come in tomorrow. Wait, you'd better sign here for the money.

(NAN signs: then she stands up and turns to go. Suddenly she staggers and is sinking down in weakness when JAMES catches her. He puts her onto a chair.)

JAMES: Nan, what's the matter?

NAN: *(After a moment.)* I'm all right... It was nothing...only a passing weakness.

JAMES: I'll see if Kate is here, I'll get you something: you wait here. *(He goes out.)*

(NAN passes her hand slowly over her forehead, looks about in a dazed way: finally her look fastens on the notes which have been left on the table. JAMES reappears.)

JAMES: Here, now, is a drop of brandy: drink that and you'll be better. *(Watches her anxiously while she drinks.)*

NAN: I'm all right, Mr. Whelan.

JAMES: Stay there a few minutes.

NAN: You're very kind.

JAMES: Kate might be inside at Brady's. She'd walk up the way with you.

NAN: I don't want that.

JAMES: Wait, I'll see.

(He goes, drawing the door out, but it is not quite shut. NAN throws a swift look over her shoulder, then bends forward quickly, takes a note from the little pile on the table. As she does this, JAMES looks back into the room—and stands—amazed. NAN puts the money carefully into the front of her cardigan, looks again at the notes on the table, picks up another, hesitates about taking it. JAMES steps forward.)

JAMES: What are you doing?

NAN: *(Frightened.)* Nothing at all.

JAMES: Nothing at all! Put back that money.

NAN: *(Putting it back.)* I was only looking at it.

JAMES: Now put back what you have there. *(A gesture.)*

NAN: *(Terrified now.)* That...that's what you gave me.

JAMES: It is not! *(Seizes her by the shoulder: shakes her roughly.)* Open your coat—put it there. *(NAN starts to cry.)* Will I take it from you? *(She opens her cardigan, puts the note on the table.)* A five-pound note!

NAN: I didn't know! I didn't mean it!

JAMES: Didn't mean it!

NAN: I would have given it back to you later... I didn't know it was five pounds.

JAMES: *(Calling.)* Moran! *(APOLLO comes in.)* Go down to the Barracks; ask Sergeant O'Sullivan to step up here.

NAN; Oh! No! No! Mr. Whelan!

APOLLO: If I might ask, what is the matter...

JAMES: You may as well ask, that woman is a common robber—taking money off my table.

NAN: I didn't mean it!

APOLLO: Excuse me a moment, if I might say it—I don't think you have a legal case in this.

JAMES: For the law you're reading?

APOLLO: I don't think you have...unless I'm mistaken, when the woman confesses herself in the wrong—

JAMES: Go for the Sergeant!

APOLLO: Excuse me. Excuse me, I wouldn't have hand or part in such an act.

JAMES: Will you go when I tell you—or will you give up your job?

APOLLO: *(Hesitates: then, with a grand gesture.)* I'll give it up!

JAMES: Give it up! *(Surprised out of his anger.)* Lad, have sense… A thing half the town is trying to get… *(Gazes at APOLLO.)* Well, boys *are* generous. And for her! *(With fury.)* She'd put her hand in your pocket the next minute.

NAN: I would not. I had no thought to do you out of your right. *(Pleading.)*

JAMES: Is my money my right?

NAN: But I would have paid it back.

JAMES: Moran, you can go out to your office.

APOLLO: If I might put forward a plea.

JAMES: You might not. *(APOLLO goes.)*

JAMES: *(Turning to NAN.)* "It will be dear to me as well" and you robbing me! "I'm grateful—very grateful"—striking at me. Now I see—the same treachery of seven years ago—I might have known—I was a fool, bitten by you a second time.

NAN: Mr. Whelan, will you listen to me?

JAMES: The Sergeant can listen.

(Turns to the telephone. NAN makes a wild dash for the door. He springs out, catches her, throws her back across the room, then, at the telephone, dials the number.)

JAMES: Yes, James Whelan speaking. Is that the Sergeant? Would you come up here… Yes, could you come this minute?… I have a person that I caught red-handed robbing me… Yes, I'll hold her here until you come.

NAN: The child, Mr. Whelan…

(Curtain.)

ACT III

The same as Act II, but the office has now a more homely and lived-in air. There are road maps and timetables on the walls and a hat-and-coat stand near the door. A second table, a small one, has been put in and is against the wall to the right front. On the wall at the back—left—there is a large framed photograph of the Silver Wings with JAMES standing beside it. It is a sunny, August day.

JAMES is seated at his table, writing. The door opens and APOLLO comes in, carrying some parcels and some rolled-up newspapers. APOLLO is very much smarter in appearance and bearing than when we saw him last: more superior than ever, but hesitant still. He leaves the parcels on the table at the right side, goes to the stand near the door, and takes down a driver's peaked cap and cashbag, puts these on and goes out, shutting the door.

A moment later, TOM comes bustling in with some more parcels. He wears a driver's cap, and has a cashbag slung across his shoulder. When he throws the parcels on the table, JAMES looks up, aggrieved at the interruption and at TOM's bearing.)

TOM: Am I up to time?

JAMES: You're before it. *(Icy.)*

TOM: That's a fault on the good side, James.

JAMES: Are these all the parcels?

TOM: There are more outside. Moran will bring the rest of them in. *(Pushes back his cap; goes to the window, stands, leaning against the window, but watching JAMES.)*

(APOLLO comes in again, pencil and book in hand, and goes to the table to check the number of parcels. JAMES continues with his work.)

APOLLO: *(Reading.)* Mrs. Mulrooney—to be called for tomorrow.

TOM: And that's Mrs. Power.

APOLLO: You needn't tell me. I'm aware of the way she makes up a parcel.

TOM: What harm when it didn't spill out on me over the floor of the bus. Some of the women beyond in Croom would have you maddened.

APOLLO: Yes, I'm sure. *(Low: a glance at JAMES's direction.)* You'd have the bus started and they'd come running down the hill—"Wait a minute." "Wait, my brother is coming." "Will you post this letter?" "Will you get me the paper in Kilbeggan?" "Wait and I'll give you a penny." That, and the engine already running on you, and Whelan so keen on saving petrol. I tell you a man has need of patience.

JAMES: *(From the table.)* I agree. *(TOM and APOLLO laugh. JAMES smiles grimly.)* Get the parcels. *(Authoritative.)*

(TOM jumps up with mock alacrity and goes quickly out of the room. APOLLO makes some entries in his book, taking the number of parcels. JAMES watches him.)

APOLLO: Yes, I thought so. Our numbers are swelling.

JAMES: You've made a good hand of the driving, Moran.

APOLLO: *(Turning round.)* That's gratifying. We all like appreciation. I'm pleased to have your good opinion.

JAMES: See that you keep it.

TOM: *(Returning with parcels.)* Mrs. Power was telling me today—

JAMES: Too fond of the talk, Carey—

TOM: You find I have failed you in my work?

JAMES: I do not. *(A pause: JAMES gets up, comes over to them.)* McGafferty's bus is off the road.

TOM: You've wiped him out! You've won the day.

JAMES: After next week it won't be running.

TOM: Good man, James. And you deserve it.

APOLLO: Congratulations. Your friends in all quarters will be pleased with these tidings. *(Stilted as ever.)*

TOM: Ah, shut up! *(Turns to JAMES.)* Sure, McGafferty hadn't a chance against you. I said that from the very beginning.

JAMES: Did you, Tom? I didn't remember.

APOLLO: This is certainly not unexpected.

JAMES: McGafferty has the shop in Croom. He won't be hard hit by this.

TOM: We're not worried about him.

APOLLO: Mr. Whelan would worry to see another man sink below the level.

TOM: True for him. *(To JAMES.)* I believe there's a soft-woman streak in you.

JAMES: There is not. *(Pause.)* You and Moran are with me from the very beginning—for this week we'll say double wages.

TOM: Well, that's handsome.

APOLLO: That is in keeping with the name you have.

TOM: You won't regret it.

JAMES: Where's the day book? *(Abrupt.)*

APOLLO: Outside, sir, I'll get it for you.

JAMES: No, I'll get it.

(JAMES goes into the outer office. APOLLO collects the parcels. TOM stands about.)

TOM: *(After a moment.)* He treats people well. I'll say that for James Whelan, excepting only Nan McClinsey.

APOLLO: Careful now. *(A glance towards the outer office.)*

TOM: He came down hard on that poor woman. It wouldn't surprise me if he regretted he had the law on her.

APOLLO: He never spoke of any regret.

TOM: There's proof for you. It wouldn't surprise me if his heart was with Nan all the time.

APOLLO: In the jail?

TOM: She's out of jail now. She has the term served.

APOLLO: But would it be concordant with his ambition? To have his heart with her, I mean, considering she has been in prison?

TOM: Don't be a fool. Yourself and ambition.

APOLLO: She's coming here, I understand.

TOM: Here! Nan McClinsey?

APOLLO: Kate said she'd tell him to take her back.

TOM: Won't the sight of her madden James now, and he blaming himself in secret. *(Pause.)* And that poor woman! Will it be pleasant for her to face back here? Would you, in her shoes, walk in again?

APOLLO: If I had a child to feed.

TOM: You mean she's starving?

(JAMES reappears.)

APOLLO: If you could be a little more careful. *(Low: long-suffering.)*

JAMES: I beg your pardon. I'm afraid I interrupt the conversation. I didn't know this was a gentlemen's club… One minute, Moran, to have those parcels checked and out of here.

APOLLO: Done, Mr. Whelan. *(Gathering up the parcels and stalking out.)*

(JAMES goes to his table. TOM brings his cashbag over to JAMES, turns the contents onto the table and hands over the check-card.)

TOM: You might count that now, and check it over. *(So casual as to be almost insolent.)*

JAMES: *(Looks at him for a moment in silence, then decides not to take offence, starts to count the money.)* You had good travelling.

TOM: You've made a success of this all right. Maybe you'll soon have more buses plying the road?

JAMES: That may be.

TOM: And McGafferty, I'll wager, helping to drive them.

JAMES: You couldn't tell.

TOM: It would be like you. I wouldn't take too much on hands if I were you. You might only harm yourself—though some people say—

JAMES: If you don't mind, we'll postpone this discussion.

TOM: There you are— *(Turning to go.)* —the fellow I always had to deal with—wouldn't take a word from people. *(Going.)*

JAMES: Tom. *(TOM turns in the doorway.)* I'm employing you now. I'm not "the fellow you always had to deal with."

TOM: And what else?

JAMES: Your employer.

(A moment's silence, then TOM goes. JAMES sits at his table, about to start work: suddenly he listens to some sound in the outer office. He grows tense: takes up his pen as if to give the appearance of being at work.)

APOLLO: *(Coming a little way in.)* That's that woman to see you, sir. *(A great show of indifference—but a little nervous.)*

JAMES: What sort of a woman? *(Very steadily.)*

APOLLO: She said to ask could she come in.

JAMES: What sort of a woman?

APOLLO: She's sandy fair—and a shawl on her. *(Then—dropping this nonsense.)* It's Nan McClinsey.

JAMES: Send her in. *(APOLLO withdraws: the next moment NAN comes in. After a moment.)* So you're out of jail now.

NAN: Yes, Mr. Whelan.

JAMES: What term did you serve?

NAN: Six weeks was the sentence.

JAMES: H'm... six weeks... with hard labour, I think.

NAN: Yes, with hard labour. It was you saw to it that I got so hard a term. *(Quietly.)*

JAMES: And I did right. What brought you here now?

NAN: The Priest told me to come.

JAMES: Yes, Father O'Connor came here this morning. About you he came: "That woman was tempted, and now she's ruined." "That may be, Father," I said. "She'll get no work if you don't give it." "There are many without work and no fault of their own." *(As if congratulating himself on his stern attitude.)*

NAN: So, you won't help me. *(Quietly.)*

JAMES: How can I help you... now you're ruined? *(Like a sudden cry.)*

NAN: If you could give me any work. *(Unmoved.)*

JAMES: Down on your knees and to scrub the floor?

NAN: I'd be glad.

JAMES: To tend the fire and clean the grate?

NAN: I would, willing.

JAMES: That fire must be lighted every morning when I come in.

NAN: And so it would.

JAMES: Or when McGafferty comes if he's before me.

NAN; Who, Mr. Whelan?

JAMES: McGafferty—from Croom—he might be here.

NAN: Is that the way? *(A shadow falls on her.)*

JAMES: I don't know. I say it may be. I'm enlarging my business. I'll be running another bus very soon. McGafferty's bus is finished now: The Silver Wings is going strong. I've been very successful. *(Great emphasis.)* We have more people than the bus can hold.

NAN: I'm glad you're happy. *(Dry.)*

JAMES: Did I say I was happy? *(Pause.)* Well, will you have it?

NAN: I will, thank you. What would you pay me?

JAMES: I don't know. We'd have to settle. Whatever is fair.

NAN: When will I start on the work, Mr. Whelan?

JAMES: I don't care when you start. *(Suddenly rough.)* I think you might as well start now. Yes, this minute! Take off your shawl and set to work. The bucket and brush are outside there. Moran will show you.

NAN: And what will I start on?

JAMES: On these boards.

NAN: Now, and you working here at the time?

JAMES: Didn't I say it? *(She turns: goes as far as the door.)* Yes. *(She stops.)* I'm taking you on—like any daily woman, sweeping and scouring to keep yourself in existence— *(Speaking out of great bitterness.)* working here until you're worn, home every night when you're tired out—and nothing else in front of you. Would you mind telling me is that Life?

NAN: I suppose it is.

JAMES: Bah! —You might as well be up in prison.

NAN: I'll have the child. I'll have my freedom.

JAMES: Freedom—h'm. Come here a minute. *(She takes a few steps towards him.)* Did they take your fingerprints?

NAN: Yes, they do always.

JAMES: And you wore prison garb?

NAN: That is the rule.

JAMES: You'll never get over the shame of that. You'll never hold up your head again. *(Pause: She is just turning away again—he stops her.)* What on earth possessed you to do what you did that day on me? *(Spoke almost against his will.)*

NAN: I wanted the money.

JAMES: Couldn't you and I have made an agreement?

NAN: How could I know?

JAMES: Couldn't you?

NAN: People in here better off than myself, and you saying how far you were above me.

JAMES: I am now. I wasn't that day. That was only talk, and well you knew it. You knew well what my feelings were that day.

NAN: I think that was why I took the money.

JAMES: That was why!

NAN: I didn't think you'd turn on me—no matter what.

JAMES: So you thought you might as well rob me!

NAN: Mr. Whelan— *(Pleading.)* —I was in a corner—there were debts. I was desperate.

JAMES: And I sitting beside you. *(Bitterly.)*

NAN: *(After a silence.)* I think you did more wrong than me.

JAMES: Without doubt. *(Hardening.)*

NAN: Sending a woman like me off to prison.

JAMES: I should have let you off scot free! You'll acknowledge yourself in the wrong before me. *(Angered.)*

NAN: Yes, I did wrong.

JAMES: But, I was worse—is that the way?

NAN: I used to be turning it over, often, in the prison, you that were kind, and knew about myself and Jack.

JAMES: This is a queer conversation.

NAN: I suppose it is. *(She turns, goes as far as the door, hesitates, comes back to him.)* That man, Bill McGafferty—is it here he'll be, or beyond in Croom?

JAMES: I couldn't tell you. He mightn't be anywhere at all. Why? *(Anger flaring.)* Are you choosing who you'll work for?

NAN: Who am I to make a choice?

JAMES: Who, indeed!

(The door is pushed open. KATE MORAN comes a little way in. She is dressed in a good, dark costume and carries a large basket, packed with parcels.)

KATE: What time do we leave?

JAMES: Leave?

KATE: I'm going to Croom. Don't you remember—I told you? *(Reproach.)*

JAMES: *(Aggravated.)* Oh, I should have remembered. I beg your pardon for forgetting. The bus for Croom leaves at 1:20.

KATE: So there's no hurry. I'm glad to see Nan back again. *(Beams on NAN.)*

JAMES: Are you, Kate? *(Fuming inwardly.)*

KATE: Ah, old friends are best. *(NAN goes out.)*

KATE: Could I put this— *(The basket.)* here while I step inside to Mrs. Brady?

JAMES: Yes—make use when it suits you of *my* office. *(A martyr—but polite.)*

KATE: That's gentle of you. James, will you look for a minute at those onions. I told that fellow to give me the very best he had. Look what he gave me! Wouldn't it try you? And I thinking I'd have them to bring to poor Mrs. Butler. But, I'm disturbing you. I'm sure I am.

JAMES: Not at all, delighted to see you. *(Forced, ironic.)* Very interesting about those onions.

(Suddenly they laugh together, his ill temper melting away. KATE laughs very merrily. She loves his moods.)

KATE: *(After a moment.)* What work will you give Nan to do here now?

JAMES: Whatever I want—sweeping or scrubbing. *(Harsh.)*

KATE: James! Won't you give her something better? *(Silence.)* I was sure you'd reinstate her. *(Silence.)* Reinstate is the word I use... I thought you'd give Nan the work she was having.

JAMES: Are you going in now to Mrs. Brady?

KATE: *(Drawing nearer to him.)* We must all forgive one another— *(Gentle.)*

JAMES: If you've business in Brady's before the bus goes—

KATE: *(Draws the chair over and sits down beside him.)* In the old days you'd never refuse me.

JAMES: When were those days?

KATE: You're in a cantankerous mood at present. Do you mean there was never friendship between us?

JAMES: I do not. But when was that time—I'd never refuse you—I was very different, I was always gentle, and very considerate? *(Grim, half humorous.)*

KATE: I couldn't follow you at all: you're too moody for me. Look at this now—that poor woman—why would you humiliate her more? Hasn't she suffered? To put her down to sweeping and scrubbing! I'm surprised you'd think of such a thing. Give her back the work she was having.

JAMES: And let her rob me?

KATE: James—that's not like you. Think shame of it.

JAMES: Whom does this place belong to, Kate?

KATE: To you, of course. I've no right to be here—only presuming on old friendship. *(Pause.)* But, my heart is ridden for poor Nan, all she has suffered. *(Pleading.)* It was only a momentary weakness. If she did wrong, so did you.

JAMES: When?

KATE: Often, for no one is blameless. And the creature so badly in need of money!

JAMES: *(In a low tone, but with passion.)* There's one sure way of winning sympathy. Get fair punishment for wrong-doing, then all the world is on your side.

(Silence.)

KATE: *(After a moment.)* So—I must tell Nan "I can't help you. My word is of no account in this place. There was a time it was different." You'll make so little of me as that—that I must tell her you refused me?

JAMES: Kate, what right have you?

KATE: No right at all. I came here asking for a favour, but if you don't grant it, I've no right to complain. Yours is the right to say yes or no. I accept your decision. I'd never raise my voice against you.

JAMES: Oh, you're a model. You were always a model... You never tried to force my hand.

KATE: James, for our friendship.

JAMES: *(After a moment.)* She believes me more in the wrong than herself—let her believe it.

KATE: Nothing matters, but forgiveness. Another man could be hard and untroubled, but not you: it isn't in your nature. I think you're tormented about her.

JAMES: Nothing torments me. I'm perfectly happy.

KATE: Oh, I beg your pardon. My mistake... I'm getting foolish.

JAMES: I'm giving her work: she should be grateful.

(TOM and APOLLO come in, in high spirits. TOM goes to where the papers have been left on the table at the right. APOLLO takes his cashbag from the rack near the door.)

TOM: *(As they come in.)* Said Bill to me not so long back, "The Silver Wings is doing badly." *(They laugh.)*

APOLLO: Hope was the father of that thought.

TOM: Said I to Bill—"So bad we're doing that every other bus is stopping." *(Turns to KATE.)* McGafferty is off the road.

APOLLO: The Silver Wings is now supreme.

KATE: Very pleasant. *(Frigid.)*

TOM: She knew it long before we did.

APOLLO: We've double wages for this week.

TOM: There's nothing here Kate doesn't know.

APOLLO: Double wages—did you ever hear the likc of that?

KATE: I did, Apollo—I often heard better. I heard of people who'd give a woman a second chance.

TOM: *(After a moment's silence.)* If I might say it, I agree.

JAMES: No one asked you. *(Hoarse.)*

TOM: It would be a great thing for Nan McClinsey—if people could forget whatever happened.

APOLLO: And this is a most auspicious moment.

JAMES: I'm well advised.

APOLLO: On the crest of your own triumph.

TOM: *(To APOLLO.)* Keep it back. *(His eloquence.)*

(NAN appears in the doorway.)

NAN: Am I to come in now, Mr. Whelan?

JAMES: Yes, come in.

(She comes in, carrying the bucket of water. She crosses the room slowly.)

APOLLO: *(As she passes him.)* I'm glad to see you. *(A little shyly.)*

TOM: Glad to see her—like that! I'm not!

(JAMES springs, rather than walks, across the room, and stands over TOM. The others hold their breath, but in a moment he regains mastery of himself.)

JAMES: Those papers should be brought to Brady's now. *(Quietly.)*

TOM: Hear that, Moran?

APOLLO: It is customary for me to take the papers, Mr. Whelan. *(Respectful.)*

JAMES: Very well.

APOLLO: And, if you please, you were to give me a letter.

JAMES: Yes, I'll get it. *(Goes out quickly, glad of the excuse to do so.)*

TOM: *(After a moment's silence.)* James would want to look out, or his temper will one day get the better of him.

KATE: That's not very customary—your mode of expression.

TOM: And why should I be customary? Is James himself?

KATE: *(To APOLLO.)* Is it you'll be driving the bus, Apollo?

APOLLO: It is my habit always to take the 1:20. *(Going, with the papers.)*

KATE: Would I have time to cross the Square before we leave?

APOLLO: You would, and plenty, unless you meet someone. *(Goes.)*

(KATE gives another look of strong disapproval at TOM, and follows APOLLO out. TOM crosses the room to where NAN, on her knees now, is starting work.)

TOM: That was a great spring James made at me. *(No reply. He bends down and taps her on the shoulder.)* Whisper now—what has made him so angry? What was it upset him? I think it was the sight of yourself. He was calm enough until you came.

NAN: That may be.

TOM: Now, I'll read you a proposition—why would James have been so angry—that day, you know, when he caught you—unless it was he cared about you? He had lost nothing.

NAN: It is better to leave things alone, Tom Carey.

TOM: That's a fool's cry. Rouse yourself, woman, and lift yourself up.

NAN: Why do you trouble yourself about me?

TOM: I'm a kind-hearted man. I am sorry for people. I was always kind-hearted.

NAN: I think you were.

TOM: It is no good. I'd be better without it. Often I think it's a kind of a curse. *(Pause.)* The women don't like it. I'd be better now if I were harder. If I were the sort of man you might read about, hard like James Whelan. *(Pause.)* Nan, you could do what you liked with Whelan still.

NAN: A woman that has been in prison!

TOM: You could make it so that he'd forget that. He's looking for marriage.

NAN: I think he'll find it, but not with me.

TOM: You wouldn't have him?

NAN: I won't be asked to have him, Tom. I see that clear. Anyway, it was never meant.

TOM: Maybe you and myself might hit it off?

NAN: We might, and we might not.

TOM: Do you think it is of wood I'm made. *(Flash.)* Or that I'm too old for you? I'm young at heart.

NAN: I think you are.

TOM: If you care for James Whelan, tell me now.

NAN: That would be queer—a man that had treated me so harshly.

TOM: Queer things have happened. *(Silence.)* So Tom can go on being kind, and James can do what he likes, to people. Where is there justice?

NAN: Don't fret yourself Tom. Nothing is worth it.

TOM: Oh, that's wisdom. But where would you see justice done?

NAN: I couldn't tell you, nor what *is* justice.

(NORA KEANE appears in the doorway and comes in.)

NORA: Could I see Mr. Whelan?

TOM: I'm sure you could if he was here. He must have gone with Kate Moran across the Square. I thought he was outside in the office. Nan, do you know will he be back?

NAN: *(Restarts to scrub.)* I don't know, Mr. Carey.

TOM: If Nan can't tell us no one could—seeing they're so friendly.

NORA: Well, I can't wait. I'll come again. Will you tell him?

TOM: Any message is better left with Nan. I'm for my dinner. *(Takes up the papers and goes out.)*

NORA: Will you tell him what I said? *(A touch of disdain.)*

NAN: What was that? I wasn't minding. *(Antagonism.)*

NORA: I'll come again later.

NAN: Who will I say?

NORA: I thought you knew me. I'm Miss Keane.

NAN: So, I'll tell him.

NORA: *(Hesitates.)* Or perhaps I'll wait. You wouldn't mind?

NAN: Why would I mind? What difference would it make to me?

(NORA sits down, watches NAN, who scrubs determinedly: then, as NAN pauses for a moment, NORA—softened—bends towards her.)

NORA: You have a boy. I often see him...a lovely boy.

NAN: He's fine and healthy.

NORA: He and I have become friendly. *(Unconsciously, she speaks in a condescending way.)*

NAN: Is that so? *(Cold.)*

(JAMES appears at the door and comes in.)

NORA: We nearly missed: I was almost going.

JAMES: That would have been a great misfortune! —for you, Miss Keane! *(This with gay, though bombastic tone—excited at sight of her, excited to see how far he can go.)*

NORA: How very witty! You're coming in. You were so slow in the beginning—but you're improving.

JAMES: Under your guidance. What did you come for?

NORA: What a question! Mightn't I have come for no earthly reason—but to see you?

JAMES: Well, there's usually some excuse offered.

(They laugh together.)

NORA: Will you come up to us this evening? Dad will be there—and some other people.

JAMES: If you'll be there, isn't that enough?

NORA: You should really get a prize!

(Again they laugh together.)

JAMES: And will you give it?

(NAN, who has given one or two contemptuous looks at JAMES, now gets slowly to her feet.)

JAMES: You needn't go, Nan. Miss Keane's not delaying.

NAN: It is the other brush I want, Mr. Whelan. *(Goes.)*

NORA: I never said I wasn't delaying.

JAMES: My mistake.

NORA: *(Serious.)* But you'd like better that I went away.

JAMES: She'll be coming back, you see.

NORA: Am I not allowed to keep her waiting? Must she not have to leave the room?

JAMES: What do you mean? ...I don't understand you, Miss Nora.

NORA: "Miss"...after all the times I've come to see you. *(Pause.)* Do I come often?

JAMES: Well, you do.

NORA: And you don't like it?

JAMES: I didn't say that.

NORA: Then you *do* like it, but you won't say—

JAMES: We're too different—

NORA: I know this. I think I know it by heart: you "worked for my father"... Why can't you ever get over that... Lots of people start that way and later forget about it... Later on they might even become partners—or run two businesses into one. *(Silence.)* Dad has no one—only me. I mean no son.

JAMES: *(After a silence.)* Some of us have no wish to become partners—or to run our business with another—

NORA: Very well, I can see that... Oh, call her back—your nice charwoman! People are better with their own kind! And I was foolish...

(She is near the door now, but JAMES, roused, intercepts her.)

JAMES: I beg your pardon. *(Low, passionate.)* I won't take that—

NORA: Well— *(Taunting.)* —will you come to my party?

JAMES: I'll be there—plain and rough though you may find me.

NORA: I never said that—but wasn't it funny the way she came back—so certain you'd have her, and you fell in and did what she wanted!

JAMES: I'll let you go on now, Miss Keane... *(Low.)* for it's no concern of mine what you call funny.

NORA: *(Delaying.)* "Plain and rough," I never called you. That is not what I feel about you... My father is a self-made man and, though now we have plenty of money, he hadn't always... He has often told me about it. *(Gently now, in a pleading way.)* I know how he grew up...the people he lived with, and I know, too, the sort he likes—simple people, so do I. Mother is different, but I am my father's daughter—don't you know that?

JAMES: If I had ever thought about it. Good morning, Miss Keane. *(He holds the door for her. NORA, defeated, looks at him and goes out. JAMES shuts the door very carefully, comes back to his table, then goes from the table to the window, and back again.)* "Funny"...the way I "fell in and did what was wanted"...

APOLLO: *(Coming in.)* Are you addressing me, Mr. Whelan?

JAMES: No, I'm not.

APOLLO: For myself—I frequently recite aloud.

JAMES: Is that so?

APOLLO: To vent my feelings to the wind.

JAMES: Dangerous habit.

APOLLO: I am very far removed from people.

(JAMES watches him quietly for a moment. APOLLO takes some papers from the drawer in the table and turns to go.)

JAMES: Don't hold yourself so lonely, Moran. *(Speaking gently.)* I was like that.

APOLLO: *(Expanding.)* For long I have known a suffering heart—and very frequently misunderstood.

JAMES: Yes, I'm sure. *(Brusque again.)* Don't leave for Croom without this letter... *(Writing.)* I'll leave it here for you when I have it ready.

APOLLO: It is not yet our scheduled time...

(Quietly: he stands at the window gazing out, sorrowfully. JAMES writes for a moment, then looks up, watches APOLLO.)

JAMES: Why this so melancholy manner?

APOLLO: I am getting accustomed to great sadness,— a certain person that used to be friendly, set my heart hoping—and now hardly sees me...

JAMES: Drop that, Apollo—picturing yourself the great brokenhearted.

APOLLO: *(Who has straightened.)* "Apollo"—*you* called me!—the old name...

JAMES: Time long ago I christened you with it...

APOLLO: That was a very long time ago.

JAMES: —A miserable slip of a young lad, coming across the fields with me on a Sunday morning...weighed down, even then, with your childish troubles... Those

Sunday mornings...myself, young then and thirsting for something...something beyond grasp that would satisfy— *(Pulls himself up.)* A young man thinks he can find it in a girl. Don't be a fool.

APOLLO: *(Far older than him.)* Now I see the man I had a wish for always.

JAMES: If you think I'm the same as I was then, you're greatly mistaken.

APOLLO: That is a matter of opinion.

JAMES: You—with your stilted way of talking! ...I'll tell you what's wisdom—have *no* regrets for anything *ever.*

APOLLO: Then, I presume, all is plain sailing?

JAMES: Is it mocking you are?

APOLLO: We can't all stay as young as you, Mr. Whelan.

JAMES: Ah, get out, Moran! and get on with the work you should be doing.

APOLLO: Is this to be the end of our conversation?

JAMES: Get out, get out! This letter has to be finished.

(APOLLO, going out, meets BILL McGAFFERTY coming in.)

APOLLO: Wait now a moment—he's very busy— *(Gesturing BILL back, turns back towards JAMES:)* A gentleman to see you, sir— *(In grandest manner: Exit.)*

JAMES: That you, Bill? Come in and wait for a minute. *(Gestures towards chair, continues writing.)*

(Enter BILL, grown heavier, more morose than when we last saw him: the cynical attitude which he then adopted has developed into a habitually dark manner. He sits down, looks slowly round the office with determined contempt: then watches JAMES, with hostile eyes. JAMES writes very slowly, giving himself time to prepare for the encounter with BILL, and deliberately conveying to BILL that he is of secondary importance.)

BILL: *(After a minute.)* Are you ready—or will I be going?

JAMES: One moment... *(Finishes slowly, puts letter on rack on the desk.)* Well, are you coming to work with me?

BILL: If we can come to an agreement, which I doubt. McGafferty is off the road. You have that all your own way now—but *not* the whole world...

JAMES: You got my message?

BILL: Otherwise I wouldn't be here.

JAMES: The note? The offer I sent you?

BILL: You made a good offer, but I want better... Partnership there might be between us.

JAMES: Never! You've got the best you'll get from me. Are you coming to work with the Silver Wings?

BILL: If I come I'll bring a certain amount of custom.

JAMES: I'll get that custom whether or no—I've won it from you.

BILL: *(Shrugs.)* True for you... So Nan McClinsey is outside, I see— *(Gestures towards outer office.)*

JAMES: That's very likely.

BILL: The impudent baggage.

JAMES: I don't think so.

BILL: That she'd have the face to come up here—standing there as cool as tomorrow. Will I tell you something about her?

JAMES: No, you needn't.

BILL: (Swift.) You know she was promised my wife.

JAMES: Your…!

BILL: *(Speaking with passion.)* She was promised to me. She promised herself and then let me down. *(Silence.)* I wouldn't look now in her direction. I wouldn't touch her. Haven't you proved her a common robber?

JAMES: Didn't I tell you *not* to speak? *(Low.)*

BILL: A woman like that can treat people badly.

KATE: *(Coming in.)* Good day to you. *(BILL nods. KATE turns to JAMES.)* I got some lettuce and tomatoes—though I don't know are they much to her liking… And is Bill coming to work here?

JAMES: No! *(Decisive. BILL looks at him in surprise.)* I made him an offer, but he didn't accept it.

BILL: *(Standing up.)* I told him something he didn't find pleasant.

KATE: A child could see that you two would never pull together.

BILL: *(To JAMES.)* I'll leave you with the people you like better. *(Goes abruptly.)*

JAMES: *(After a silence.)* Nan was going to marry Bill McGafferty.

KATE: She was at one time—the poor creature. *(Casual.)*

JAMES: You never told me!

KATE: *(Very dignified.)* If I didn't tell you, James, that must be I didn't think it of interest. It was beneath your notice. *(Rallying his pride.)*

JAMES: Oh, I see. *(Grim.)*

KATE: For you had left all that behind you… *(Pause.)*

JAMES: *(In changed tone.)* Kate, my mother isn't so well today.

KATE: *(Taking his lead.)* So I'm to go and see her?

JAMES: If you would.

KATE: As soon as I get back from Croom—or *(Very gently.)* I'll put Croom off if you'd like that.

JAMES: Why would you? *(Appreciation.)*

KATE: Don't you know me? *(Affection.)*

JAMES: If I had any sense at all. *(Roused now.)*

KATE: Yes, but you haven't. I know that well.

JAMES: And I think you're very glad. *(Patching it, gallantly.)*

KATE: Maybe it's better.

JAMES: Aye, far better; for we can stay good friends always.

KATE: *(Sadly.)* Like people are saying since the world started, trying to make out they're pleased with the way things are for them. *(NAN reappears, coming in quietly, brush in hand.)* Now, I'll put my parcels in the bus. *(Goes out with some of her parcels, but leaves the basket.)*

JAMES: *(To NAN.)* Have you got whatever it was you went out for? *(Quiet now: watches her, but no longer with excitement.)*

NAN: The brush I wanted, Mr. Whelan. *(Crosses the room, about to start work, hesitates: comes back to JAMES.)* Did Bill tell you I'm not honest?

JAMES: Honest! *(Stares at her.)* McGafferty too!

NAN: *(Passionate.)* Mr. Whelan, I did no wrong to him!

JAMES: Nor to me—is that the way?

NAN: I took nothing from him. Will you believe me?

JAMES: How can I believe you?

NAN: Bill and I were friendly once.

JAMES: *(Hardening.)* Is that so?

NAN: After Jack died I had no one—

JAMES: You had made your choice away from me.

NAN: And you forgot me.

JAMES: I didn't, Nan.

NAN: Until you saw me here again.

JAMES: You're mistaken. *(Very gently.)*

NAN: Bill was kind to me in the beginning, and we got friendly. But I was afraid *now* he might turn you against me—

JAMES: Would that matter?

NAN: If I was to lose my work it would.

JAMES: Oh, I see. *(Hardening again.)*

NAN: I never liked him.

JAMES: *(Flashing.)* You were only going to marry him!

NAN: I never cared for him at all.

JAMES: A man and woman don't go that far without something.

NAN: He pestered me and, in the end, for the child's sake, I said I'd have him. But I couldn't bear it. I couldn't bring myself to face it. When I told him that, Bill was angry.

JAMES: He had a right to be, seeing you had promised.

NAN: The morning after we parted friendship he accused me. I had sent a young lad down to Bill's yard for potatoes—for I had a custom to get them from Bill when we were friendly. The boy came back—McGafferty wanted me very urgent. I took Jackie with me... Bill said he missed money out of his office. There was no one but myself could have taken it. *(Silence.)*

JAMES: Well, did he prove it?

NAN: No one could prove it either way. There was only my word against his. I never laid eyes on that money. I knew nothing of it. Do you believe me?

JAMES: *(After an instant.)* Yes, I believe you.

NAN: *(Then—after a moment.)* Bill said if I'd have him, we'd forget it.

JAMES: What! Blackmailed you?

NAN: *(Passionate.)* That was the start of all my trouble—I don't believe I'd ever have thought to touch your money...only...only seeing how easy it could be done...or said about you.

JAMES: Why didn't you tell me this before?

NAN: That another accused me! *(A silence.)*

JAMES: *(Gets up, moves about restlessly, comes back to her.)* You might leave this now— *(The scrubbing.)*

NAN: Leave it—you mean—?

JAMES: Of course, you were in the wrong with me. I'm not taking that back.

NAN: I suppose you're not—

JAMES: But, all the same, leave this now. And after dinner we'll see how you'd do in the outer office.

NAN: Oh—Mr. Whelan— *(Moved.)*

JAMES: And I think we'll forget all that happened. From this day out we'll forget all about it. *(Carried away.)* Will we, Nan?

NAN: Forget all about it. I suppose *you* will.

(A dead silence.)

JAMES: So that's it now.

(A pause: he watches her.)

NAN: Am I to put these things away? *(The bucket, etc.)*

JAMES: I suppose so— *(Abruptly. Exit.)*

KATE: *(Outside.)* Now I think I have everything. *(She comes in, taking her basket.)*

NAN: I'm to mind the books—in the outer office. *(To KATE.)*

KATE: You don't tell me! *(Alarm.)*

NAN: I thought you were a friend to me?

KATE: And I am so, and glad of this—but—

NAN: You needn't worry.

APOLLO: *(Hurries in.)* The letter for Croom! *(Goes to JAMES's table.)* All is lost! He has it with him.

KATE: What is it, Apollo?

APOLLO: I'm not to leave without his letter. But the bus must leave this very minute. I'm on the horns of a dilemma.

KATE: Why didn't you ask him for it? He's outside there, with Bill, this minute.

APOLLO: Mr. Whelan doesn't take kindly to interruption. He went up to Bill McGafferty. He appeared somewhat heated. I hesitated to interrupt their conversation.

KATE: Get out now and get the letter.

APOLLO: *(Turns to NAN.)* Would it be wise? Could you tell me to ask him for it—or to wait? Which, in your opinion, is the better method?

NAN: Where is Bill?

KATE: *(Looking out the window.)* Outside there—and James is angry. God grant he won't lose his temper.

APOLLO: Would I go out and intervene? Would that be well? Make this letter excuse, and come between them?

KATE: *(At the window—very uneasy.)* Maybe—maybe. I don't know—they might be better left alone.

NAN: Is it to Bill he's talking now?

APOLLO: As I told you.

KATE: *(At the window.)* Oh! Oh! My gracious! Mother of God! What came on him!

(APOLLO springs to the window.)

NAN: What is it, Apollo?

APOLLO: He knocked Bill down.

KATE: Such a thing to happen—on the street.

APOLLO: Flat on the pavement!

KATE: Keep back, Apollo! Nan, keep away! He wouldn't like we were looking.

APOLLO: This is a very unforeseen occurrence.

NAN: Bill will make trouble.

KATE: I'm sure you're at the bottom of it. *(Angrily.)*

APOLLO: Mr. Whelan will rise above all misadventure. *(Calming her.)*

KATE: Miss Keane is there.

APOLLO: Where is she?

KATE: Keep back, Apollo. She's on the outskirts of the crowd.

APOLLO: If I could see her.

NAN: Has a crowd gathered?

APOLLO: *(On tiptoe.)* Not very many. Miss Keane must have been crossing the Square at the wrong minute. To his great misfortune, he was seen by her at a disadvantage.

NAN: He wasn't the one to be knocked down— *(Dry.)* and never will.

KATE: What was it about? *(To NAN, angrily.)*

NAN: I couldn't tell you.

APOLLO: Bill must have been coming in to see him. "I think we'll talk outside"—in a voice of low passion— *(Melodramatic.)* So much I heard—

KATE: What happened, Tom?

TOM: McGafferty got what he deserved, and I never felt so near to James.

KATE: But what will be the outcome of it? *(Near to tears.)*

NAN: *(At the window.)* Bill is up. Mr. Whelan and he are talking now.

APOLLO: Kate, come on. The bus will be leaving.

KATE: How could I go to Croom at such a moment?

APOLLO: The bus can't be late—no matter what happens.

TOM: *(To NAN.)* Is he talking to Bill McGafferty?

NAN: No, they have parted.

TOM: Did they part friendly?

NAN: No, I don't think so.

TOM: James will carry this off all right, I tell you. They'll be partners likely before long.

KATE: How can that be? Oh, my goodness, what will it lead to?

APOLLO: Kate, I'm going.

JAMES: *(Appearing.)* You should be gone already. *(Quiet.)*

(TOM winks at NAN and slips out.)

APOLLO: I understood I was to take a message.

JAMES: Why didn't you come and ask me for it?

APOLLO: It appeared that you were occupied.

JAMES: You had only to say— "I beg your pardon"—

KATE: James—what happened? *(Unable to wait longer.)*

JAMES: *(To APOLLO.)* Buses must leave up to the minute.

APOLLO: I'm sorry I failed you at such a moment. I hesitated to intrude.

JAMES: You didn't fail me! *(In sudden acknowledgement.)* I know that.

(APOLLO goes out.)

KATE: I won't go to Croom this day!

JAMES: Why not, Kate?

KATE: I will not go—I'm too upset.

JAMES: That isn't like you. *(Gentle.)* Well, go down to my mother. Tell her it's nothing.

KATE: Could I say that?

JAMES: There's a good woman. Don't let her be worried.

KATE: What did he say to make you so angry?

JAMES: Go on now.

KATE: Oh, James—why couldn't you keep your temper!

JAMES: Let you not mind—

KATE: *(Breaking down.)* How can I help but mind if you're in trouble? ...James, anger is horrid. *(Pleading.)* Let there be friendship.

JAMES: My mother would be glad to see you. *(Gentle now.)*

KATE: I'm in your way. I'm no help to you at a time like this.

JAMES: You are, great help—if you'd stay with her.

KATE: I will, so. I'll tell her it will all blow over.

JAMES: Yes, that's right.

(He has got her out: comes back to the table, stands there with the quietness of a man after violent action. NAN watches him.)

TOM: *(Reappearing.)* He's going to prosecute you, James. *(Excited.)* "Prosecute away" says you. *(Comes over.)* I'd like it was myself had done that.

JAMES: That you, Carey.

TOM: That fellow needed knocking down. My hand to you, he did so.

JAMES: Hardly a matter for congratulation.

NAN: What will it mean?

TOM: Ah! 'Twill mean nothing. Nothing at all but a fine to pay—or not to pay. There's Tom O'Reilly above...fined every other week, and the devil a penny out of his pocket. Anyway, it was very well worth it. *(Goes to the door.)* He's outside here—talking still. *(Goes out.)*

JAMES: *(After a moment.)* It means—if I didn't pay that fine I'd go to prison. Does that give you satisfaction?

NAN: I don't feel that way at all.

JAMES: You have reason. *(A silence: a look of gratitude from her.)* Bill withdrew that charge against you.

NAN: That's very easy.

JAMES: But whether or no, I didn't believe him. *(But quite detached from her.)*

NAN: *(Moves over to him.)* I'm grateful that you sided with me. *(Gentle: her first real approach to him.)*

JAMES: That's all so. *(Quietly.)*

NAN: Is that all? *(Watching.)*

JAMES: I think so, Nan. *(Pause.)* When you come back after dinner, Moran will show the books to you. I won't be here myself this evening.

NAN: *(After a silence.)* I knew this would be all between us. *(With a certain pride. Then she turns and goes out.)*

(JAMES stands quite still, at his table.)

TOM: *(Looking in again.)* He's getting sorry. I don't think you'll hear much more about it.

(NORA appears in the doorway. TOM turns and sees her.)

TOM: I beg your pardon. *(Withdraws.)*

JAMES: Yes, you want me?

NORA: If you're not busy.

JAMES: Please come in.

NORA: Whatever happened?

JAMES: I think you saw.

NORA: Yes, you knocked him down. *(Nervous: not sure how she'll be taken. Suddenly—flashes.)* Daddy would say—"Cherchez la femme." That means—"Find the woman." *(A laugh—showing contempt.)*

JAMES: I know what it means. I've that much French. *(A silence: she is ashamed.)* What have *you* against me?

NORA: So that's it now. *(Lightly.)* I've something against you.

JAMES: You seem to have.

NORA: I was wondering if I'd come in—or go on home.

JAMES: And you came in.

NORA: I may as well go on, I think.

JAMES: It might be better.

NORA: You'll come tonight—in spite of this. *(A taunt.)*

JAMES: Why wouldn't I come? Wasn't that settled? *(His pride up.)* Sit down, please. *(Almost rough. He sits down. She does not.)* There's likely to be a summons against me. Bill has every right to have me fined... Possibly we might make it up... He's the type of man I am myself—rough and tumble, the sort that might give a blow to another—any minute when he's angry. *(A pause.)* What happened outside—that's a thing remote altogether from your life... Well, *am I wanted* at *your* party?

NORA: Yes, you're wanted. *(Low.)*

JAMES: You should think a little while about that.

NORA: There's no need.

JAMES: Sometimes I warn a person of the risk they take, but if they take it I won't be sorry for them later... I mightn't even remember there's any reason for being sorry.

NORA: There'd be no reason. *(Low.)*

JAMES: *(Won now.)* Oh, but you're foolish! You, so fresh and dainty! *(Takes her hands: draws her to him.)* Am I to tell your father I'm as good a man as himself?

NORA: No. Say you're better. *(Throws her arms round his neck.)*

JAMES: And that his daughter is going to be my wife? *(NORA agrees—waits to be kissed. JAMES smiles at her, but lets her release him again—then takes her hands and kisses them.)* When we have his permission we'll do more... *(NORA laughs delightedly at him.)* Now I'll let you go on, I think.

(They stand up. He goes with her to the door—seeing her out; moves to the window, watches her across the yard; lifts his hand in response to a wave from her. Turns from the window. KATE comes in.)

KATE: Your mother's asleep.

JAMES: That's a good thing. *(Absently.)*

KATE: James, I was thinking you could settle with Bill if you'd take him right.

JAMES: Yes, I suppose so.

KATE: *(Looks sharply at him.)* Miss Keane was here.

JAMES: She was, Kate.

KATE: She called in to see you.

JAMES: She called to see me.

KATE: That was nice and friendly.

JAMES: Very friendly.

KATE: *(After a moment.)* Since you don't want me, I'll go on.

JAMES: *(Swings round.)* Nora Keane and I are getting married.

KATE: So! *(Checks a gasp, goes to him with outstretched hands.)* Isn't that what I always wanted. God bless you now. I'm glad for you. I am indeed. *(Now talking quickly and too much.)* And this should make your mother happy—to have you settled… And John Keane will be pleased, for he'd know a good man when he'd see one. You'll be no foolish husband, you'll make her into a sensible woman…she that might have been…different.

JAMES: Tell me—are you sorry for her? *(Hoarse: unsure of himself.)*

KATE: Sorry! Oh, James, you're humble. I'm amazed! Isn't she the lucky girl! And now you are insured for the future.

JAMES: Insured? How so?

KATE: You are, indeed, against anything foolish… Once you make the choice you'll abide by it—and I so often afraid you'd do something foolish.

JAMES: She's very fond of me now, Kate—

KATE: And you of her… *(A door slams: a silence. JAMES turns his head and looks out of the window.)* What is that?

JAMES: Nan—going to her dinner… I thought she had gone already… Nan Bowers—McClinsey, I mean… *(A pause.)*

KATE: *(Moves a little uneasily.)* Nora Keane is very pretty—with her fair hair, and her blue eyes.

JAMES: *(Gives her a look of contempt.)* Fair hair, blue eyes—that doesn't describe her. Her eyes are a very unusual colour. *(Soaring.)*

KATE: Oh! Are they?

JAMES: And I'd call her hair more brown than fair…

KATE: Oh! I see.

JAMES: *(After a moment's silence.)* But, I'd like that things were well with Nan… I was thinking she might get married to Tom Carey…

KATE: No one could say what might happen— *(Dry.)*

JAMES: I'd like that things were well with her.

KATE: So's everyone could be very happy—and everything right in the world again. *(A little bitterly, but with tenderness.)* I might as well have gone to Croom this day.

JAMES: Oh! No! *(Impetuous.)* I'm glad you're here—to tell you about this.

KATE: To tell me about it! *(Gently.)*

(KATE looks at JAMES, but with his head thrown back, he is gazing into his own future.)

(Curtain.)

MINT THEATER COMPANY produces worthwhile plays from the past that have been lost or forgotten. These neglected plays offer special and specific rewards; it is our mission to bring new vitality to these plays and to foster new life for them.

Under the leadership of Jonathan Bank as Artistic Director, Mint has secured a place in the crowded theatrical landscape of New York City. We have received Special Obie and Drama Desk Awards recognizing the importance of our mission and our success in fulfilling it. The *Wall Street Journal* describes Mint as "one of the most consistently interesting companies in town."

Our process of excavation, reclamation, and preservation makes an important contribution to the art form and its enthusiasts. Scholars have the chance to come into contact with historically significant work that they've studied on the page but never experienced on the stage. Local theatergoers have the opportunity to see plays that would otherwise be unavailable to them, while theatergoers elsewhere may also have that opportunity in productions inspired by our success. Important plays with valuable lessons to teach—plays that have been discarded or ignored—are now read, studied, performed, discussed, written about, and enjoyed as a result of our work.

Educating our audience about the context in which a play was originally created and how it was first received is an essential part of what we do. Our "EnrichMINT Events" enhance the experience of our audience and help to foster an ongoing dialogue around a play—post-performance discussions feature world-class scholars discussing complex topics in an accessible way and are always free and open to the general public.

We not only produce lost plays, but we are also their advocates. We publish our work and distribute our books, free of charge to libraries, theaters, and universities. Our catalogue of books now includes an anthology of seven plays entitled *Worthy But Neglected: Plays of the Mint Theater* plus four volumes in our *Reclaimed* series, each featuring the work of a single author: Harley Granville Barker, St. John Hankin, Arthur Schnitzler, and Teresa Deevy.